THE FROZEN SHIP

THE
FROZEN SHIP

THE HISTORIES AND TALES
OF POLAR EXPLORATION

SARAH MOSS

BlueBridge

Jacket design by Stefan Killen Design

Cover art top by Royal Geographic Society, London (The "Endurance" frozen in the ice.)

Cover art bottom by Art Resource, New York (Caspar David Friedrich [1774-1840], The Polar Sea [Das Eismeer]. 1823-1824. Oil on canvas.)

Published in Great Britain by Signal Books Limited, Oxford.

Interior images: John Torrington, courtesy John Geiger; Bodleian Library, Oxford; private collection

The publishers would like to thank Broken Jaw Press Inc. of Canada for permission to reprint "For John Torrington" by Jennifer Footman. (http://www.library.utoronto.ca/canpoetry/footman/poems.htm)

Library of Congress Cataloging-in-Publication Data

Moss, Sarah.
  The frozen ship : the histories and tales of Polar exploration / Sarah Moss.
    p. cm.
  Includes index.
  ISBN 1-933346-03-5
  1. Polar regions—Discovery and exploration. 2. Polar regions—Description and travel. I. Title.

  G590.M69 2006
  910.911—dc22
      2006016403

Published in North America by

BlueBridge
An imprint of
United Tribes Media Inc.
240 West 35th Street, Suite 500
New York, NY 10001

www.bluebridgebooks.com

Printed in the United States of America

10 9 8 7 6 5 4 3 2 1

CONTENTS

"It was two miles beyond the entrance of this canal that a ship made its appearance about noon. The sun shone brightly at this time and a gentle breeze blew from the north. At first, some intervening icebergs prevented Captain Warrens from distinctly seeing any thing except her masts, but he was struck with the strange manner in which her sails were disposed, and with the dismantled aspect of her yards and rigging. She continued to go before the wind for a few furlongs, and then, grounding upon the low icebergs, remained motionless.

. . . On approaching he observed that her hull was miserably weather-beaten, and that not a soul appeared upon the deck, which was covered with snow to a considerable depth. He hailed her crew several times, but no answer was returned. Previous to stepping on board, an open port-hole near the main chains caught his eye, and on looking into it, he perceived a man reclining back in a chair, with writing materials on a small table before him, but the feebleness of the light made everything very indistinct. The party, therefore, went up on deck, and having removed the hatchway, which they found closed, they descended to the cabin. They first came to the apartment which Captain Warrens had viewed through the port hole. A tremor seized him as he entered it. Its inmate retained his former position and seemed to be insensible to the presence of strangers. He was found to be a corpse, and a green damp mould had covered his cheeks and forehead and veiled his open eye-balls. He held a pen in his hand, and a log-book lay before him, and the last sentence in its unfinished page ran thus: '11th Nov. 1762. We have now been enclosed in the ice seventy days. The fire went out yesterday, and our Master has been trying ever since to kindle it again, but without success. His wife died this morning. There is no relief. . .'

Captain Warrens and his seamen hurried from the spot without uttering a word. On entering the principal cabin, the first object that attracted their attention was the dead body of a female reclining on a bed in an attitude of deep interest and attention. Her countenance retained the freshness of life, and a contraction of the limbs alone showed that her form was inanimate. Seated on the floor, in one corner of the room, was the corpse of an apparently young man holding a steel in one hand and a flint in the other, as if in the act of striking fire upon some tinder which lay beside him.

In the fore part of the vessel several sailors were found lying dead in their berths, and the body of a dog was crouched at the bottom of the gangway stairs. Neither provisions nor fuel could be discovered any where, but Captain Warrens was prevented by the superstitious prejudices of his seamen from examining the vessel as minutely as he wished to have done."

George Powell Thomas, "The Frozen Ship," *Colburn's United Service Magazine and Naval and Military Journal,* 1847.

PREFACE

"Face to face with real death one does not think of the things that torment the bad people in the tracts, and fill the good people with bliss. I might have speculated on my chances of going to Heaven; but candidly I did not care. I could not have wept if I had tried. I had no wish to review the evils of my past. But the past did seem to have been a bit wasted . . . I wanted those years over again. What fun I would have had with them: what glorious fun! It was a pity. . . . And then quite naturally and no doubt disappointingly to those who would like to read of my last agonies (for who would not give pleasure by his death?) I fell asleep."

Apsley Cherry-Garrard, *The Worst Journey in the World*

"In Bjorn Jonsson's account of Lik-Lodin, who lived about the middle of the eleventh century, we read that he was in the habit of sailing to the northern ubygder or waste places in the summer, and bringing back the bodies of those who had been wrecked in the drift-ice. He found them in caves and crevices, and with them runes telling of the disasters they had met with. Again, the Sturlunga Saga, speaking of Ingemund the priest who perished in a cave in east Greenland, tells us that wax tablets and runes were found, recording the circumstances in which he met his death."

Helge Instad, *Land under the Pole Star*

The frozen ship of *Colburn's Magazine* is emblematic of the modern fascination for writing about polar exploration and travel. As the enduring and immense popularity of books about Arctic and Antarctic disasters demonstrates, the far north and south are places of death, where heroes go to test their heroism to its sublunary limits. More than that, they are places where the limits of heroism are recorded, written into the landscape and into the body and onto the notebooks or the wax tablets that lie beside the body. The frozen ship preserves for us a better past, a corner of the world in which it is still 1762 or

1913 or "about the middle of eleventh century." The frozen landscapes of these texts offer a kind of cryogenic time-travel, a way for the armchair explorer to visit the heroes of a fantasy past. The frozen ship sails on, but we can visit for a while.

Like any fantasy, this is complicated and revealing, and it is these complications and revelations as well as the fantasy itself that I wish to explore. The Arctic is not of course a "space of death" but a place to live for many thousand people. Uninhabited Antarctica is even more obviously a blank canvas for our own greatest hopes and fears. The glimpses of the past we sometimes see in the ice, north and south, are not necessarily windows into the heroism of a nobler and better past; sometimes they may be enduring evidence of incompetence, inequality or merely the awfulness of some lives in 1762 or 1913 or the middle of the eleventh century. Apsley Cherry-Garrard's uncompromising title and relentless understanding of his readers forces us to confront both our own motives as readers, those who "would like to read of [his] last agonies" and his own refusal of the hero's role. Despite participating in Robert Falcon Scott's iconic expedition, Cherry-Garrard doesn't want to die nobly, he is not a person in a tract. He wishes he'd had more fun. And so, very possibly, did Ingemund the priest and the Master of the frozen ship and his exquisitely dead wife. But the literary poles, the Arctic and Antarctic of the unashamedly metropolitan readers that most of us are, are not made of fun and sleep and regret for the past. These imaginary polar spaces are black-and-white landscapes in which the great explorers prove themselves, and us, by fighting on to the bitter end, striving, seeking, finding and not yielding even to death itself.

From the beginning of the European presence in the Arctic over a thousand years ago, the capacity and compulsion of the dying to document the progress of starvation, exposure, and despair has produced a distinctive and unsettling genre of writing. This is not just a book about Arctic and Antarctic travel and exploration—there are many of those. I have not been to the Arctic or Antarctic and have no claim to frostbite of my own. This is as much about the literature of polar travel, about why polar explorers continue to write as the last candle gutters and the frost-bitten hands jerk the pencil stub, and about why and how we consume their writing.

I have tried to be sensitive to the issues involved, but this is not either a book about first or subsequent encounters between European travelers and the Inuit. The term "Inuit" is itself problematic. It has been used to replace "Eskimo," a Native American term of abuse for the First Nations peoples of the Arctic, but both "Inuit" and "Eskimo" are used to lump together communities with different histories, cultures, languages and traditions. I use "Inuit" here because the writers with whom I am concerned thought in terms of a single indigenous Arctic people, and because the use of the term by some First Nations organizations provides some justification for it.

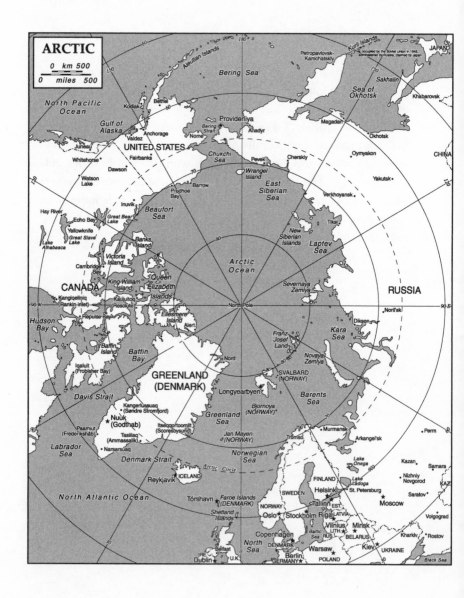

A Brief History of Polar Exploration

In the Western imagination the Arctic has always been a strange and beautiful place just over the horizon, just out of sight of the outer reaches of the continents, just off the edge of most of our maps. It lies there, close, part of the geographic imagination, and yet beyond familiarity, out of reach of the daily productions of culture and society. From the beginning of anything that might be recognized as European culture, the Arctic is present, an integral part of how Europeans imagine their continent, and yet known only for its strangeness and inaccessibility. It is "land" that is actually frozen water, land in constant and seasonal flux that resists the kind of mapping by which Europeans navigate the rest of the continent. Scandinavians— themselves regarded as odd by early imperial centers at Rome, Athens and Constantinople—are used to long winter nights and long summer days, but a space at whose heart there is one six-month day and one six-month night cannot quite seem like part of humanity's planet. There are, of course, people to whom the Arctic with all its unearthly strangenesses is home, and until late in the twentieth century visiting Europeans often regarded Inuit cultures as little more than extraordinary survival strategies. Strange waves and beams of colored light sweep down from the sky when the aurora borealis appears and, even during the day, distortions of light make vision untrustworthy, presenting travelers with several suns or a coastline far below the horizon. In practical ways at least as much as in the imagination, it is a place where none of the usual rules apply. You can put one foot in front of the other for weeks and still find that your only progress is backwards because the ice is moving south faster than you can walk north. You can survey a mountain range and then find that it is a small cairn magnified by a trick of the polar light. It is doubly hard to navigate because, the closer we approach to the pole, the still axis of the spinning world, the clearer it becomes that it is not at all still, that the spinning world wobbles. To quote from Barry Lopez's *Arctic Dreams*,

> Tectonic activity, the gravitational pull of the moon, and the continuous transport of sediments from one place to another by rivers cause the earth to wobble slightly, and its axis to shift as it does so. If the North Pole were a scribing stylus, it would trace a line every 428 days in the shape of an irregular circle, with a diameter varying from 25 to 30 feet.

The Geographic North Pole is "the average position of the center of the circle," but the ice upon which this point is located is constantly shifting, as are the other North Poles. Lopez remarks that the North Magnetic Pole moved some 400 miles between its discovery in 1831 and 1985, and the North Geomagnetic Pole is 500 miles east of that. There is also the Pole of Relative Inaccessibility, the point at the geographic center of the Arctic (the South Pole of Relative Inaccessibility is the point furthest from the coasts of Antarctica). There is no final point on the earth's surface at which it can be said that one is at the North Pole. The axis wobbles, the poles move in relation to each other, and the point around which our planet's magnetic field is arranged is not the same as its axis. We need to believe in the fixity of the North and South Poles because it holds up our maps in all sorts of ways, but polar travel undermines that belief and the whole cartographic and navigational system sometimes threatens to collapse. Occasionally stray icebergs have wandered down towards metropolitan Scandinavia and one or two kayaking Inuit have appeared, astonishingly, on the coasts of Aberdeenshire, but for the most part the Arctic is a place that we must seek to encounter. It underlies or outlies much of the cultural imagination but very rarely intrudes in visible or measurable ways. And we have sought it almost from the beginning of recorded history.

The first—distinctly shadowy—indication of European awareness of the Arctic is conventionally said to be the voyage of Pytheas of Massalia, a Greek pilot or perhaps nobleman who circumnavigated Britain, probably in the fourth century BCE. Either in the course of this voyage or on a subsequent occasion, he sailed north from the northernmost part of Britain for six days, until he reached a place called Thule where people lived on berries and millet because it was too cold for agriculture or animal husbandry. They also made mead from honey, which rather complicates the attempt to identify Thule. A further day's sailing took him to a frozen sea where the summer nights were less than three hours long. This place has been variously identified as the Shetland Islands (which would take six days to reach only in exceptionally difficult conditions, and is much more than one day away from any sea ice), Iceland (which was uninhabited then and has never had any bees), Spitzbergen (far too far to reach in six days and also not inhabited by bees) and Greenland (again, too far away). Pytheas' own account does not survive and is known only through the work of Polybius, a later Greek geographer who was critical of his predecessor and keen to undermine his claims to veracity. In this context, it is difficult to say more about Pytheas than that he brought some awareness of the Arctic into metropolitan Europe several centuries before the next recorded journeys, but the very fact of this uncertain account's survival speaks to the power of the idea of the Arctic from a very early date. The following travelers initiated an ongoing tradition in polar travel and exploration writing.

The next people to head for the Arctic systematically and leave some record of their journeys were Celtic monks seeking isolated hermitages in the seventh and eighth centuries. Some of them, by following the path of Arctic geese that passed over their monastery at the mouth of the Shannon, certainly preceded the Vikings to Iceland, where their presence is reflected in place names. Again, this is not well documented, but the construction of the Arctic as the ultimate place for retreat and reflection is important. The idea of the Celtic hermitage, an isolated and bleakly beautiful place for a solitary to live in prayer and meditation on the western fringes of northern Europe, remains powerful through centuries of literary and popular accounts of these places. Whether the monks really reached much beyond Iceland or not, the point is that the Arctic already feels like the end of a quest for unworldly peace, an intensification of the silence and wildness of Celtic retreats. This early medieval tradition of imagining the Arctic is difficult to analyze because the sources are abstruse and ambiguous, but its afterlife is enduring; even nineteenth- and twentieth-century military accounts of polar travel assume that the landscape engenders meditative awe. In the writings of the Vikings who followed these monks northwest, of course the mood changes and we encounter the first ambitious heroes of polar exploration. The major genres of polar literature were established a thousand years ago.

Meanwhile, the existence of Antarctica was inferred by the second-century Alexandrian scholar Ptolemy, whose work eventually filtered into Europe via Arabic geographers in the fifteenth century. Maps based on Ptolemy's were the basis of most fifteenth- and sixteenth-century voyages by Europeans, which explains why spectacularly successful sailing was not usually matched by even vaguely realistic ideas about the geographic relationships between starting points and destinations. Ptolemy imagined a large Southern Continent filling most of the southern hemisphere, a counterweight to Europe and Asia. Since no one knew anything about it and it was not thought to offer any prospects of trade or colonization, the Southern Continent was largely ignored for many centuries.

As the Spanish and Portuguese exploitation of South America and the East Indies began to transform those countries and their places in the perpetual European power struggle, British sailors became increasingly interested in finding shipping routes to the fabled wealth of Asia. There were few specific ideas about the place, often called "Cataya," that they were seeking, but the houses were supposedly roofed with gold, beautiful girls dressed in rich silks awaited the sailors under perfumed trees, and there were tables piled with delicious sweetmeats on gold and silver platters. This fantasy is loosely based on the writing of Marco Polo, now usually regarded as fictional. It is hard and perhaps pointless to correlate early modern ideas of geography with our own understanding of the globe, but Cataya was thought to lie east of the Holy Land and west of the Atlantic. The problem was that the Portuguese had established the route around the Cape of Good Hope as theirs, leaving the Spanish to claim the southwest passage around Cape Horn. The English accordingly had to look north, and the campaign to reach the luxurious profusion of the Pacific by sailing along the north coast of North America or across the top of Siberia was fought relentlessly for the next three hundred years. The search for a Northeast or Northwest Passage was a remarkable triumph of greed over experience, and it killed thousands of strong and healthy young men in slow and messy ways without achieving anything more lucrative than better cartography.

Heading North
The first few British Arctic voyages of the 1550s gave a clear indication of how destructive this enduring cultural obsession was to be. Sebastian Cabot, the first governor of Elizabeth I's Merchant Adventurers of England, dispatched an expedition commanded by Hugh Willoughby, with Richard Chancellor commanding the second ship. The ships were separated in a storm off the Norwegian coast, but both continued northeast. Willoughby crossed the Barents Sea before trying to over-winter in Novaya Zemlya, where he and all his crew died of cold and starvation. Chancellor landed near Archangel, from whence he made his way by sledge towards Moscow. He was well received at the court of Ivan the Terrible, and established the Muscovy Company, which continued to trade long after Chancellor's death in a shipwreck in 1556.

Martin Frobisher was the next to head north on an official expedition, and he also established precedents for catastrophe in Arctic exploration. Known for ruthless activities as a pirate as well as for having friends in high places at the Elizabethan court, Frobisher made three voyages—in 1576, 1577 and 1578—to the North American Arctic (he sailed along the coast of Greenland but could not land because there was too much ice). On the first one, he leaned out of his ship to grab an Inuit man in a canoe who had come to trade with the sailors. The man was so distressed that, according to Frobisher's sixteenth-century biographer Captain Beste, he bit his tongue in half, and died shortly after arriving in England. Frobisher also took home some pieces of black rock, which glistened like gold after being dropped into a fire. To quote the Arctic historian David Mountfield, "Men have never been able to resist the lure of gold even when the incidental difficulties attending its acquisition are larger than the likely profits," and this unconvincing black rock from the high Arctic was no exception.

Queen Elizabeth herself funded another expedition of three ships, despite the suspicion of several prominent geologists, and then chose to believe the few people who remained convinced (or at least vocal) about the gold. She sent a further fifteen ships carrying miners and 120 colonists, many of whom were taken out of prison for the purpose. The second expedition kidnapped a young Inuit woman and her baby, who died on the voyage home. The third one encountered storms and crashing ice which threatened the ships, and turned around rather than explore Hudson Bay. Despite the conditions, Frobisher carried hundreds of tons of worthless black rock back to England, where his sponsor was thrown into prison for wasting public funds while Frobisher retired to live a gentleman's life in his native Yorkshire. The combination of greed for gold, astonishing daring on the high seas and inconsistent judicial administration makes the whole episode seem stereotypically Elizabethan.

Explorers and Survivors

Next came John Davis, in the 1580s, after whom the Davis Strait between Greenland and the North American Arctic archipelago is named. Like many successful explorers who did not harm the natives and brought back most of their own men without untoward events, he is rarely discussed, but Davis accurately mapped all of the west coast of Greenland and some of the east as well as a surprisingly large part of the archipelago. He also reported the cod fishing grounds off Newfoundland.

Another of the names that now feature on the Arctic map is that of the Dutch Willem Barents, who in 1594 was able to sail through the Kara Sea. It was an unusually mild year—this achievement was not repeated for two centuries—but Barents could not know that and returned the following year to explore the waters north of Spitzbergen. The conditions were normal this year, and Barents' ship was crushed in the ice, leaving him with the appalling prospect of attempting to survive the winter in northern Novaya Zemlya with minimal equipment and provisions. He and his crew built a house out of driftwood, which had a chimney, a basic under-floor heating system and a Turkish bath made of wine barrels. Two died of malnutrition and cold and everyone else suffered badly, hunted by polar bears and harassed by foxes, but when June came fourteen survivors set off on a 1000-mile journey across the Arctic seas in open boats. Barents and two others died on the voyage, but the rest were back in Amsterdam four months later and dined out on their stories for the rest of their lives. Shortly afterwards, the Dutch established control of the East Indies and lost interest in the northern trading routes.

At the beginning of the seventeenth century, Henry Hudson was employed by the Muscovy Company to sail due north, across the pole to Asia. He passed Spitzbergen and made 80°, a farthest north that endured for over a century. His second voyage attempted a more conventional Northeast passage but returned home after the crew mutinied, which happened again on his third voyage, now in the pay of the Dutch East India Company. Hudson resolved this mutiny by turning to look for the Northwest Passage instead, and in 1609 sailed up the Hudson River past what is now New York City to Albany. It was pleasant but it was conspicuously not the North-west Passage, and on his next voyage Hudson, accompanied by his young son, sailed through the daunting straits into the bay that bears his name. Here the final mutiny of his career took place. Hudson, the little boy and five loyal crew members were abandoned in an open boat without oars or any equipment or provisions. Death would have come slowly. Four of the mutineers died in clashes with the Inuit and one starved to death, but the others reached home and, despite being sentenced to death, were allowed to live. One of them, Bylot, went on to captain William Baffin's remarkable voyage of 1616, which—although the map does not survive—charted Baffin Bay and Lancaster Sound, which is in fact the opening of the (almost always unnavigable) Northwest Passage.

During the later part of the seventeenth century, the political upheavals of the English Civil War, Cromwell's Protectorate and the Restoration left few national and military resources for polar exploration, and it was not until the middle decades of the eighteenth century that the Arctic became a focus of British attention again. By then, the Hudson's Bay Company (HBC), which had been chartered in 1670, was able to rival the Admiralty in funding and organizing expeditions, and was often more efficient and successful because of excellent local knowledge and readiness to make use of Inuit and Native American expertise. HBC trappers and voyageurs mapped vast tracts of what is now northeast Canada, but the Company was even more secretive and wary of state intervention than most big businesses, and most of this knowledge was not available to the Admiralty or anyone else. Like the Navy, the HBC imposed censorship on all letters and claimed ownership of all other manuscripts written by employees, so there were few leaks and no cooperation. This infuriated some English speculators who, bitterly resentful of the HBC's regional monopoly on trade, alleged that the company was concealing tracts of fertile land, orchards, rolling hills and (of course) gold behind the Arctic coastline. The main proponent of these allegations, Arthur Dobbs, eventually funded a private expedition which found no immediate evidence of these sunny pastures—in fact, when they tried to toast the king on the anniversary of his coronation, the wine allegedly froze as they poured it into glasses—but did, inevitably, manage to construe some of what their local First Nations informants told them to indicate that there were rivers of silver and fields of gold just a few miles further west. The view, then, that the Arctic conceals sources of unimaginable wealth is inaugurated early in the sixteenth century and, in changing form, continues to this day with the questionable interest in polar oil reserves.

The Far South

Meanwhile, the first systematic investigations of the Far South were beginning. The Spanish had been crossing the South Pacific since the early 1600s, but with much of South America to subjugate and plunder they had not spent much time mapping islands or looking for the great Southern Continent. Some private Dutch explorers, eager to break the monopoly of the Dutch East India Company, had visited parts of the coast of Australia, New Zealand and New Guinea, although they had not explored in enough detail to realize that the three countries were separate. In the second half of the eighteenth century, French explorers, keen to make up for losing Canada to the British and anxious for an empire to rival the Dutch and Spanish, began to make detailed surveys of the South Seas and mapped most of the major islands. Many of these sailors glimpsed icebergs and Antarctic mirages, and their discoveries eliminated some current ideas about the vast size of the Southern Continent, but it was not until the spectacular and culturally transformative voyages of Captain James Cook that there was any systematic survey of Antarctica itself.

Cook, who spent ten years in merchant shipping before joining the Navy, rose rapidly through the ranks until, in 1768, he was commissioned to lead an expedition to observe the transit of Venus across the sun and to explore the Southern Continent. On this first voyage, he surveyed the coast of New Zealand and the east coast of Australia and spent three months in Tahiti and the Society Islands. One of his greatest achievements was the defeat of scurvy, which killed as many as 80 percent of sailors on some voyages and only a few individuals on his. The general health and welfare of his crew were better than a similar population could have expected over the same period at home.

These priorities stood Cook in good stead on his second voyage, on which the *Resolution* and the *Adventure* spent the winters of 1773, 1774 and 1775 circumnavigating Antarctica and passing the intervening summers in the islands of the South Pacific (which was a great relief to the crew). It is no exaggeration to say that this widely publicized experience of life in Hawaii and Tahiti changed Western

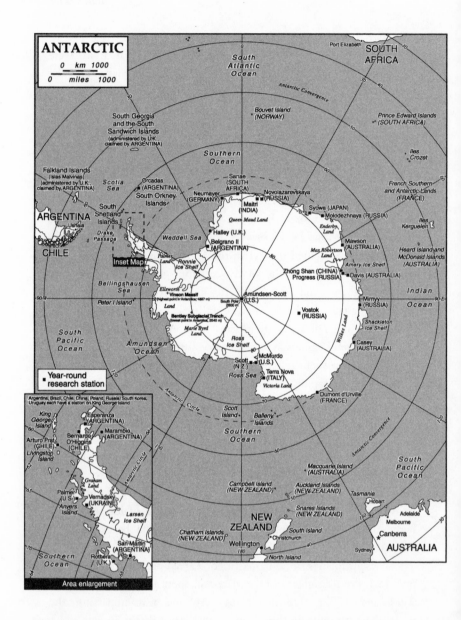

culture forever, and re-drew the popular image of earthly paradise to one that most of us would still recognize, with white sand, turquoise water and palm trees. This was an extraordinary voyage and an immense achievement, particularly as only four of the crew of 112 died in the course of the expedition, but Cook was rarely within seventy miles of the Antarctic coast and did not see the continent itself. Ice blocked his way, and he was determined not to get stuck. Cook's final voyage, which left England in 1776, charted the North Pacific, including nearly all of the Alaskan coastline and the Bering Sea. It seems fitting that, before he was killed in a misunderstanding in Hawaii in 1778, Cook was the first European to see the easternmost point of Asia and the westernmost point of North America at the same time from the middle of Bering Strait. The globe took on its modern form.

Cook's discoveries were confirmed and occasionally elaborated by the French Jean-François de Galaup, Comte de La Pérouse, who circumnavigated the world starting in 1785. At the beginning of the nineteenth century, European and American whaling ships began to descend on the South Atlantic in their thousands. These whalers certainly made innumerable discoveries, and many are known to have sailed far into the Antarctic ice in search of seals. Because of the need to keep good hunting grounds secret, and because they were paid to kill as many seals as possible rather than to explore, most of their findings are undocumented, although the firm owned and run by the Enderby brothers encouraged and paid their captains to explore and happily publicized the results.

There is still controversy about whether British sealers, American sealers or the Russian expedition of 1819–21 led by Fabian von Bellingshausen were the first to set foot on the Antarctic landmass, but it is enough to say that there was a growing Western awareness of the potential scientific importance of Antarctica. In any case, the hunters slaughtered so many whales and seals that three years after the frenzy began the population was so low that sealing was no longer worth the journey. It was unnervingly easy to kill these animals because they knew few predators and had never encountered humans. The ecological damage to the polar regions was unprecedented until the twentieth century, and it is interesting that many of the whalers, who knew more about Antarctica and its flora and fauna than anyone else, were well aware that they were reducing the populations far faster than they could regenerate. Then as now, economic necessity was used to justify environmental destruction.

In Search of the Northwest Passage
Meanwhile, the end of the Napoleonic Wars meant that the British Navy had the resources and the time to return to the quest for the Northwest Passage. The beginning of the nineteenth century was auspicious for Arctic exploration for several reasons. Huge numbers of naval officers, laid off on half pay with the cessation of hostilities, were keen to return to work in the ships now standing idle in dock and to prove themselves worthy of promotion. The government was always seeking new markets for British goods and new sources of raw materials, and the new secretary to the Admiralty, John Barrow, who served from 1804 to 1845, was an ardent polar enthusiast. Constant technological advances meant that there was always hope of the next ingenious piece of equipment, and it seemed politic to reinforce English possessions in Canada as Russian influence spread south from Alaska and the United States gazed interestedly across the undefended border. A young whaling captain, William Scoresby, whose own work on Arctic geography anticipated many of the "discoveries" of the next century, wrote to Barrow in 1817, telling him that he had seen less ice in the Greenland seas in the last two years than in recorded memory and that there had never been a better time for Arctic exploration. Barrow needed little encouragement, and the next year sent out one pair of ships under the command of David Buchan and John Franklin, to pass between Greenland and Spitzbergen, past the pole and on to the Bering Strait, and another pair, commanded by John Ross and Edward Parry, to look for the Northwest Passage in the Davis Strait between West Greenland and Canada. Other ships were sent to the Bering Strait to await the successful expedition.

The immense expectations surrounding these expeditions came to nothing. Buchan and Franklin were beset in ice just north of Spitzbergen and barely escaped, while Ross, sailing westwards through Lancaster Sound, insisted that he saw "a chain of mountains" blocking the way. Parry and the other officers saw no such thing, and were sure that the open sea ahead must be the opening of the long-sought-after passage (which it was). Ross was unbending; he named his mountain range—the Croker Mountains—and turned for home. The mountains in fact do not exist and the most probable explanation is that Ross saw a mirage of the sort that frequently misleads polar travelers. But there was gossip that Ross was afraid and invented his mountains in order to go home, and the Admiralty decided to resolve the issue by sending another expedition, this time led by the young and ambitious Parry, to establish the relationship between the Croker Mountains and the Northwest Passage. There was no officer over thirty on either ship, so they had everything to gain and the mood was intensely hopeful. A "fresh gale" sent the *Hecla* and the *Griper* scudding up Lancaster Sound, and sounding after sounding could not reach the sea bed. Very quickly, they passed Ross' furthest west and knew that the Croker Mountains were not there. The compasses sawed about and became useless, a sign that the magnetic pole was very close but not a help to navigation through the uncharted, stormbound archipelago.

On September 4, 1819, Parry passed the meridian of 110 west from Greenwich, the official definition of the Northwest Passage. But ice blocked the way west, and Parry soon had to accept that the ships would have to winter off Melville Island (see Part Two for an account of that winter). The following summer brought no relief—the ice was thicker in August than it had been the previous November—and Parry sailed reluctantly for home. In his next expedition, 1821–23, Parry tried to find a parallel way around the islands further south, but again the ice was impregnable and one of his ships, the *Fury*, was crushed. Parry left the *Fury's* stores piled on the beach where they supplied distressed explorers for decades to come and, packing everyone into the *Hecla*, headed south. His final expedition, a remarkable attempt on the North Pole by sledge, met a similar end when it became clear that however hard his exhausted men struggled north, the southward drift of the pack ice they were crossing meant that they would never move fast enough to achieve their goal before fatigue and winter set in. Nevertheless, Parry established a new furthest north which was not exceeded for fifty years.

Catastrophe in Canada

As secretary to the Admiralty, Barrow's greatest hopes were of the sailing expeditions seeking a sea route from the Atlantic to the Pacific, but he also sent out several land expeditions to chart Canada's northern-running rivers, which should, he assumed, end in an open Arctic sea. Most of these involved some cooperation with the Hudson's Bay Company and therefore depended heavily on Native American guides. John Franklin made the most famous of these journeys in 1819–22, which is well known mostly because of his later career but also because he wrote a compelling book about it. On returning from Spitzbergen, Franklin was sent to travel overland to the Great Slave Lake and then along the Coppermine River to the Arctic Ocean, where he hoped to meet Parry on his way through the Northwest Passage. Since the Navy had no expertise in wilderness trekking and a great reluctance to incur any avoidable expense, the HBC and the North West Company were required to provide assistance. It rapidly became clear that promises made in London carried little weight in the northern wilderness. The winter of 1819 was unusually harsh, and Native American and European fur traders on the brink of starvation were not very interested in an English gentleman and explorer.

The portly and sedentary Franklin was an odd choice for the mission. He insisted on taking a great deal of equipment but proved quite unable to carry much at all himself (in fact, he often had to be carried) and was constantly obliged to abandon provisions and content himself with isolated traders' undertakings to send them after him. He was so unused to snowshoes that he left footprints marked in blood across miles of snow. Despite increasingly clear evidence that the expedition's collapsing food supplies could not possibly suffice,

Franklin pressed on in the stubborn hope that some of the promises would be kept and some game would be shot. In a country where everyone was starving, this could not happen. The expedition split and split again and ended with death by starvation, insanity, murder and cannibalism. Franklin himself and a few others survived on rotten deer skins, lichen and their own leather shoes. From all points of view the expedition was catastrophic, as much because of the Admiralty's meanness as anything Franklin did or omitted to do, but Franklin's account of heroic survival was an instant bestseller which made a national hero of its author.

Franklin's second Arctic expedition, in 1825–27 was an entirely successful journey down the Mackenzie River. Having chosen his own companions and designed his own equipment, Franklin was able to spend the winters in comfort in stone houses and the summers charting thousands of miles of river and coastline. Somewhat unfairly, this well-planned and properly executed expedition is remembered mainly because Franklin departed knowing that he was leaving his first wife, Eleanor Porden, in the final stages of tuberculosis. It was not a happy marriage—she was a feminist and a poet, and he was a conservative Evangelical—and they both seem to have been relieved by the separation, but, as they had both expected, she died a few days after he left.

Stuck in the Ice

In 1829, John Ross, still in deep disfavor with the Navy, led an expedition funded by Felix Booth, the gin merchant and sheriff of the City of London, to have yet another look for the Northwest Passage. The ship was stuck in the ice for three years, but Ross' nephew James Clark Ross was able to locate the North Magnetic Pole in 1831 and built a cairn where, as he put it, "Nature had erected no monument to denote the spot which she had chosen as the center of one of her great and dark powers." The expedition formed a good relationship with the local Inuit, and the first winter seems to have been cheerful enough. But the mood darkened when the second winter brought no prospect of release. The *Victory*, the first steamship in the Arctic (which was so inefficient that it had to be used as a sailing ship), was abandoned, and the crew began to suffer badly from cold and diminishing food supplies. Ross had insisted on a diet involving as much fresh meat and fish as possible and limited alcohol, so his crew had more resistance to scurvy than most. Even so, by the time they were rescued by a whaling ship that Ross himself had once commanded, malnutrition was taking a severe toll. Ross' war wounds from twenty years earlier were opening up, and his men were too weak to bury the few who died. Nevertheless, Ross was knighted for bringing most of his men back from such a potentially disastrous expedition.

Back in 1828 the British Parliament, recognizing that wherever it lay, the Northwest Passage was not going to transform the national economy and that Arctic exploration involved immense expenditure and high death rates for no practical gain, had repealed the Act setting out rewards for progress towards the Northwest Passage and the North Pole. This brought the end of official expeditions for twenty years, but in the meantime, three Hudson's Bay Company employees, George Back, Peter Warren Dease and Thomas Simpson, mapped most of Canada's northern rivers and Arctic coast. They were followed by Dr. John Rae, another HBC man, who filled in the remaining blanks in the northeast and was thus ideally placed to offer the first sensible suggestions when Franklin went missing in the area in 1847.

Imperial Ambitions

Now that enough was known about the Arctic to make it clear that no one's fantasies of endless riches would be fulfilled there, international attention turned instead to the Antarctic. Russia, France, the United States and Britain competed enthusiastically for "discoveries," and there were several spats about who had seen or set foot on particular pieces of land first. Some of this fervor was a rational if, to modern eyes, distasteful interest in whaling, which was lucrative and increasingly difficult in the north as stocks fell, hunted to the verge of extinction. As the nineteenth century progressed, jostling for imperial status and power became a more important motive, and here the terms which were to dominate polar exploration until the end of the Cold War first appear. Whatever explorers' real sensitivities were, until the accession of Queen Victoria the rhetoric of exploration had been more concerned with expanding the total of human knowledge and engaging in science for its own sake than with nation-building.

As the British and French empires expanded and the Russians were concerned to affirm their presence in the Pacific, the United States began to assert itself as an international power. The sketched outlines of Antarctica made a good forum for the competition for national prestige. Following the Russian circumnavigation of Antarctica led by Bellingshausen, the French Dumont d'Urville spent two summers in Antarctica in 1837 and 1838, trying to sail further south than anyone else. (Earlier in his career, he had recognized the newly discovered Venus de Milo and, prevented by his captain from shipping it home, had persuaded the French ambassador to Constantinople to buy it for the nation.) He kept running into the huge American expedition led by Charles Wilkes, which was remarkably badly equipped and financed and, apart from the sighting and naming of Wilkes Land, achieved little beyond the survival of nearly all the participants—which was no small feat under the circumstances.

Spurred on by these voyages and by the growing popular and scientific interest in magnetism, the Admiralty sent James Clark Ross, commanding the *Erebus* and the *Terror*, to find the South Magnetic Pole in 1839. Having changed direction to avoid direct competition with Wilkes and d'Urville, Ross sailed easily through the pack ice and was astounded to find himself approaching a spectacular mountain landscape where he had expected only ice. The expedition moved south along the strange and eerily silent land, naming glaciers, promontories and mountains as they passed, until they came to Mount Terror and Mount Erebus, which was erupting in spectacular fashion. A small party landed on a rocky outcrop and carried out a ceremony, "taking possession of these newly discovered lands, in the name of our Most Gracious Sovereign, Queen Victoria." This moment, with the small group of huddled men planting a flag on some rocks on the shore of a continent they had barely seen and whose size they could not guess and then claiming that it belonged to a monarch in a crinoline on the other side of the world, sometimes seems to epitomize both the strange confidence and the dependence on symbolism of nineteenth-century exploration.

Ross expected to find an archipelago to match that of the Northwest Passage, but he found only mile after mile of solid ice cliffs. Winter was drawing on and at last, reluctantly, he turned north to Tasmania, then governed by John Franklin. After a winter of recreation there, Ross returned to very different Antarctic conditions. His ships were badly battered by the ice, winter came early and he headed for the Falkland Islands with both ships in need of repair. The third winter was no better, but Ross had charted huge swathes of previously unimagined land. By establishing some kind of British primacy in the coastal areas closest to the South Pole, he had also begun to set the scene for the dramas of Scott, Shackleton and Amundsen seventy years later.

"Scandinavian Ascendancy"

The next great polar event was Franklin's final expedition, John Barrow's swan-song to the Arctic and the Northwest Passage to which he had devoted his career as secretary to the Admiralty. It was the beginning of a sequence of British and American Arctic disasters which were unprecedented and subsequently unequaled.

It is probably an oversimplification, but an irresistible one, to say that the Arctic ceased to be a place of horror and catastrophe again when the "Scandinavian ascendancy" of the late nineteenth and early twentieth centuries began. The Swedish Baron A. E. Nordenskjold led the first of many detailed and successful Nordic explorations of Greenland's ice cap, and in 1878 he ran a meticulously planned international steamship expedition which passed successfully and uneventfully through the Northeast Passage. Ten years later, his protégé Fridtjof Nansen and four companions skied across Greenland. Their food supplies proved inadequate, and the journey ended with a ridiculously dangerous cruise down the fjord in an overgrown basket, but overall the expedition was a great success and confirmed Nansen's view that Inuit survival skills, intensive and detailed planning and small, democratically organized groups made for far safer and more successful journeys than the traditional Anglo-American military expeditions. It is hard to imagine better public proof of this than his subsequent polar drift in the *Fram* (see Part Two) and indeed Roald Amundsen's sledge journey to the South Pole—while Robert Falcon Scott's expeditions seem to give ample proof of the inferiority of British Arctic methodology.

Race to the Poles

By the beginning of the twentieth century, the race to the poles had started. No one now expected to find a column of black stone rising from an open sea, much less a sun-soaked land of flowers and fruit, at 90°. Those who sought the poles knew that there would be no way of knowing them when they saw them and that nothing but repeated scientific observations of latitude and longitude would make one particular step on the blizzard-scoured snow different from all the others. In the event, even this proved an overestimate of the moment's significance, as both Robert E. Peary and Amundsen had to walk a grid of a mile or two around the spot suggested by their calculations to be reasonably sure of having set foot on the poles themselves, and even then it was entirely possible that they had only come within a few feet of the goal. As it became most concrete, most physically demanding, the mission had also achieved an abstract and formal quality. All those who wanted to be first at the North and South Poles wanted personal fame and national heroism, and the governments that funded them wanted enhanced prestige for their nation-states, but nobody expected any concrete or tangible benefits of any description to result from "bagging" a pole. It was an exercise in mathematics and public relations that seemed to have little to do with the starvation and frostbite on the ground.

The American naval engineer Peary was determined to be the first person to set foot on the North Pole, and he devoted his life to this ambition. He made several attempts between 1890 and 1909, learning from each one until he developed a distinctive technique which combined the Anglo-American use of large numbers of people to relay food and supplies across the ice with the Scandinavian respect for Inuit survival skills. All of Peary's toes had been amputated as a result of severe frostbite on an earlier expedition, but by 1908, aware of Norwegian and Italian expeditions towards the pole and fearful of the rivalry of his old colleague Dr. Frederick Cook, Peary was becoming desperate. The conditions were good, and Peary sent his supporters back as planned, leaving himself, his African American servant Matthew Henson and four unnamed Inuit guides to cover the last miles. On April 6, 1909, Peary claimed that this group reached a point within two miles of the North Pole. He reported that, having made observations to demonstrate this fact, they kept going north until further observations showed that they were now going south, and then tacked around until Peary felt able to assert, "I had passed over or very near the point where north and south and east and west blend into one."

Peary came home triumphant to find that Frederick Cook had announced his own attainment of the pole a year earlier. The controversy is still not resolved beyond dispute, but it is generally thought that Cook was probably lying and that Peary probably was not. (Most of those who doubted his word did so on the prejudiced assumption that his only witnesses were not white and therefore intrinsically unreliable and/or incapable of understanding what the pole was and how it was identified.) Another possibility, espoused by some well-regarded historians of exploration, is that they were both lying.

Amundsen's expedition to the South Pole was altogether more straightforward and similarly well-planned. He had borrowed Nansen's *Fram*, telling Nansen and everyone else, including his crew, that he was going north until they were far out at sea. Amundsen knew that Scott was also planning an attempt on the South Pole but (probably) believed Scott's gentlemanly protestations that he was really only there for the science and had a merely incidental interest in such vulgarities as the pole. While Scott struggled with last-minute changes of plan and the difficulties of using ponies, Amundsen's team of skiers with dog-sledges made excellent progress, even although it turned out that their chosen route involved ascending the fearful Axel Heiberg Glacier. Undeterred by the blizzards and heavy snowfall that kept Scott and his men immured in their tents and starving, Amundsen's party continued swiftly and efficiently towards the South Pole and reached a point within a few miles of it on December 14, 1911. They paced a grid a generous twelve miles across, planted the Norwegian flag in the middle of it and returned to their base camp six weeks later, "men and animals all hale and hearty."

This energetic and professional approach to polar exploration persisted surprisingly long, despite the advent of the First World War. The Australian Douglas Mawson, who had been on Shackleton's first expedition, set out to research the evolution of penguins and Antarctica's fossils which were believed (rightly) to be of immense importance to geology. As is inevitable, Mawson's expedition (1911–14) is remembered more for its disasters than its successes. Crossing what are now the Mertz and Ninnis glaciers, one of Mawson's two companions, Ninnis, suddenly vanished with a team of dogs and the sledge carrying nearly all the expedition's food and equipment. He had fallen into a crevasse so deep that Mawson could not see the bottom of it, leaving his companions to make a frantic 300-mile dash back to their base in hopes of arriving before the little remaining food ran out and the few dogs were eaten. Mertz died in the sleeping bag he was sharing with Mawson, and Mawson crept and staggered on, arriving in time to see his relief ship disappearing over the horizon and leaving him to survive another Antarctic winter (which he did, going on to help found the Scott Polar Research Institute in Cambridge after the war).

Shackleton's Expedition

The last expedition before the war closed in and the whole business began to seem anachronistically recreational was Shackleton's. Ernest Shackleton had been on Scott's first expedition, from which he was sent home against his will because of ill health, and had been back to the Antarctic several times since. In 1914 he set out again, planning to cross the Antarctic continent from the Weddell Sea to the Ross Sea. He found that funds for the Imperial Trans-Antarctic Expedition were relatively easy to raise from private subscribers and the Royal Geographical Society, and departed with two ships in August 1914. Britain declared war on Germany as he was leaving, and Shackleton immediately telegraphed the Admiralty offering the entire expedition to the military campaign. It was Winston Churchill who telegraphed back, "Proceed."

Shackleton proceeded until his ship, the *Endurance*, was beset in the ice in January 1915. The *Endurance* was not built like the *Fram*, and the ice eventually destroyed her, crushing and twisting the huge beams as the crew watched in consternation. Shackleton had plans in place for an evacuation, and he and his men crossed the pack ice towards open water, using dogs and sledges to drag two small boats across the disintegrating ice. This was ice travel at its most dangerous. The ice was opening and closing all the time, threatening to drop men and sledges into the black water below, but there was not enough open water for the boats which would have been crushed between the floes. In April they were at last able to launch the boats and, rowing by day and sleeping on ice floes by night, reached Elephant Island. It might have been possible to try to winter there, but Shackleton was worried by the state of his crew, already seriously weakened by trauma, cold and hunger. Taking five of the fittest for companions, he set out in one of the open little boats for the island of South Georgia, where there was a whaling station, the nearest source of help.

This voyage of 800 miles across the most dangerous seas in the world has become the most famous achievement in polar exploration and, like Bligh's return home after the mutiny on the *Bounty* or Barents' men's return from Spitzbergen, it seems like the attainment of the impossible. On reaching the island, the men had still to climb cliffs and cross uncharted mountains to reach the whalers, who offered them tea and a devastating response to Shackleton's eager, "Tell me, when was the war over?" It still took Shackleton four attempts and nearly five months to get back to his men, but in the end he rescued all of them and was able to send them home, where they were immediately dispatched to the trenches in northern France.

Expeditions, of course, continued after the First World War and after the Second, through the Cold War (where the Arctic proximity of the U.S.A. and the U.S.S.R. was a source of great anxiety) and on into the twenty-first century. But Shackleton, who refused to take a radio transmitter for fear of interference of any kind from home, and whose receiver oddly failed to work, was the last for whom the polar regions were entirely separate from the rest of the world, and therefore the last for whom polar values and ideology could be completely set apart from those at home. Shackleton's valuation of his men's lives above all else had no place in the battlefields of the First World War, where a generation of men was obliterated.

When scientists and explorers returned to the high latitudes after the Second World War, they were experimenting with aeroplanes, which were intrinsically no harder to fly over the poles than over the English Channel or the Midwest and could, at least in theory, reach embattled travelers with food and medical supplies in a matter of hours. Shackleton is conventionally seen as the last in the "Age of Heroism," but of course heroism of all kinds continues in the Antarctic as everywhere else, and it would be foolish to give weight to nostalgia for the days when polar exploration was—and celebrated being—male, white and frequently dead. Shackleton's voyage, like most of the awe-inspiring feats of polar explorers, was a response to a nasty and dangerous situation that neither he nor any other sane person would choose to encounter.

As Jennie Darlington's *My Antarctic Honeymoon* and other writing suggest, the Arctic and Antarctic may have offered a dubious escape to some men who found it difficult to cope with the demands of everyday routines and relationships, but in the age of air travel and then snowmobiles, submarines, jeeps of various kinds, helicopters and at last global positioning systems, satellite navigation and e-mail, such escapes have become more and more specious. Modern Antarctic bases and Arctic oil and military stations have cinemas, fast food outlets and shops as well as flush toilets and central heating.

It was, of course, always a fantasy that the polar regions are qualitatively different from the rest of the world, as anyone who has lived and worked within the Arctic Circle can confirm. It is space like any other, inhabited by human beings like any other and being destroyed by human beings like everywhere else on earth. The story that begins with Pytheas bringing the Arctic into metropolitan and imperial geography ends with the melting of the ice caps and the redundancy of Inuit survival techniques. The polar regions will soon look like everywhere else, and ice will no longer signify our planet's axis.

Writing on Ice

Writing about the Arctic and Antarctic has been popular at least since the expansion of English print culture in the eighteenth century and probably long before that. The Norse influence on very early English writing meant that there was constant awareness of the landscapes of the far north even though it is hard to clarify any specifically Arctic references. In the early modern period, there were two, closely related compendia of travel writing which were very widely read and used as sources by writers including Shakespeare, Thomas More, Milton and Jonathan Swift. Both Hakluyt's *Principal Navigations, Voyages, Traffiques and Discoveries of the English Nation* and Samuel Purchas' *Purchas his Pilgrims*, devote significant space to the polar regions, and both were popular as sixteenth- and seventeenth-century recreational reading as well as influencing major writers. By the eighteenth century, travel writing was outselling everything but religious and devotional works, so that book buyers were spending more on travel books than they were on fiction. By the beginnings of English Romanticism in the 1790s, the Arctic and, in a different way, the Antarctic, were taking on a definite cultural role, broadly related to that period's interest in landscape and wilderness (see Part Six).

For the Victorians in England and for their contemporaries in North America, Arctic literature was a recognizable genre increasingly exploited by novelists and poets. From Charlotte Bronte's fascination for Parry and the polar fantasy scenes in *Jane Eyre* to some truly dreadful adventure books for boys, the Arctic began to figure in the English Victorian imagination as a place where mettle could be tested and personal worth affirmed. The disappearance of the Franklin expedition (in 1847) and the aftermath of that disappearance both complicated and entrenched this view, for Lady Jane Franklin's public campaigns for apparently endless research into her husband's death kept Arctic exploration in the headlines, at least until it was displaced by the Crimea. It was through the Franklin disaster that Dickens, Wilkie Collins and Tennyson came to write about the far north, in all cases presenting it as a testing ground for upper-class Victorian heroic masculinity. Ian Stone, writing in *The Dickensian* of 1987, quotes from a contribution to Dickens' widely read periodical *Household Words*:

> For three hundred years the Arctic seas have now been visited by European sailors; their narratives supply some of the finest modern instances of human energy and daring, bent on a noble undertaking, and associated constantly with kindness, generosity and simple piety. The history of Arctic enterprise is stainless as the Arctic snows, clean to the core as an ice mountain.

This theme of the Arctic's literal and metaphorical cleanliness is developed in George Macdonald's children's book, *At the Back of the North Wind* (see Part Six). It is with this kind of writing that the Arctic begins to look like a sacred land of English chivalry, testing ground and churchyard combined. Arctic deaths now start to feel like martyrdoms simply because anyone who was there was assumed to be serving his country by definition, by being an Englishman striving to be in the Arctic. It is a typical popular elision of physical challenges and difficulties with moral triumph, reflected in Tennyson's epitaph for Franklin:

> Not here! The white North has thy bones; and thou
> Heroic sailor-soul,
> Art passing on a happier voyage now
> Toward no earthly pole.

The Arctic becomes a kind of prototype for Heaven, the scene of the ultimate Victorian quest narrative.

Much of the writing coming out of Robert Falcon Scott's journeys in the Antarctic can be seen to continue this tradition in a deeply conservative way. Antarctica can be less problematically assimilated into a quest narrative because no one has ever lived there. Nineteenth-century accounts of Arctic survival against all the odds or eventual, inevitable but heroic defeat by unbelievably difficult conditions are always to some extent undermined by the continuing progress of Inuit cultures and societies in precisely the same locations and conditions. Antarctica on the other hand lends itself much more readily to representations of an almost entirely metaphorical landscape, where extreme cold is simply a challenge to planning/moral fiber and storms are sent to define the limits of travelers' ability to cope. In the years after the First World War the minimalist aesthetic of Antarctica combined with this abstract understanding of the place to make it appealing to Modernist writers and painters, but in Scott's journal and his subsequent hagiography, Antarctica figures mostly as the stage setting for an "artistic, Christian" progress towards a glorious martyrdom for men who were too good for the post-war world. T. S. Eliot is probably invoking both the modernist and traditional readings of the Far South in Section V of *The Waste Land* where he borrows Shackleton's image of a spectral extra presence on the final march:

> Who is the third who walks always beside you?
> When I count, there are only you and I together
> But when I look ahead up the white road
> There is always another one walking beside you

All three of the men racing across South Georgia to bring help for those left behind had a constant sense of a fourth person accompanying them, but in Eliot's poem this "other one" seems to figure as an absence or a displacement, one of many of *The Waste Land*'s images of departed meaning.

Over the last century, literary representations and ways of imagining the polar regions have become increasingly diverse, and the most marked change is the development of an entire genre of Canadian Arctic literature. This is beyond the scope of this book, but twentieth-century Canadian writing shows a growing engagement with the far north, reflected in the interests of Margaret Atwood, Mordecai Richler, Aritha von Herk and Rudy Wiebe among others. While *The Frozen Ship* is primarily concerned with ways of imagining the polar regions as both alien and remote, this Canadian genre is broadly interested in the Arctic as part of Canada's present and future national identity (see, for example, Margaret Atwood's *Wilderness Tips* and *Strange Things: The Malevolent North in Canadian Literature* and John Moss' *Enduring Dreams*).

There is also a growing Australian literature on Antarctica, much of it with a post-colonial consciousness of the British sense of historical ownership of a place that is much closer to Australia. Nearly all European Antarctic expeditions made their final ports of call either there or in New Zealand, and in both places there is an increasing literary interest in the relationship between Antarctica and post-colonial national identities.

Much of the most recent Antarctic writing is still dominated by Scott just as Arctic literature continues to be powered by the Franklin expedition and its afterlives. It is clear that these two men and their flawed expeditions are as central to a post-modern, post-colonial polar canon as they were to the Boy's Own writers on polar heroes. Disaster remains compelling to the most and least sophisticated writers.

PART ONE

Making a Home

Nearly all polar travel writing is concerned with journeys starting and ending at home in Europe or North America, and lasting (or intended to last) no more than a year or two. These journeys are typically undertaken by groups of men, who regard the time spent in the highest latitudes as outside and alien to "ordinary life." Some, like Fridtjof Nansen and Richard Byrd, long for their homes and families even as they achieve extraordinary things, while others—Captain Oates of Scott's Antarctic Expedition and Charles Francis Hall looking for Franklin, for example—glory in the boys-only freedom from domesticity and certain kinds of social convention. All of them leave their homes and families and head north or south in order to achieve something specific—like finding the South Pole or Franklin, or proving that polar currents, glaciers or penguins behave in a certain way. When they return, or die in the attempt, they have failed or succeeded but in either case, the journey is concluded; it was an episode set apart from daily life.

This is part of the appeal of polar travel writing, which has much in common with the quest narrative. The travelers and explorers in this section take a more radical and imaginative approach to the strange spaces at the top and bottom of the world. Eerily confident that ideology will triumph over time and tide, they leave everything they have ever known and set out to establish forms of domesticity on the polar ice. For most of them, the expectation is that the very strangeness of the Arctic, the dark winter days and light summer nights, the aurora borealis, the surreal structures of icebergs, indicate a kind of Promised Land in which daily life will be mysteriously different and better. The daily round will be transformed and glorified by extraordinary surroundings far from the pressures and stresses of life in the home country, and beside this the inconveniences of cold, distance and shortages of food count for nothing.

It is not surprising that this compelling but unworldly vision seems to be founded in the experiences of early medieval Irish anchorites, who combined remarkable navigation skills and seamanship with a desire for hermitages in the North Atlantic archipelago. This fantasy of the remote, windswept little house overlooking the Arctic seas in which one will be able to be as God intended is a surprisingly pervasive tradition. It can be seen to connect poets from the early Saxon *Seafarer* ("the cry of the gannet was all of my gladness/The call of the curlew, not the laughter of men") to the popular 1990s American television drama *Northern Exposure*. It is a vision of the far North as old as the English language. Nevertheless, the Celtic monks were quickly overtaken by Nordic (Viking) communities emigrating westwards, first to Iceland, then to Greenland and finally to North America. The settlement of Iceland, which had previously been uninhabited, was straightforward, and most modern Icelanders are descended from the tenth-century emigrants. The next step west began an extraordinary and unresolved story which is central to the cultural history of the Far North.

I
Medieval Norse Sagas and the Pagan Prophetess

Graenlendiga Saga and *Eirik's Saga*, published together as *The Vinland Sagas*, provide detailed accounts of the Viking colonization of Greenland. The sagas are rarely in any way novelistic or biographical, their purpose being to chart the inauguration and development of the Icelandic nation, but they are certainly a crucial part of the Western literature of the Arctic and they fascinated later writers from Coleridge through W. H. Auden to Seamus Heaney. Part of the appeal of the Vinland Sagas, the records of the medieval Norse colonization of parts of Greenland and North America, is that the plain style and minimalist approach to narrative gives the impression of people who simply thought of things—killing the neighbors or founding a colony in Greenland—and did them. There is very rarely any account of deliberation or doubt, and most interactions are described with an ellipsis that leaves much to the imagination. This literary style as much as anything else may be responsible for the enduring image of ultra-masculine Vikings whose daring deeds know no limits, and since Nordic polar travelers in the late nineteenth and early twentieth centuries saw themselves acting out their Viking heritage, the sagas are in some ways fundamental to the most successful polar expeditions in history.

Iceland in the tenth century was a democracy of hill-farmers, who met at an annual Thing (parliament) where grievances accumulated over the previous year were resolved and penalties determined. Exile was often used to free the country from persistent trouble-makers. In about 960, according to *Eirik's Saga*, "a man called Thorvald" and his son Eirik the Red "left their home in Jaederen, in Norway, because of some killings and went to Iceland" where they settled in the south. Here Eirik killed two men and was banished to the west, where a feud between him and some neighbors ensued. Eirik was banished again. He prepared his ship for a long voyage and told his supporters that he was going in search of the land that had been seen to the west by sailors blown off-course. The voyage, around the year 985, was successful. To quote the saga:

He found the country he was seeking and made land . . . he sailed south down the coast to find out if the country were habitable there. He spent the first winter on Eirik's Island, which lies near the middle of the Eastern Settlement. In the spring he went to Eiriksfjord, where he decided to make his home. That summer he explored the wilderness to the west and gave names to many of the landmarks there. . . . He spent the second winter on Eiriks Holme, off Hvarks Peak. The third summer he sailed all the way north to Snaefell. . . . Then he turned back and spent the third winter on Eirik's Island, off the mouth of Eiriksfjord.

He sailed back to Iceland the following summer and put in at Breidafjord. He named the country he had discovered Greenland, for he said that people would be much more tempted to go there if it had an attractive name. . . . Next summer he set off to colonize Greenland. . . . In the summer in which Eirik the Red set off to colonize Greenland, twenty-five ships sailed from Breidafjord and Borgarfjord, but only fourteen reached there; some were driven back and some were lost at sea.

Despite the difficult voyage, which meant that contact with Iceland and Norway was unreliable, the colony seems to have been stable and successful until the beginning of the sixteenth century. The hill-farms clustered around two settlements, Esterbyggd or the Eastern Settlement, just west of the southern tip of Greenland, and Vestrebyggd or the Western Settlement, several hundred miles further up the west coast. (It is thought that the east coast was inaccessible because of ice.) The colonists were pagan for a few years after leaving Iceland, and there is a fascinating account in *Eirik's Saga* of the visit to Herjolfsness (in Esterbyggd) of a prophetess clad in white cat's fur:

There was a woman in the settlement who was called Thorbjorg; she was a prophetess, and was known as the Little Sybil. She had had nine sisters, but she was the only one left alive. It was her custom in winter to attend feasts. . . .

Thorkel invited her to his house and prepared a good reception for her, as was the custom when such women were being received. A high-seat was made ready for her with a cushion on it, which had to be stuffed with hen's feathers.

She arrived in the evening with the man who had been sent to escort her. She was dressed like this: she wore a blue mantel fastened with straps and adorned with stones all the way down to the hem. She had a necklace of glass beads. On her head she wore a black lambskin hood lined with white cat's-fur. She carried a staff with a brass-bound knob studded with stones. She wore a belt made of touchwood, from which hung a huge pouch, and in this she kept the charms she needed for her witchcraft. On her feet were hairy calfskin shoes with long thick laces which had large tin buttons on the ends. She wore catskin gloves, with the white fur inside.

When she entered the room everyone felt obliged to proffer respectful greetings, to which she responded according to her opinion of each person. . . .

Later that evening the tables were set up; and this is what the prophetess had for her meal; she was given a gruel made from goat's milk, and a main dish of hearts from the various kinds of animals that were available there. She used a brass spoon, and a knife with a walrus-tusk handle bound with two rings of copper; the blade had a broken point.

This is one of very few surviving accounts of Nordic paganism, which either vanished very quickly with the arrival of Christianity or, more likely, was not described by the priests and monks who wrote most of the sagas. This compellingly strange vignette stands almost in isolation, and it also gives unusual detail about contemporary social life. When Eirik married, his wife Thjodhild "refused to live with him" until he converted to Christianity. The priest who arrived a few years later initiated widespread conversion, although archaeological evidence suggests that pagan beliefs coexisted with Christianity, at least as a last resort or back-up, until the end of the colony. Still, over the next centuries several letters from a succession of popes attest to their spasmodic concern for the people (and the tithes, i.e., church taxes) of the remote Gardar see, and by around 1200 a cruciform cathedral was built at Gardar in the center of the Eastern Settlement. To quote from historian Kristen Seaver's *The Frozen Echo*:

> Though no match for the ambitious ecclesiastical edifices going up elsewhere in Europe at that time, Gardar cathedral distinguished itself by size and shape from the surrounding stone-and-turf houses. It was built of blocks of the local red sandstone, which had a handsome pattern of white dots and circles, and it had moulded soapstone trim. Huge sandstone slabs paved the way from the sacristy to the main door of the episcopal dwelling. We also know that the cathedral had a separate bell tower and windows of opaque, greenish glass.

As Seaver suggests, compared to Durham or Salisbury which were built at the same time, Gardar cathedral sounds primitive, but it was larger and more complex than any subsequent building in Greenland until the late nineteenth century, and it was built at a time when everyone in the settlement was engaged in subsistence farming of difficult land and would have been hard pressed to spare time and materials. Access to technology was limited, there was very little wood, and nearly all metal had to be imported on the rare ships that also brought more basic commodities. Life in Greenland was clearly demanding, but probably no more so than elsewhere in medieval Northern Europe. At the high point of the mid-thirteenth century, the combined population of the two settlements was around 6,000. For the first centuries of the colony, the settlers probably encountered no Inuit, for the climate was relatively warm and the colonies a long way south of where the Inuit seem to have been concentrated at the time. The Norse seem not to have acquired Inuit survival skills or hunting techniques, but there is no evidence that they suffered significantly from this lack. The settlers supported themselves with a modified version of the subsistence fishing and farming practiced all around the North Atlantic into the twentieth century. Unlike the Norwegians, Icelanders and Faroese, the Norse Greenlanders grew no wheat and very little other grain, and engaged in seasonal hunting of seals to eat and animals whose pelts could be traded.

Subsistence was a full-time activity and even the clergy at the cathedral also worked the farms, but there is no evidence from graveyards or homesteads that the diet was routinely inadequate, and mortality seems to have been low compared to contemporary Britain and Scandinavia. It was not a complex or leisured society, but ecclesiastical and secular artifacts demonstrate high levels of craftsmanship. Although it is not clear how efficiently tithes and taxes were collected, at its most prosperous the economy was producing enough of a surplus that tax collectors in Norway and Rome, if not Greenland, expected taxes to be paid. Many small churches as well as the cathedral were built and maintained over several centuries, which would not have happened in a community always struggling to survive. Generations upon generations were born, married and buried, engaged in arts and crafts, farming and hunting, worship and politics taking for granted that southern Greenland was, and always would be, an ordinary part of the Nordic community. Their houses were extremely commodious for the Middle Ages, with running water, saunas and cellars in the permafrost which made admirable refrigerators. There is, in short, no obvious explanation of the complete and abrupt disappearance of the Norse Greenlanders from written record around the beginning of the fifteenth century.

Awareness of strange tidings from Greenland filtered slowly into plague-stricken Northern Europe. Few texts survive—perhaps, amid the devastation of the Black Death, no one cared enough to write about lost peripheral communities—and for most of the following centuries the fate of the Norse Greenlanders was an alarming mystery. We do know with reasonable certainty that in 1341 a priest called Ivar Bardarson was sent from the Bergen diocese in Norway to investigate a falling-off in the payment of tithes and other taxes. He arrived at the Eastern Settlement to find the church struggling to maintain the power it held elsewhere in Europe. There were few, elderly clergy ministering to a very scattered population of independent farmers, and tithes were difficult to collect partly because money had never figured in the Greenlandic economy, which depended on bartering more useful commodities. Excavating in the 1930s, Poul Norlund found walrus skulls ritually arranged in the graveyards at Gardar and Herjolfsness and burial places inside the church at Herjolfsness, presumably those of the clergy, containing amulets and boxes of food—odd finds in a place which had allegedly been Christian for several centuries, and ones which Norlund interpreted to mean that, deprived of any contact with the metropolis, the Greenlandic community had "regressed into primitivism." It is equally possible that Greenlandic Christianity had always retained pre-Christian elements, especially in the absence of much episcopal supervision, and a degeneration of the relationship between the Norse settlers and the Norwegian administration need not indicate any deterioration in the viability of the Greenland community itself. However, when he eventually sailed up to the Western Settlement, Ivar Bardarson found an eerie scene. He saw the houses along the coast from the sea, and as the ships approached the sailors could see animals grazing around the small farms. Drawing closer, they saw racks where fish were drying, but "there are left some horses, goats, cattle and sheep, all feral, and no people either Christian or heathen." All the buildings were intact and seemingly inhabited and the big church at Stensness still furnished, but there was no sign of anyone present or recently departed.

There are several puzzling aspects of this mystery: the description specifies "horses, goats, cattle and sheep," of which, as Kristen Seaver points out, only goats and sheep would have stood any chance of surviving a winter without byres and dried fodder. This suggests that, if the colonists had gone, they had left no more than a few weeks before Bardarson arrived. Furthermore, there is clear archaeological evidence that at least some of the farms in the Western Settlement were inhabited for several decades after Ivar Bardarson left Greenland in about 1350, although this evidence too points to fairly sudden desertion. At one farm, archaeologists found a larder still stocked with a wide range of fish and game, and a goat's knuckle, two soapstone shards and a small silver shield engraved with a Scottish coat of arms used by the Campbells in the mid-fourteenth century. The idea of contact between Greenland and Western Scotland seems surprising, but it is not incredible. If we think of the geography of the North Atlantic in terms of an archipelago rather than a continent and outlying islands, it seems sensible that sailors would progress from the Scottish mainland to the Orkneys, on to the Shetlands and then the Faroes and then either up to Iceland and across or straight to southern Greenland (which is a long way west but not far north of Scotland). Such voyages would have been secret because there was a Norwegian monopoly on trade with Greenland, but the fact that they happened undermines the suggestion that the Western Settlement was dying out before or even for some decades after Bardarson and his companions found it deserted. It is quite possible that the inhabitants of the Western Settlement knew a tax collector when they saw one and evaded him accordingly, hiding in the hills until he went away. Nevertheless, Bardarson's account was accepted in Norway, and there is no documentary evidence of further visits to the west until eighteenth-century travelers went to see the ruins.

The Eastern Settlement, according to both official documents and archaeological findings, lasted longer: the last ships known to have visited left Norway in 1406. It is important that this was a private voyage, and the last official supply ship had sailed around forty years earlier, for the erosion of Norwegian state infrastructure by plague and climatic deterioration meant that the colony was slipping from metropolitan control, and undocumented, illegal voyages, made under the reasonably plausible excuse of drifting off course from Iceland, became more flagrant. One result of this loosening of connections between the Norse Greenlanders and their Norwegian governors was that very little was written in Norway about Greenland and anything that was written in Greenland disappeared along with the Greenlanders. It is frustrating that this lapse into silence precedes the disappearance of the settlement, for we are left with no stories at all about the colony's decline and fall. Thirteenth-century sagas tell of thriving communities and memorable parties, and the next tale is of abandoned homesteads and desolate settlements. It is precisely this silence that makes the story of the Norse Greenlanders so attractive to later writers on the Arctic.

The last ships, then, sailed under Thorstein Olafsson, the most important of the group of young Icelandic noblemen. They stayed at the Eastern Settlement for four years, and Thorstein married Sigrid Bjornsdatter, the daughter of another wealthy Icelander, at the church in Hvalsey in 1408. The very fact of contracting an extremely important dynastic marriage there suggests that it was taken for granted that Greenland was part of the dynamic Nordic society of the day. Three banns were published, and more people were present in the church than lived within a day's journey of Hvalsey; people with the time and resources to undertake long journeys merely for pleasure are not on the brink of extinction. In 1410, Thorstein and his cohorts left Greenland and the Icelandic chroniclers had no further interest in recording what happened there.

The next document relating to the colony is a letter sent in 1448 from Pope Nicholas V to unnamed bishops in Iceland (contact between Iceland and Rome had broken down when the Black Death reached Iceland in 1410), requesting funding to choose and consecrate another bishop of Gardar. It was fifty years since the death of the previous incumbent and nearly a century since a bishop had last set foot in Greenland. The money was not forthcoming and no contact with Greenland was attempted. There are few further accounts of visits to Greenland between Thorstein's departure in 1410 and the arrival of Hans Egede in 1721. One is by "John Greenlander," an English sailor who "drifted" to the west coast while fishing for cod in the 1530s. This was printed in Danish in 1624, and to quote Hans Egede's 1745 version:

> He narrowly escaped being cast away, and lost with Ship and Crew upon the dreadful Rocks of Greenland, by getting in at last to a fine Bay, which contained many Islands, where he happily came to an Anchor under a desert Island; and it was not long before he spied several other Islands not far off, that were inhabited; which for fear of the Inhabitants, he for a while did not dare to approach; till at last he

pluck'd up a good Heart, and sending his Boat on Shore, went to the next House, which seem'd but very small and mean. Here he found all the Accoutrements, necessary to fit out a Fishing-Booth, or small Hut, made up of Stones, to dry Fish therein, as it is customary in Iceland. There laid a dead Body of a Man, extended upon the Ground, with his Face downwards; a Cap sewed together on his Head; the rest of his cloathing was made partly of coarse cloth, and partly of Seal-Skin; an old rusty Knife was found at his Side, which the Captain took, in order to shew it to his Friends at his Return home to Iceland, to serve for a Token of what he had seen.

There are intriguing gaps in this fourth-hand, twice-translated account. Were the "inhabitants" of the "several other islands" visible, or was their presence only inferred from the houses? If they were there, were they Inuit or Norse? How old was the man, and was there any clue about the cause of death? Less importantly for the archaeologists, but equally odd to the reader, did John Greenlander leave the body lying face down by the fish-drying rack, having had a good look at his clothes? In much Arctic writing the fact that nothing decomposes forms part of the fascination, for food and even faces look much the same after a century or two of freezing. This is not the case in southern Greenland, where summer temperatures are quite high enough to allow decomposition. The man cannot have been there for very long, and yet it seems there was no one to bury him. There is, of course, no reason to treat this shadowy and laconic account as factually reliable, but it is the only one available and it certainly had an impact on its readers. The story is so effective in its strangeness that one can see why archaeologists treat it with caution—it seems too much like fiction—but in accounting for the European mythology of the Arctic it is important. The mysterious John may have been the last European person to see these buildings for four hundred years, by which time most of them were hollows in the ground and fallen walls.

As mentioned, Martin Frobisher and John Davis sailed along the Greenland coast in the 1570s and 1580s, but made only limited explorations. In 1605–06 James Hall was sent by the king of Denmark to Greenland with instructions to explore its west coast. When Captain W. A. Graah set off from Copenhagen in 1828, he still carried naval instructions based on the assumption that he would find the Norse Greenlanders thriving—an indication of how long the myth persisted in the national consciousness. Graah went to the east coast because the last expedition to look in the west, James Hall's, had made it hard to return. One can see why Hall's behavior (quoted here in Graah's account) gave rise to a certain amount of local hostility:

> Hall. . . seized four of the natives, who, however, made so desperate a resistance, that he found it necessary to put one of them to death, in order to intimidate the rest, who thereupon quietly submitted to be conveyed on board. Their countrymen, meanwhile, assembled about the ship, apparently with the intent of preventing its departure. They that were dispersed, however, by a discharge of musketry and cannon, and the ship sailed with the three captives.

Not surprisingly, Admiral Lindenow's Danish expedition in 1607 found that "the natives showed signs of hostility and seemed determined to prevent him landing." Someone sent on shore who "had hoped by means of presents to conciliate the natives" was immediately stabbed to death. It seems quite possible that it was this incident which gave rise to the idea that the Norse Greenlanders had been massacred by the Inuit (which was the received version of most nineteenth-century historians). In fact, there is no record anywhere in the history of foreign presence in the Arctic of any Inuit group making an unprovoked attack on anyone, and little archaeological evidence of violence. Further expeditions in the 1650s and 1670s were blocked by ice, suggesting that there was some climate change towards the likely end of the Norse colonization period in the early seventeenth century, and the next person to seek the site of the lost colonies was Hans Egede in 1721, followed by the Moravian mission of the 1730s. Egede landed on Greenland's southwest coast, and there founded the new settlement of Godthåb (now Nuuk).

These missionaries were not only fascinated but motivated by the vanished Norse settlement. They felt called by God to find and resurrect the colony, to repopulate the deserted farms and reconsecrate the empty churches, to create again an Arctic homeland far from the anxieties of nationhood and sovereignty racking contemporary Scandinavia.

II
Full of Fruit: Hans Egede's Greenland

Hans Egede was born in 1686 and grew up on the Lofoten Islands off the northwest coast of Norway. People there lived by the same mixture of subsistence farming and fishing that sustained isolated farmsteads and villages all around the North Atlantic from Wales to Greenland, but it was a harsher environment than most, with little fertile land, long, hard winters of almost complete darkness and a long, hard journey to even the smallest centers of commerce and culture. It was probably a good training for his vocation, for soon after his ordination as a Lutheran pastor, Egede began to hear an insistent call to go to Greenland. He had read about the lost Norse colonies and become convinced that the communities were still there, albeit cut off from communication with the rest of Europe for two hundred years. Egede was particularly concerned that the Norse Greenlanders had had no contact with the church for so long, and worried about the souls of those who must have folk memories of Christianity but had no one to guide them in the ways of salvation. He became convinced that God was calling him to find them and bring them into the Lutheran fold.

As with all Arctic travel, finding funding proved the most difficult part of the whole enterprise, but Egede eventually persuaded the king of Denmark (of which Norway was then part) to finance the beginning of a mission on the understanding that he would combine evangelizing with trade. Denmark still had a monopoly on trade with Greenland, which was used only for fishing, and the Danish administration had high hopes of a fur trade to rival that of the Hudson's Bay Company. Needless to say, this never materialized, but Egede knew how to cash in on royal ambitions, and wrote an effective dedication to his published account of the mission:

> The poor Greenlanders have a Right to claim your Protection, as well as the Kingdoms of Denmark and Norway; and are in Hopes of enjoying, one Day, the greatest Blessings under Your happy Reign. . . .

When the poor Greenlanders shall have learned to know and worship
God, as their Creator and Redeemer, then they will likewise learn to
acknowledge and honour a Christian Sovereign as their King and Ruler.

Egede was convinced that this double domestication, bringing
Greenland back under Danish rule and Lutheran ideology, and
allowing Danish families to make homes there, would turn Greenland
back into the Elysium he was sure it had once been. Other travelers
believed that battling through the ice might bring them to somewhere
flowing with milk and honey (usually seekers of the Northwest
Passage who hoped for a marvelous and exotic Orient just across the
Bering Strait), but Egede and his colleague David Crantz were alone
in their conviction that faith could transfigure the frozen Arctic into
a land of profusion. Egede wrote excitedly:

Nicolas Zenetur, a Venetian by Birth, who served the King of Denmark
in the Quality of a Sea Captain, is said by chance to have been driven
upon the Coast of Greenland in the Year 1380; and to have seen that
same Dominican Convent. His Relation is alledged by Kircherus in
the following Words: "Here is also a Dominican Convent to be seen,
dedicated to St. Thomas, in whose Neighborhood there is a Vulcano
of a Mountain that spews Fire, and at the Foot thereof a Well of
burning-hot Water. This hot Water is not only conveyed by Pipes into
the Convent, and through all the Cells of the Friars, to keep them
warm, as with us the Rooms are heated by Stoves of Wood-Fire or
other Fuel; but here they also boil and bake their Meat and Bread
with the same. This Vulcano, or fiery Mountain, throws out such a
Quantity of Pumice-Stone, that it hath furnished Materials for the
Construction of the whole Convent: There are also fine Gardens,
which reap great Benefit from this hot Water, adorn'd with all Sorts
of Flowers, and full of Fruit. And after the River has watered these
Gardens, it empties itself into the adjoining Bay, which causes it never
to freeze; and great Numbers of Fish and Sea-Fowl flock thither,
which yields plentiful Provision for the Nourishment of the
Inhabitants."

The 1930s archaeologist Poul Norlund described finding the remains of what may very well have been a convent by the only hot springs in Greenland, opposite the island of Unartok, although there are no active volcanoes there. The existence or otherwise of the garden cannot be determined, but in Iceland, where farmland is laced with hot springs, this has only really affected agriculture since greenhouses became available in the twentieth century. Much, if not all, of this account is clearly exaggerated and perhaps fantastic. The presentation of most of it as a quotation demonstrates Egede's need to lend weight to the idea of the Arctic utopia, implying that other authorities support his view of Greenland's untapped potential. The emphasis on the ease of this life in the Far North is characteristic: "with us the rooms are heated by stoves," whose fuel must be painstakingly gathered, but here not the rooms but the people are much more tenderly "kept warm" by the land itself, which also provides the means of cooking as well as the food. There is no mention of human agency or effort in the planting or cultivation of the luxurious gardens either; the profusion of fruit and flowers is presented as almost naturally occurring, "reaping benefit" from the river which waters them before conveniently "emptying itself" in such a way as to provide yet further "plentiful provision" for the happy dwellers. (In fact, the only fruits that occur naturally in Greenland are small mountain berries such as bilberries and cranberries, which have a very short season and would certainly not thrive on hot water; anything else would need to be imported and planted even if it then grew well without further effort on the part of the monks and nuns.) The land has even spontaneously "furnished materials" for the building of the "whole convent," phrasing which suddenly reveals the peculiarity of the appreciation of Arctic land, for it is not clear where else building materials would come from, or where and how land offers, or even *furnishes*, material for less than a whole building. Even the Gardar cathedral was built of local stone.

Helge Ingstad, an eminent Norse archaeologist, offers an equally enchanted but very different reading of the same place, suggesting a more conventional form of Arctic romanticism also inspired by the lost colonies:

An Arctic nunnery. Here women walked in the black, voluminous habit and white coif of the Benedictine order.... What was the daily life, what were the thoughts of the women who dwelt here in the shadow of the inland ice?

We don't know. Women lived here for several hundred years, busy with their affairs, and we know nothing about them. We have found some ruins on the grassland, a few little objects handled by the women, and a number of skeletons; no more . . .

. . . The monks did not choose the smiling landscape for their house, but the wildest and bleakest, under steep mountains with scree at their foot and ice-scoured walls. It was in their shadow that they had built the little monastery of stone and turf.... They turned their minds to sea and mountain, stone and earth: a step on the stair to God.

Ingstad's account is as fully engaged as Egede's, but what Ingstad celebrates is the heroism of any enactment of ordinary life in this place so strange and distant that it seems to be on the way out of the world. The women dressed in the same clothes as Benedictines across Europe from Denmark to Spain, they were busy with their quiet lives despite "the shadow of the inland ice." The monastery, very close by, leads the ascetic monks to be absorbed in the land as a prototype of absorption into God, as a fitting prelude to eternal life. There is no profusion here, no fantastic provision of fruit and game, but an equally exotic Arctic sublime. Egede recognizes the aesthetic appeal of the icy landscape, but he remains convinced that it is a modern aberration, superseding the plenteous land that was enjoyed by the Norse Greenlanders and that will return if only the deserted settlements can be found and repopulated:

As to the Nature of the Soil, we are informed by ancient Histories, that the Greenland Colonies bred a Number of Cattle which afforded them Milk, Butter and Cheese in such abundance, that a great Quantity thereof was brought over to Norway, and for its prime and particular Goodness was set apart for the King's Kitchin, which was practiced until the reign of Queen Margaret. We also read in these Histories, that some Parts of the Country yielded the choicest Wheat-Corn, and in the Dales or Valleys the Oak-Trees brought forth Acorns, of the Bigness of an Apple, very good to eat. The Woods afforded Plenty of Game of Rein Deer, Hares &c. for the Sport of Huntsmen. The Rivers, Bays and the Seas furnished an infinite Number of Fishes, Seals, Morses and Whales; of which all the Inhabitants made a considerable Trade and Commerce. And, though the Country at present cannot boast of the same Plenty and Richness, as it lies destitute of Colonies, Cattle and uncultivated; yet I do not doubt, but the old dwelling Places, formerly inhabited and manured by the ancient Norway Colonies, might recover their former Fertility, if they were again peopled with Men and Cattle.

Despite Egede's "histories," most of this has no known historical or geographical basis; it is mythmaking. Milk, butter and cheese were sent to Norway in lieu of taxes because the Greenlanders, almost all of whom were subsistence farmers, used no money. Far from being abundant, dairy produce was one of very few portable commodities in Greenland and could ill be spared, which was rarely a problem because contact with Norway was spasmodic and the relationship between the two countries tenuous even before the plague reached mainland Scandinavia. Grain has always been very difficult to grow north of about 60°, and by the time Thorstein got to Greenland in 1406, no one there could recognize bread. There are no oak trees, only, in the south, a low bushy scrub that bears no fruit but withstands the winter winds, and the plants that do grow, far from bringing forth acorns like apples, are smaller and much slower-growing than their continental counterparts. There are few reindeer in western Greenland, where there is little for them to eat. Far from enjoying a sporting hunt through the woods, dwellers in Greenland, whether European or Inuit, have always been hampered by the lack of wood more than almost anything else. Occasionally, highly prized pieces of driftwood from Siberia and North America appear on the shore, where they are gathered and used and re-used for years. The furnishing of the rivers, bays and seas with infinite stocks of fish and marine mammals was as seasonal in the Middle Ages as in Egede's day, and both the medieval Norse and the eighteenth-century missionaries rapidly discovered that even seasonal plenty only appears in good years (the average summer temperature of the seas off southern Greenland is 1.8°C; the kidneys of adult cod fail at 2°C). "A considerable trade and commerce" is at least a hopeful exaggeration on the part of Egede. Trade in Greenland never reached the levels of trade in Arctic North America, and even in the best years it fell a long way short of covering the mission's expenses. It is, then, crucial that this Arctic land of milk and honey is lost to the present of Egede's text, that this is a fantasy of a past that may be recoverable in a millennial future. A passage from the journal of Egede's son, Poul, makes the distinction between the Promised Land and the discovered territory very clear (as quoted by David Crantz):

> Mr. Poul Egede in his journal of Jan. 7, 1738, records the following amazing effects of the cold at Disko: "The ice and hoar-frost reaches thro' the chimney to the stove's mouth, without being thawed by the fire in the day-time. Over the chimney is an arch of frost with little holes, through which the smoke discharges itself. . . . Beds are often froze to the bed-stead. The linen is frozen in the drawers. The upper-eider-down-bed and the pillows are quite stiff with frost an inch thick from the breath. The flesh barrels must be hewn in pieces to get out the meat. . . .

This is one of the most vivid accounts of cold in Arctic writing. Many eighteenth- and nineteenth-century travelers record storing alcohol in their sleeping bags in vain attempts to stop it from freezing, but such travelers are just passing through, suffering for a few months or—usually inadvertently—years for the sake of money, science or England. The missionaries were trying to live there and, more distinctively yet, expecting the experience to be if not pleasant, then at least immediately rewarding. Unlike the traders and explorers whose descriptions figure elsewhere, the missionaries took their wives and children, produced more children, built schools and churches as well as shelters and trading posts. They sought, and founded, a homeland rather than an aesthetic experience or a chance to prove manhood or a point further north than anyone else. Egede's family and friends were the only people to have eiderdown beds and linen drawers in Greenland and so far north, and it is these trappings of familiar domesticity that make Poul's account of the cold so arresting and such a stark contrast to his father's vision of the lost country. One expects to find frozen sleeping bags, tents stiff with ice and clothes that need to be thawed before the explorers can put them on in the morning in polar travel narratives—the thrill of *schadenfreude* is arguably one of the reasons for reading the genre in the first place. But this is different and quite literally closer to home—it seems that the next thing to freeze must be the fire in the hearth.

Certainly, these belated inhabitants cannot boast of the plenty and richness in which Egede's imagined forebears revel. His own description of cold is less bitter but no easier to reconcile with the vanished plenty:

> Besides the frightful Ice that covers the whole Face of the Land, the Sea is almost choak'd with it, some flat and large Fields of Ice, or Bay-Ice, as they call it, and some huge and prodigious Mountains, of an astonishing Bigness, lying as deep under Water as they soar high in the Air. These are pieces of the Ice-Mountains of the Land, which lie near the Sea, and bursting, tumble down into the Sea and are carried off. They represent to the Beholders, afar off, many odd and strange Figures, some of Churches, Castles with Spires and Turrets; others you would take to be Ships under Sail; and many have been deluded by them, thinking they were real Ships, and going to board them. Nor does their Figure and Shape alone surprize, but also their Diversity of Colours pleases the Sight, for some are like white Crystal, others blue as Sapphires; and others again Green as Emeralds.

There are several striking features of this account, not least the emeralds which are an obvious source for Coleridge's "Rime of the

Ancient Mariner" ("And ice mast high came floating by/As green as emerald"), but in context it is most startling that only ten pages separate this from "The Greenland colonies bred a number of cattle . . . ," for the contrast makes clear just how profound an effect the conversion, or re-conversion, of the Greenlanders, is expected to have. The devoutly hoped consummation of this missionary narrative will convert a land covered with frightful ice and a sea choked with prodigious mountains into fertile pastures and woods affording plenty of game for the sport of huntsmen for, Egede reasons, "if the Produce and Commodities of *Greenland* were formerly reckoned of that Importance, that they were deem'd sufficient to maintain the King's Table: Why not also at present? provided *Greenland* may by Settlements and Improvement retrieve its former Abundance, which is not impossible."

Egede does not delight in the sublime strangeness of this frozen world; there is no sense of excitement or climax about such a bizarre landscape. The "figure and shape" of these cathedrals in ice "surprises," while the "diversity of colours" merely "pleases the sight." The ice, like the persistent failure of the locals to produce any folk-memories of their Viking origins, is a difficulty that only reinforces Egede's conviction. It is precisely because this place is so difficult that the missionaries know it is right; the hallucinatory qualities inherent in the land itself, where icebergs mimic ships and buildings and curtains of green light sing in the sky, are the basis of their recognition of the potential Promised Land.

Faced with the Inuit community and no particular evidence of the lost colonists, Egede eventually decided that, although they did not know it, the Inuit had absorbed some of the Vikings' traditions and culture. To the end of his life, he held to the belief that the colonists were still there, farming and fishing at the other side of Greenland which he could not reach either overland or by sea because of the ice. Evidence of the ruins was greeted by the assertion that everyone had always known that the Western Settlement had been abandoned, but Egede remained convinced that the Eastern Settlement was still running smoothly, somewhere just out of sight behind the next range of hills. He devoted himself to the conversion and "education" of the Inuit, striving to learn Greenlandic Inuktitut so he could preach and translate the Bible, and traveling tirelessly up and down the coast in all weathers. In practice, Egede's understanding of the language was such that his translation apparently remains utterly incomprehensible, and it was his children, growing up in the mission, who became bilingual and were later able to explain Lutheranism in terms that made sense to the Inuit. It is also these children who inspired one of Egede's surprising literary afterlives, a children's book by Eve Garnett (otherwise best known for *The Family at One End Street*) called *To Greenland's Icy Mountains*, which offers a very thoroughly researched account of Egede's life and an imaginative reconstruction of his children's upbringing at the mission.

After a few years, Egede's Lutheran mission was joined by a Moravian one, whose official chronicler, David Crantz, records a visit to the Eastern Settlement. Crantz was interested in the Norse colonies, but since the Moravians (who had had some success in establishing missions to the Native Americans) were there to save the Inuit rather than the medieval Norse, his approach is more measured than Egede's. He writes:

> Then I landed and walked up the valley for a league, to see some ruins of the old Norwegians, by the side of a great lake of fresh water; but these relics of antiquity were now nothing but a great square heap of stones, grown over with high grass. The valley seemed to me to be full two leagues long, and one broad. In the middle flows a little brook, which here and there halts and sports in little ponds. The adjacent hills do not ascend all at once so hastily as those by the sea, and are beautified with a good deal of grass, moss and bushes, and present a prospect like Vogelsberg in Wetteravia.

There is a sense of movement here rare in descriptions of Arctic landscape. The little brook (and the adjective "little" is unusual in accounts of Arctic scenery which usually tend to concentrate on grandeur and magnificence) flows, halts and, most charmingly, sports in little ponds. There is perhaps an echo of the psalmist's "little hills rejoicing on every side." The very hills surrounding this pretty, well-appointed valley refrain from "ascending all at once too hastily." They are adorned with a wider range of greenery than is found elsewhere in a usually monochrome landscape, and they offer to the homesick gaze a "prospect"—the word comes from the vocabulary of the eighteenth-century picturesque—just like the one left behind in Wetteravia. This combination of the lost home and the Promised Land is typical of eighteenth- and nineteenth-century hopes for new territories. Early American literature describes the landscapes of the East Coast in such terms when those disillusioned with eighteenth-century England looked westwards for a new life, and in the nineteenth century they are applied to Australia and New Zealand, but in both cases there really were new social and economic opportunities for those who felt that Europe had failed them. Greenland may have offered the ideological and spiritual satisfactions of a successful mission in circumstances of physical hardship, but the fantastic abundance of the missionaries' imagination had never been there.

III
Secret Runes: Searching for the Colonists, 1800–2000

There is no contemporary writing that offers any clue about what happened between 1410 and around 1540, but recent archaeology has more to offer. In the 1930s, excavating the graveyard at Herjolfsness, Poul Norlund found clothes perfectly preserved by water and frost. These clothes are of very distinctive styles fashionable in Northern Europe in the late fifteenth century. They are intricately made, requiring dozens of labor-intensive button-holes, pleats and panels, even an early form of zip fastening, and they seem to have been worn by ordinary men and women on the farms. Like the grand wedding at Hvalsey at the beginning of the fifteenth century, this expenditure of resources does not suggest a community struggling to survive. Norlund also found thin Rhenish stoneware at a farm in Herjolfsness, of a style and intricacy that cannot possibly predate the late fifteenth century. This attests to direct trade with western Europe where the clothes only demonstrate contact—it is easy to copy clothes, or even to design them on the basis of a verbal description, but the ceramics must have come on a ship and something must have been given in return.

Such finds have been one of the most puzzling aspects of the disappearance of the Norse Greenlanders, for it seems that active international trade and flourishing contacts around the North Atlantic should indicate a thriving community with a secure future. However, foreign ships could carry aggressive men as well as consumer durables. Both Kirsten Seaver and Helge Ingstad compare the abandoned farmsteads and burnt churches of Greenland with those of coastal Iceland, where the crews of British fishing vessels took advantage of the communities' isolation to loot houses and churches, raping and murdering some of the inhabitants and abducting others as forced labor, during the fifteenth and sixteenth centuries. If increasing competence in ship-building and navigation allowed such men to reach the coasts of Greenland—and the enormous quantities of cod circulating in medieval Europe suggest that they did—then the men may well have given or traded ceramics, described or modeled fashions and, when the fancy took them and they thought they could get away with it, looted and fired churches, slaughtered or stolen farm animals and abducted or killed a significant proportion of the youngest and strongest people.

The findings of Anne Stine Ingstad, a North Atlantic archaeologist who excavated in North America as well as Greenland in the 1960s, reveal a sustained Norse presence at L'Anse aux Meadows in Newfoundland, not very far west of western Greenland. This leads Ingstad to suggest that the young and active may have left Greenland for what is now Canada, leaving the old to die out slowly, a pattern that can still be seen in small communities in northern Norway and that leaves similar evidence of eerily deserted and apparently viable settlements. An earlier generation of scholars, led by Poul Norlund, had considered that the bones from Herjolfsness showed a population rendered infertile and diseased by malnutrition and inbreeding (Norlund came to the conclusion that "These men made a planned attempt to live the life of Europe, Christian, ordered and civilized, beyond the limits that nature had set to such a life"), but the application of modern scientific methods to those bodies contradicts this, demonstrating that even the last people to be buried in Greenland were taller and stronger than elsewhere in Europe. A certain amount of inbreeding was inevitable among such remote communities, but there is some recent evidence that, within limits, this accelerates biological adaptation to a specific environment. The pattern of deaths does not suggest any epidemics, for most of the graves in the churchyards are of old people and there are very few bodies that were not given a proper burial. Isolated victims of epidemic and massacre would usually be left where they fell. Although the Black Death raged in Scandinavia and killed more than half the population of Iceland in the twelfth and thirteenth centuries, it is unlikely that the plague could have reached Greenland given the length of the voyage: everyone on an infected ship even from Iceland would have died before reaching Greenland.

The very early conclusion that feuds had broken out with the Inuit and the Inuit had won is extremely improbable for several reasons. Inuit oral tradition, which carried the story of the Frobisher voyages for at least three hundred years, offers nothing to suggest any sustained disputes at all, although the one story that does survive relates both violence and mutual support. Inuit history has its legends and its factual accounts like any other kind of history, and this enticingly strange tale is usually told as legend; to quote from Frederica de Laguna's memoir:

> In olden times Norsemen lived on Inugsuk, and they have left a cairn and the ruin of a big house; at Qagsserssuaq lived Eskimos at the same time. Once the anqakoa [shaman] flew from Qagsserssuaq over Inugsuk, and saw that the Norsemen were in their house. So he returned home and said to his countrymen: "Tonight we will all go to Inugsuk, kill the Norsemen and take all the things they have." They immediately set off with their sledges and came to Inugsuk, where the people were just retiring to rest. They had taken off their clothes, as they used to sleep naked. Some were already entirely unclothed, while others still had their boots and dogskin trousers on. Then the Eskimos forced their way into the house and killed them all with their bows, with the exception of three, who fled. One of them, who was quite naked, fled to a place not far from Augpilagtoq, but on the way the soles of his feet and his back were frostbitten. When he reached the Eskimo settlement and sought refuge in one of the houses, the skin of his back being frozen, went to pieces as it rubbed against the entrance passage. The angakoq there could not do anything to help him because he was a Norseman, and his cure could only help Eskimos, and so he died. The other two, a man and his wife, fled to a steep cliff some miles south of Upernivik, where they climbed up and turned into stone; the cliff is still called Qavdlunarssuit (the Norsemen); but the figures have fallen down. When the Norsemen were killed the Eskimos were about to share the spoils. The angakoq took a big chest standing in an outhouse; but he was too tired and had no dogs; so he had to work all night dragging the chest to Qagsserssuaq. But when he got home and opened the lid, it only contained a recently dead Norseman in a white dress.

Nevertheless, there is compelling evidence of good relations and mutually beneficial trade. During the earlier years of the colony, there was probably almost no contact between the Norse and the Inuit, since the relatively warm climate meant that the Inuit found the best hunting and fishing grounds far to the north of the colonies. But as the "mini Ice Age" of 1400–1700 took hold (the one that saw horses, carriages and barbecues on the solidly frozen Thames during the reign of Elizabeth I), the Inuit moved south. At the same time, the colony flourished and Norse hunting parties ventured into the very far North, where they left cairns, hides and rune stones recording their presence north of Upernivik at 72° 57′.

In the 1920s, the Danish archaeologist Therkel Matthiassen excavated some medieval Inuit settlements in northern Greenland. He was assisted by Frederica de Laguna, a 22-year-old American who went on to start the Anthropology Department at Bryn Mawr. They found some remarkable toys and carvings in the midden of an Inuit settlement dating from the thirteenth century in Inugsuk, over a thousand kilometers north of the main Norse settlement at Gardar. Frederica de Laguna published a personal account of her first field trip forty years later:

> The most spectacular find was a wooden doll, which I came upon. It was only about two inches high, and had unfortunately been burnt about the feet.... The waist was very small, the hips flaring, so that it must have been a woman with a garment fitting closely about the waist and full at the hips. The headdress was the most curious of all, for it was apparently made of a separate piece of material which fell below the shoulders in front and behind, giving the woman the appearance of a nun. If anything was clear, it was that the woman was not an Eskimo at all! . . . The more we think about it, the more wonderful it seems that such a doll should have been found.

She and Matthiassen went on to find a lump of church bell metal, a fragment of woven woollen cloth (this thousands of miles from the nearest sheep), another doll, a carving of a very Nordic face and, perhaps the most startling, a spinning top made from a carved checkers counter. Even further north, Erik Holtved, excavating in

1935–37, found a piece of a chain mail coat and a beautifully carved chess piece among other Norse finds in an ancient Inuit settlement. There is parallel evidence in the ruined Norse farmsteads, where several Inuit carvings and artifacts have been found. It is clear that, whatever occasional local and individual tensions there may have been, there was sustained amicable and fruitful contact between the Inuit and the Norse settlers.

The Norse Greenlanders, then, were not exterminated by the Inuit. They were not malnourished, although it may have been getting harder to grow their accustomed range of crops. There were no significant epidemics. Looters probably made life rather difficult for those living in places that were visible and readily accessible from the sea, and regular supplies from Norway dried up decades before the colonies' disappearance (though, on the other hand, so did the demands for taxes and tithes). Some Norse Greenlanders certainly lived in North America for a while, although if the numbers were significant it is surprising that they died out without trace. Farming methods which were sustainable over centuries in Scandinavia caused erosion in the dry and wind-scoured land of southern Greenland. Although there were sophisticated irrigation systems in place, some farms probably became steadily less productive. While it seems likely that most of these explanations have some validity, none is sufficient in itself, and even in combination they seem somewhat inadequate.

In the end, it is simply not known what became of the Norse Greenlanders or why. Partly because of this mysterious ending, the story is one of the origins of later interest in the Arctic. The fantasy of the homeland is always fundamental to ideas of elsewhere, of unknown destinations, and here, it seems, is a homeland that was indeed a refuge from the political complexities of high medieval Europe, a real alternative to life in the metropolis. The story of the Norse Greenlanders, disappearing glamorously and perhaps unnaturally into the Arctic mists after five centuries of apparent prosperity, offers a compelling mixture of homeliness and strangeness, a kind of domestic Gothic that has enduring appeal.

PART TWO

The Long Dark Night

M ost conventional polar travelers, imagining the Arctic and Antarctic as places to endure more than inhabit, have tried to minimize the time spent there during the winter, and over-wintering is mainly a feature of pre-twentieth-century expeditions when the return voyage took too long to complete in one year. Once internal combustion engines made it possible to get to and from the High Arctic in one season, visitors preferred to go for the summer and return as the ice and darkness began to close in. The hazards for seventeenth-, eighteenth- and nineteenth-century sailors through the winter were terrifying. Because the sea freezes along the Arctic coasts, it was necessary to get ships into the right place and position for the next few months before the moment when the freeze set in, a date which, even in the same latitude, could range across several months from year to year. At best, the ship and all its inhabitants were then stuck until the ice melted in spring (although there were springs in which this never happened). At worst, the unpredictable movement of the ice would crush the ship or tear it apart. For obvious reasons, little is known about most of the expeditions to which it is assumed this happened.

There were many lesser physical perils. It was extremely difficult to keep a frozen ship warm enough for survival, much less comfort, and the attempt necessitated using a large proportion of the ship's storage capacity for fuel, displacing food and drink. The challenges of lighting were even greater, and posed a serious and fearsome fire hazard. There was no hope of any fresh food at all, making everyone dependent on the vagaries of early food preservation techniques. Scurvy and other forms of malnutrition were endemic and starvation frequent. A reliable water supply was hard to secure, since melting snow caused condensation problems that had water streaming down the walls and soaking clothes and bed linen which then froze.

The social problems were even worse, and at least as dangerous. Captains struggled to stop the crew realizing that there was, in fact, almost nothing to do until summer. Naval ships were crewed on the (not unreasonable) assumption that the crew was needed for sailing, so when the ship was frozen in place most of them were entirely redundant although unable to leave. In the absence of drinking water and the presence of large quantities of rum, they were also frequently drunk, as well as bored, starving and resentful of the officers' superior living conditions. The ways in which explorers passed the winter tell more about the cultures of exploration, and the relationship between society at home and on the ice, than all the achievements and disasters of the summer.

Mindful of the potential for social breakdown, most captains of over-wintering expeditions, at least from the nineteenth century onwards, insisted that the men went outside at least once a day, and many required daily scrubbing of the decks and washing of clothes in an attempt to use up energy and avoid scurvy, which was thought (conveniently) to result from indolence and untidiness. Some, such as Parry, went to the lengths of printing the ship's "newspapers" and providing costumes for plays to keep everyone active and entertained. Daily dancing on deck was compulsory on some ships; it helped the crew to sleep and limited their interest in more disruptive activities. Even on the most determinedly cheerful and well-organized ships, after several weeks of complete darkness and unbelievable cold, amid the strange silence of a frozen landscape long abandoned by birds and animals, these activities began to seem surreal. There are many obviously amateur sketches by under-occupied sailors, showing officers in dress uniform processing solemnly across enormous, empty two-dimensional landscapes to commemorate some royal non-event and pass a few hours, or showing tiny stick figures engaged in a ball game, wrapped in furs and occupying a minute area of the ice that stretches blankly to the dark horizon. It is hard to know whether to be moved or appalled by those who, stocking the ships in preparation for several grueling and desperate years, thought to include toy printing presses and women's clothes for dressing up when the earth shut down for the winter and there was no food and nothing to do.

Inevitably, in hard years or on ships that were under-equipped or ravaged by disease or had a captain whose morale-raising capacities were limited, despair set in. Little or no artificial light was available below decks, whatever the officers had, and even if there had been any natural light outside there were no portholes for the crew. Ventilation was almost non-existent below the waterline, so that even near the fires or stoves in the crew's quarters, condensation was so bad that the slight warmth was hardly worth it. If food ran low, energy levels plummeted and there was no reason to leave the cramped and fetid quarters for the frozen darkness above. The vulnerable went mad, the weak fell sick and died, and the strong found unmentionable ways of passing the time. No wonder that officers and captains resorted to the ridiculous to stave off the nihilism and anarchy that waited for pauses in the endless round of organized jollity. This section looks at the first two voyages of Sir William Edward Parry, whose Arctic winters with the *Hecla* and the *Griper* were famously successful, Fridjhof Nansen's very likeable account of winter aboard a very different ship a hundred years later, and Admiral Richard Byrd's unusually frank account of solitude and despair in the Antarctic.

IV

Sir William Edward Parry: "The Utmost Regularity and Good Order"

"On the evening of the 24th, being Christmas-eve, the ship's companies were amused by the officers performing the two farces of 'A Roland for an Oliver' and the 'Mayor of Garratt.' On Christmas-day, divine service on board the Fury was attended by the officers and crews of both ships. A certain increase was also made in the allowance of provisions, to enable the people to partake of Christmas festivities to the utmost extent which our situation and means would allow; and the day was marked by the most cheerful hilarity, accompanied by the utmost regularity and good order."

Sir William Edward Parry was regarded with a mixture of dislike and respect by most of his contemporaries in the upper echelons of the early-nineteenth-century British Navy. Conspicuously pious, publicly affectionate towards his equally pious wife and given to a patronizing (rather than brutal) view of his crew, Parry can seem to epitomize the most priggish aspects of upper-class Victorian patriarchy. It is quite impossible that his voyages were really as orderly and cheerful as his published accounts suggest, although it is equally impossible to find an unofficial version of the expeditions, since it was a condition of joining naval expeditions at this date that any written accounts or records should be handed over to the Admiralty on returning.

Parry was sent on three voyages in search of the Northwest Passage between 1819 and 1825, and an attempt to reach the North Pole in the summer of 1827. He had no particular personal interest in the Arctic, but he was interested in ascending the naval hierarchy as fast as possible and he was well respected because he had a high regard for the letter of naval protocol and brought nearly all of his men and (more importantly as far as the Admiralty was concerned) his ships and their equipment home safely at the end. Somewhat unfairly, this greatest strength was also perceived as his greatest weakness, and Parry was famed among later explorers for twice turning back on the point of finding the Passage, once because he felt that his crew's strength and energy were exhausted and once because he had abandoned one of his two ships, the *Fury*, after it was crushed in the ice. He gave up his attempt to reach the Pole at 82° 45" after realizing that the sledge party was drifting south faster than it could drag the equipment north, and that the summer was half over. Some at the Admiralty thought that Parry had failed to display the zeal and determination that carried other captains through greater disasters. Possibly he had, but he had also come back, which is more than can be said for many of those who soldiered on, including the folk-heroes Scott and Franklin.

Parry's prose reflects his aloofness from the traditional cultures of polar exploration. His determination that all should be seen to be well, and under control, on all occasions, precluded any heroic rhetoric about striving to overcome great obstacles or succeeding against all odds or persisting bravely in the face of danger. Great obstacles ought to have been foreseen and avoided; it would not be sensible to attempt something that was more likely to fail than not, and no responsible captain led his men into danger. It is an attitude that should be immensely sympathetic after volume after volume of nineteenth-century upper-class gentlemen merrily setting off across the ice in tweeds with a small hamper from Fortnum and Mason and a suicidal readiness to die in the national interest, but the lack of excitement that made Parry a cautious and responsible leader also makes him dull to read. His descriptions of the aurora read like municipal reports on suburban street lighting, even when prefaced with the observation that "these were among the most remarkable instances of this phenomenon in my experience."The goriest episodes appear unremarkable in Parry's plodding prose, as in this account of a fire in the instrument store:

> In their anxiety to save the dipping needle, which was standing close to the stove, and of which they knew the value, they immediately ran out with it; and Smith, not having time to put on his gloves, had his fingers in half an hour so benumbed and the animation so completely suspended, that on his being taken on board by Mr Edwards, and

having his hands plunged into a basin of cold water, the surface of the water was immediately frozen by the intense cold thus communicated to it; and, not withstanding the most humane and unremitting attention paid to them by the medical gentlemen, it was found necessary, some time after, to resort to the amputation of a part of four fingers on one hand and three on the other.

Because he wintered north of the area frequented by the Hudson's Bay Company, Parry spent time with Inuit groups who had never encountered Europeans before, but he recounts this experience by religiously comparing their behavior, domestic arrangements and attitude to their "superiors" against those of the "deserving poor" (i.e., hard-working, respectful, unpoliticized poor) in England. Parry is most interesting to read when he least intends to be. It is the casual remarks on the day-to-day running of the ship that give a startling glimpse of the social reality of nineteenth-century polar exploration.

Most of these seem to be intended to show off Parry's fatherly attitude to his crew (he later wrote an almost unreadable collection of meditations entitled *Thoughts on the Parental Nature of God*), and even to the nineteenth-century ear the sanctimonious note would probably have been clear. For example, an account of a gale during the first voyage concludes, "The people were carefully kept on board during this and every high wind throughout the winter, to avoid the possibility of frost-bites." The passive voice makes it seem as if the identity of those doing the careful keeping is irrelevant; the point is that on Parry's ships these things simply happen. The economy of the voyage is such that it is natural that "the people" are cared for. The problem with this and all such heavy-handed remarks is that it immediately becomes clear that it is not natural at all because if it were, Parry would feel no need to point it out, or at least not so often. This remark also seems to suggest that the sailors, left to their own devices in the matter of going for walks in an Arctic gale, would lack the sense to come in from the cold. One might also say that the term "the people" is revealing as the term used by most political regimes to designate those without power. We see these attitudes in more detail when Parry describes other measures to protect the sailors from illness in both his first and second voyages:

> The daily proportion of lime-juice and sugar was mixed together, and, with a proper quantity of water, was drank [sic] by each man in presence of an officer appointed to attend to this duty. This latter precaution may appear to have been unnecessary, to those who are not aware how much sailors resemble children in all those points in which their own health and comfort are concerned.
>
> Our people were sent out to walk for exercise whenever the weather was favourable, and the duties of the ship did not afford them sufficient employment; care being taken to keep them together, under an officer, and to furnish them with proper arms. Finger-posts were also erected, as before, in various parts of the island near the bay, for the purpose of directing persons to the ships if surprised by snow-drifts.

Most crews wintering in the Arctic would have profited from more policing than they had and, whatever dismay is caused by his prose, nearly all Parry's "people" came home in good health, if without a few fingers. Nevertheless, these accounts are troubling because of the assumption that "our people" cannot even be allowed to manage their own bodies. Clearly, a good expedition leader will make sure that people are not allowed to harm each other and perhaps also that they are compelled to help each other, but the step from this to forced medication and exercise is a large one, and Parry's immense satisfaction with his arrangements should not blind us to the politics of these voyages. Parry's concern for—or interference with—his crew was not limited to their physical welfare, and his provision for their morals and their morale can seem enlightened, sinister or merely pragmatic. It begins a tradition in polar exploration which ends with the First World War and Scott's disaster:

> Under circumstances of leisure and inactivity, such as we were now in, and with every prospect of its continuance for a very large part of

the year, I was desirous of finding some amusement for the men during this long and tedious interval. I proposed, therefore, to the officers to get up a Play occasionally on board the Hecla, as the readiest means of preserving among our crews that cheerfulness and good humour which had hitherto subsisted . . . . In these amusements I gladly undertook a part myself, considering that an example of cheerfulness, by giving direct countenance to everything that could contribute to it, was not the least essential part of my duty, under the peculiar circumstances in which we were placed.

In order still further to promote good-humour among ourselves, as well as to furnish amusing occupation, during the hours of constant darkness, we set on foot a weekly newspaper . . . under the promise that it was to be supported by original contributions from the officers of the two ships: and, though some objection may, perhaps, be raised against a paper of this kind being generally resorted to in ships of war, I was too well acquainted with the discretion, as well as the excellent dispositions of my officers, to apprehend any unpleasant consequences from a measure of this kind . . . .

The nature of the "unpleasant consequences" is not obvious. Parry may fear that officers with weaker dispositions and less discretion might make fools of themselves and lose the respect of their subordinates, or perhaps that they would disclose information about their colleagues that would undermine their authority. In any case, he is quite clear that his are nice ships on which the presses can be allowed to roll without fear. (Although there is no thought that the men themselves might be allowed to write.) No one will publish anything unpleasant or subversive and everyone will, under orders, exhibit cheerfulness and good humour because it is their duty to do so. By the time the first winter of his second voyage came around, Parry was even better prepared:

While care was thus taken to adopt all the physical means within our reach, for the maintenance of health and comfort among the crews, recourse was also had to some of a moral nature, which experience has shewn to be useful auxiliaries in the promotion of these desirable objects. It would, perhaps, indeed be less difficult to imagine a situation in which cheerfulness is more likely to be desired, or less likely to be maintained, than among a set of persons (and those persons seamen too,) secluded for an uncertain and indefinite period from the rest of the world; having little or no employment but that which is in a manner created to prevent idleness, and subject to a degree of tedious monotony ill according to their usual habits . . . . The astonishing effects produced by the passions of the mind, in inducing or removing scorbutic symptoms, are too well known to need confirmation, or to admit doubt . . . . As a source therefore of rational amusement to the men, soon after our arrival, I proposed to Captain Lyon and the officers of both ships once more to set on foot a series of theatrical entertainments . . . some preparation having been made for this previous to leaving England, every thing was soon arranged for performing a play on board the Fury once a fortnight. In this, as in more important matters, our former experience gave many useful hints. Our theatre was now laid out on a larger and more commodious scale, its decorations much improved and, what was no less essential both to actors and audience, a more efficient plan adopted for warming it, by which we succeeded in keeping the temperature several degrees above zero on each night of the performance throughout the winter.*

★ While on the subject of our plays, I cannot omit to mention that just before we left England, a large and handsome phantasmagoria or magic lantern had been presented to me for the use of the Expedition, by a lady who persisted in keeping her name a secret to those whom she was thus serving. This apparatus, which was excellent of its kind, was frequently resorted to during this and the succeeding winter; and I am happy to avail myself of this mode, the only one in my power, of thanking our benefactress and assuring her that her present afforded a fund of amusement fully answering her kind intentions.

Parry manages to make these activities sound a little sinister because his prose style is so much at odds with his subject matter that it almost seems to constitute an ulterior motive on its own. The characteristic weighty passive tense ("while care was thus taken" . . . "a more efficient plan adopted") and the ponderous double negatives ("it would, perhaps, indeed be less difficult to imagine a situation in which cheerfulness is more likely to be desired . . .") bury the image of people dressing up, playing and watching a magic lantern *for fun*. Of course, it is not really for fun but because people who believe they are having fun, or at least engaging in *rational amusements*, are less likely to get scurvy and incommode the Navy by dying. The view that scurvy, which invariably affected the crew much more than the officers, was caused by lax morals and poor hygiene had been around for more than a century, but it is interesting that Parry grew mustard and cress by the stoves as well as deploying "the passions of the mind." It suggests that he may have been fully aware of the other advantages of keeping everyone busy.

Parry was relentless in his desire to fill all of everyone's time. Particularly when there really was nothing at all that needed doing, the sailors had a strict timetable of early rising, prayers, cleaning and washing, meals, marches, dancing on deck, more prayers and early bedtime. On the second voyage Parry set up a school so that every man could learn to read the Bible. He took great satisfaction in the sight of all the sailors sitting quietly in neat rows: "I made a point of visiting the school occasionally during the winter, by way of encouraging the men in this praiseworthy occupation, and I can safely say that I have seldom experienced feelings of higher gratification than in this rare and interesting sight." The singing and dancing were particularly important, since they used up a great deal of energy and generated the impression of good cheer, but as Parry remarks, "It is scarcely necessary to add, that the evening occupations of the officers were of a more rational kind than those which engaged the attention of the men." The question raised by all this is what kind of "rational occupations" "the men" might have found had their energies not been quite so thoroughly diverted. It is not a question Parry ever appears to contemplate, but it sometimes seems that in winter, all his own energies on all three of his sea voyages were consumed by the endeavor not to find out. This was probably prudent.

Our New Acquaintance

On Parry's second voyage, the ships spent the winter close to an Inuit community that seemed to have had little or no previous contact with Europeans. Parry was intrigued by the Inuit and keen to adopt the correct scientific vocabulary to describe them, but quite unable to absorb the idea that a set of moral criteria different from those of middle-class evangelicals in nineteenth-century England might be useful:

> We found our new acquaintance as desirous of pleasing us, as we were ready to be pleased; so that we were soon on good terms with them all. While we were engaged in examining every part of their huts, their whole behavior was in the highest degree orderly, respectful and good humoured. They eagerly received the various articles that were given to them, either in exchange for their own commodities or as presents, but on no occasion importuned us for anything.

This is not a historical disability: James Cook in the 1770s was entirely comfortable with the idea that the Tahitians might have a great deal to teach him about politics as well as geography, and Samuel Hearne spent much of the 1780s learning cartography and survival skills from Native American and Inuit groups. But Parry sounds rather as Mr. Brocklehurst from *Jane Eyre* might if deposited in an Inuit village one winter (which is surprising, since he was one of Bronte's childhood heroes). "Pleasing behavior" on the part of the Inuit involves perfect conformity to Parry's very specific views of the ideal comportment of subordinates. They must be grateful for what they are given without indicating any interest in anything that is not offered—an impression that seems more likely to result from weak communication than real feeling—and there is no space for any idea of interaction except through material objects.

This is exactly the relationship that nineteenth-century conservative evangelicals typically sought with the indigent. They were happy to be charitable to those whose best efforts to help themselves had failed through no fault of their own, as long as the charity was received with unquestioning gratitude and without the expectation of anything further. Asking for things automatically rendered the poor undeserving of them. The deserving poor were by definition those who strove ceaselessly to support themselves but were entirely passive when this failed, and this is exactly how Parry chose to see the Inuit. Since, as on nearly all Arctic expeditions, none of the British spoke any Inuktitut and none of the Inuit spoke any English, Parry is free to interpret all speech and behavior exactly as he wishes. It is not surprising that he finds the ideal Victorian peasant wearing *kamiker* and spending the winter eating seal in *iglus* on Melville Island.

> The Esquimaux went out to endeavour to catch seals as usual, but returned unsuccessful after several hours labour. As it was now evident that their own exertions were not at all times sufficient to procure them food at this season, and that neither indolence nor any idea of dependence on our charity induced them to relax in those exertions, it became incumbent upon us carefully to attend to their wants, and by a timely and judicious application of resources we had set aside for their use, to prevent any absolute suffering among them. We therefore sent out a good meal of bread-dust for each individual, to be divided in due proportion among all the huts.

Again, there is the emphatic reference to duty (rather than goodwill or sympathy) as the proper motivation for this munificence. It became *incumbent* upon "us," not friendly or even charitable, to "apply" only those "resources" already set aside for the purpose. Parry writes as if his readers are waiting for the chance to accuse him of encouraging laziness or squandering resources on the undeserving. It is an anxiety typical of the mid-nineteenth century that generosity on the part of the elite might destabilize the whole economy. Since Parry has seen evidence that the utmost exertion is unavailing, then it might just about be acceptable judiciously to prevent "absolute suffering," which presumably means starving to death, since the Inuit families are already eating scraps of leather. The culmination of the "bread dust" (presumably powdered biscuit of some kind) would be funny without the thought of the starving families visiting ships full of plum pudding and frozen sides of beef and being sent home with some "bread dust" to share between sixty. The humorlessness of the compromise between charity and keeping to the letter of the law is typically effective and typically depressing.

V
Comforts and Good Cheer: Nansen Goes North

Fridtjof Nansen is probably the most likeable of famous polar explorers, although amiability is not one of the more obvious characteristics of the group. Born in Oslo in 1861 into a middle-class professional family, Nansen learned to ski before he could walk and assumed from the beginning that travel and survival skills learned in the Norwegian winter and from the Sami and Inuit would be transferable to Arctic science and exploration. He devoted his professional life to polar exploration and led several successful expeditions between the 1880s and 1920s, but his most famous journey was the *Fram*'s voyage across the polar ice cap between 1893 and 1896. This was scientifically important because Nansen, having observed the movement of driftwood from Siberia to the west coast of Greenland, surmised that there must be a current in the polar ice cap. His methodology was revolutionary: rather than fighting the cold and preparing to suffer while observing the movements of ice through the Arctic winter, Nansen designed and commissioned a small ship, the *Fram*, intended to withstand the most powerful movements of ice. He provisioned it to keep a small number of people well-fed and happy for several years and then deliberately got it frozen into the ice at the beginning of winter. Getting stuck had been disastrous for most British naval Arctic expeditions, which depended on fishing and hunting to survive beyond the anticipated number of weeks in the ice, and it was also psychologically very difficult for men who could not see and did not know that the ice itself was moving and feared being permanently imprisoned on failing ships in the polar ice. This did sometimes happen, and one of the things that alerted Nansen to the polar drift was the way wreckage would appear on the ice thousands of miles from where a ship was known to have been crushed or abandoned.

Arctic experts of the British and American navies, who had controlled almost all polar travel for decades, met Nansen's theories with disdain. Given the public resources and human lives these men had expended on expeditions based on the idea that exploration means fighting difficult terrain and weather with all the technological and military equipment available, one can understand their hostility to the idea that holing up in as much comfort as possible for a few years might be more effective. As their successors would scorn Amundsen's methods of Antarctic travel a few years later, so they regarded Nansen, another Norwegian civilian with big ideas, with little short of horror. Admiral Sir Francis Leopold M'Clintock, then the grandfather of English polar exploration, was characteristically sharp, concluding his response to Nansen's address to the Royal Geographical Society: "I wish the doctor full and speedy success. But it will be a great relief to his many friends in England when he returns, and more particularly to those who have had experience of the dangers at all times inseparable from Arctic navigation, even in regions not quite so far north." American general Adolphus Washington Greely (whose own achievements in these matters are chronicled in Part Three) wrote excoriating articles damning Nansen's lunacy: "Arctic exploration is sufficiently credited with rashness and danger in its legitimate and sanctioned methods, without bearing the burden of Dr. Nansen's illogical scheme of self-destruction." Typically, Nansen quotes these remarks without comment and without reference to the disasters encountered by his critics. His only reference to them comes much later, when the *Fram* was beset by moving ice:

> Friday, October 13th. Now we are in the very midst of what the prophets would have us dread so much. The ice is pressing and packing round us with a noise like thunder. It is piling itself up into long walls, and heaps high enough to reach a good way up the *Fram's* rigging; in fact, it is trying its very utmost to grind the *Fram* into powder. But here we sit quite tranquil, not even going up to look at all the hurly-burly, but just chatting and laughing, as usual.

Applications for funding from international organizations having failed, the Norwegian government and king paid most of the cost of the expedition and the *Fram*, although Nansen had to make up the rest himself on the eve of departure.

The *Fram* was a happy ship from the beginning. Nansen had chosen his crew for their congeniality as much as their survival skills, and in the Norway of the 1890s there was no habit of calling some people officers and some people crew. His account of the expedition, *Farthest North*, makes delightful reading after the miserable valor of frozen and starving English Victorians. Nansen certainly has a strong sense of patriotism and links his achievements to the nineteenth-century renaissance of Norway as a nation-state, but, although this is partly born of nostalgia for the Viking empire, it seems respectably energetic more than bombastic. He repeatedly describes the *Fram*'s voyage as a continuation of early medieval Nordic adventuring and compares his own aims to the achievements of the Vikings.

This sense that the polar ice cap is both the spiritual home and the national destiny of Norwegian travelers is shared with Hans Egede, and is clearly a powerful idea in Arctic literature. Since living in Norway is much better training for living in the high Arctic than living in London or Chicago, events tend to reinforce this feeling. Nansen treated his expedition like ordinary life as far as he possibly could. Like Parry, he was constantly aware that the social structure of life on board would be crucial to success or failure, but the contrast with Parry in terms of writing as well as welfare could not be greater. Much of this, of course, should be ascribed to the difference between the social structures of 1820s London and 1890s Norway, but even so, the differences are telling. In place of Parry's fanfare about the "rational amusements" of the officers, Nansen remarks simply, "A good library was of great importance to an expedition like ours, and thanks to publishers and friends both in our own and in other countries we were very well supplied in this respect."

A Happy Ship

The expedition had a difficult start, for although Nansen had known that the *Fram* was much better designed to withstand ice than perform well in blue water sailing, he had not realized quite how uncomfortable and alarming the voyage up to the ice might be. The swell was enormous, and the *Fram* rolled and skidded from wave to wave, apparently threatening to capsize at every moment. But by late September 1893 they had sailed to 78.5° North—further than they had dared hope—and, encountering solid pack ice to the north, worked their way in as far as possible and then settled down for the winter. Like Parry's men, the *Fram's* crew immediately established a daily routine, intended to give shape and purpose to otherwise undifferentiated time, but they were very different kinds of routine:

> We all turned out at eight, and breakfasted on hard bread (both rye and wheat), cheese (Dutch clove cheese, Cheddar, Gruyere . . .), corned beef or corned mutton, luncheon ham or Chicago tinned ham or bacon, cod caviar, anchovy roe; also oatmeal biscuits or English ship-biscuits—with orange marmalade or Frame Food jelly. Three times a week we had fresh-baked bread as well, and often cake of some kind. As for our beverages we begun by having coffee and chocolate day about; but afterwards had coffee only two days a week, tea two and chocolate three.
>
> After breakfast some men went to attend to the dogs . . . others went all to their different tasks. Each took his turn of a week in the galley—helping the cook to wash up, lay the table and wait. . . . Some of us would take a turn on the floe to get some fresh air, and to examine the state of the ice. . . . At one o' clock all were assembled for dinner, which generally consisted of three courses. . . . With the meat we always had potatoes and either green vegetables or macaroni. I think we were all agreed that the fare was good. . . . As a rule, stories and jokes circulated at table along with the bock-beer.
>
> After dinner the smokers of our company would march off, well fed and contented, into the galley, which was the smoking room as well as the kitchen. . . . Afterwards came, for most of us, a short siesta. Then each went to his work again until we were summoned to supper at six o'clock. . . . Afterwards there was again smoking in the galley, while the saloon was transformed into a silent reading-room . . . . At half-past seven or eight cards or other games were brought out, and we played well on into the night. . . . About midnight we turned in, and then the night watch was set. Each man went on for

an hour. Their most trying work on watch seems to have been writing their diaries and looking out . . . for any signs of bears at hand.

The interest in bears is culinary rather than zoological. A great deal of Nansen's narrative relates to food, partly because, having much more of it available, he was able to rely on it almost exclusively to structure and pass the hours of the six-month polar night. Where Parry used work and exercise and Byrd used his meteorological observations to make sure that similar things happened at similar times every 24 hours despite the unbroken darkness, Nansen arranged the life of the *Fram* around cooking and eating. It is not clear whether this was a conscious decision, but his occasional expressions of dismay over the rapid weight gain of his crew suggest not. In this case, it seems likely that Nansen is being more straightforward than most polar captains about the centrality food assumes in closed communities. In other expedition narratives, one tends to read intense anxiety about the next—or last—meal as the natural result of food shortage, but Nansen shows how such concern relates also to other kinds of shortage. On the ice there is no money to earn or spend by way of self-affirmation or proof of status, and food can work as a replacement, particularly when cooking and hunting are undertaken by everyone so a pseudo-economic hierarchy can develop. Usually, and particularly on smaller expeditions where everyone knew everything about everyone, there was little physical affection to offer reassurance and pleasure, so eating was perhaps the best source of physical gratification and consolation. Planning, cooking and eating three or four meals, each consisting of three or four courses, would also pass enormous amounts of time in a relatively interesting and creative, if self-indulgent, way. The thought and planning Nansen gave to food paid off in conviviality as well as nutrition, and he was well aware of its capacity to replace all sorts of currencies:

Sunday, November 5th. A great race on the ice was advertised for today. The course was measured, marked off and decorated with flags. The cook had prepared the prizes—cakes, numbered and properly graduated in size. The expectation was great; but it turned out that, from excessive training during the last few days, the whole crew were so stiff in the legs that they were not able to move. We got our prizes all the same. One man was blindfolded, and he decided who was to have each cake as it was pointed at. This just arrangement met with general approbation, and we all thought it a pleasanter way of getting the prizes than running half-a-mile for them.

The first day the sun returns has him commenting anxiously,

Monday, Feb 19th... The way we are laying on flesh is getting serious. Several of us are like prize pigs, and the bulge of the cook Juell's cheeks, not to mention another part of his body, is quite alarming. I saw him in profile today and wondered how he would ever manage to carry such a corporation over the ice if we should have to turn out one of these fine days. Must begin to think of a course of short rations now.

The punning on "corporation" and the coy "another part of his body" show Nansen's wry amusement at running a polar expedition whose main problem is excessive weight gain, but there is also anxiety here. The term "short rations" invokes military customs of food distribution rather than healthy living, and there is a disgusted note in "prize pigs," as if the expedition has become morally as well as nutritionally over-indulged. The image of Juell carrying "such a corporation" across the ice plays into the Anglo-American naval establishment's sneer that Nansen's expedition was bourgeois and amateur, for in the original Norwegian as well as in English "corporation" is more often a word for a business than for a body. It is as if, should the *Fram*'s cozy middle-class drawing room suddenly tip the crew out into the world of "real" exploration, Juell will be literally unable to carry his commercial background across the terrain that separates the men from the boys. Nansen fought others' accusations that he was not doing polar exploration properly if his crew were not suffering, but it was nevertheless an anxiety that preyed on him even during the winter he spent living in a snow-covered hut on the beach at 80° N. His attitude to the *Fram* and her crew during the first winter is clearly complicated and ambiguous, veering between smugness, self-deprecation and shame:

Monday, December 25th. Christmas Day. Thermometer at -38 C. below zero. I took a walk south in the beautiful light of the full moon. At a newly made crack I went through the fresh ice with one leg and got soaked; but such an accident matters very little in this frost. The water immediately stiffens into ice; it does not make one very cold, and one feels dry again soon.

They will be thinking much of us just now at home and giving many a pitying sigh over all the hardships we are enduring in this cold, cheerless, icy region. But I am afraid their compassion would cool if they could look in upon us, hear the merriment that goes on, and see all our comforts and good cheer. They can hardly be better off at home. I myself have certainly never lived a more sybaritic life, and have never had more reason to fear the consequences it brings in its train. Just listen to today's dinner menu:

1. Ox-tail soup;

2. Fish-pudding, with potatoes and melted butter;

3. Roast of reindeer, with peas, French beans, potatoes, and cranberry jam;

4. Cloudberries with cream;

5. Cake and marzipan (a welcome present from the baker to the expedition; we blessed that man).

And along with all this that Ringnes bock-beer which is so famous in our part of the world. Was this the sort of dinner for men who are to be hardened against the horrors of the Arctic night?

Every one had eaten so much that supper had to be skipped altogether. Later in the evening coffee was served, with pine-apple preserve, gingerbread, vanilla-cakes, cocoanut macaroons, and various other cakes, all the work of our excellent cook, Juell; and we ended up with figs, almonds, and raisins.

Now let us have the breakfast, just to complete the day: coffee, freshly baked bread, beautiful Danish butter, Christmas cake, Cheddar cheese, clove-cheese, tongue, corned beef, and marmalade. And if anyone thinks this is a specially good breakfast because it is Christmas Day, he is wrong. It is just what we have always, with the addition of the cake, which is not part of the every day diet.

Add now to this good cheer our strongly built, safe house, our comfortable saloon, lighted up with the large petroleum lamp and several small ones (when we have no electric light), constant gaiety, card-playing, and books in any quantity, with or without illustrations, good and entertaining reading, and then a good sound sleep—what more could one wish?

Nansen's pleasure in the "good cheer" and "sybaritic life" waned as his frustration and "fear of the consequences"—which still seem to be as much moral as physical—grew. He was bored and missed his wife desperately: "Monday, March 26th .... The sun mounts up and bathes the ice-plain with its radiance. Spring is coming, but brings no joys with it. Here it is as lonely and cold as ever. One's soul freezes. Seven more years of such life—or say only four—how will the soul appear then? And she . . . ? If I dared to let my longings loose—to let my soul thaw. Ah! I long more than I dare confess."

These longings are clearly, at least in part, sexual, but nonetheless emotionally debilitating. Nansen felt guilty about "letting" his emotional needs affect his commitment to the expedition, but his mood swings made it harder and harder to be as cheerful as everyone needed him to be. As spring advanced, he began to plan in earnest an attempt on the North Pole, which had been at the back of his mind since first undertaking the expedition.

Nothing to Write About

The idea was that Nansen and one other man would try to reach the North Pole by dog-sledging while the others remained on the *Fram*, charting her route across the top of the polar ice cap. Nansen had set up depots along the course of his proposed route back, and did not expect to meet his ship and crew again until they were all back in Norway. In the spring of 1895, Nansen and Fredrik Johansen left the *Fram* and set off due north with 25 dogs and two sledges. They reached 86° 10" north with much less trouble than any earlier expeditions. The trip was certainly hard and often worrying, but they had enough dogs to pull food and equipment, and as they ate the food, lightening the load, they killed the dogs one by one and fed them to the surviving animals. It was a very efficient form of polar travel, but did mean that the equation between dogs and food had to be kept in very careful balance—no point in having more food than the surviving dogs could pull or more dogs than the remaining food could sustain—and supplies of both began to run low long before they approached the North Pole.

Nansen and Johansen turned back, and reached open sea near Franz Josef Land with two dogs still alive. Reluctantly, they killed these and set off in kayaks, killing polar bear and seals to eat along the way. By late August, the weather was worsening rapidly and progress was so slow that there was little hope of reaching Spitzbergen that year. They resigned themselves to wintering where they were, and began to shoot as many animals as possible. Most of the bears they encountered were females with cubs, and these passages do not make edifying reading:

A she-bear, with two large cubs, was going up the shore; they had just passed close by our door. I aimed at the she-bear, but, in my haste, I missed her. She started and looked around; and as she turned her broad side to me I sent a bullet through her chest. She gave a fearful roar, and all three started off down the shore. There the mother dropped in a pool on the ice, but the young ones ran on, and rushed into the sea, dashing up the foam as they went, and began to swim out. I hastened down to the mother, who was striving and striving to get out of the pool, but in vain. To save ourselves the labour of dragging the heavy animal out, I waited until she had drawn herself up on the edge, and then put an end to her existence. Meanwhile the young ones had reached a piece of ice. It was very close quarters for two, and only just large enough to hold them; but there they sat balancing and dipping up and down in the waves. Every now and then one of them fell off, but patiently clambered up again. They cried plaintively and incessantly, and kept looking towards land, unable to understand why their mother was so long in coming. The wind was still high, and they drifted quickly out to sea. . . .

Nansen and Johansen launched the kayaks and chased the cubs back towards the hut:

From the very first it was evident how much better the bear that first went into the water swam, although it was the smallest and thinnest. It waited, however, patiently for the other, and kept it company; but at last the pace of the latter became too slow for its companion, who struck out for the shore, the distance between the two growing greater and greater. They had kept incessantly turning their heads to look anxiously at us, and now the one that was left behind looked round even more helplessly than before. While I set off after the first bear, Johansen watched the second, and we drove them ashore by our den and shot them there.

The combination of the anthropomorphic descriptions of the bears' behavior and the relentlessness of Nansen and Johansen's desire to kill them makes such accounts distressing in a way that a simple description of hunting out of necessity might not be. Calling the female bear "the mother" brings images of human mothers and babies to mind, and calling the cubs' attempts to survive "patient" and their cries for their dead mother "plaintive and incessant" gives them human emotions and characteristics that sit oddly with Nansen's unsporting determination to kill female bears with young. The imaginative projection of "unable to understand why their mother was so long in coming" (there is no way of knowing what bears understand) and the description of one bear "keeping the other company" (are bears reassured by company?) makes this seem much less like a zoological account of animal behavior and much more like

murder. The "anxious" and "helpless" expressions on the faces of the
bear cubs confirm this, for these distinctly unscientific words present
the bears as most human, most emotionally like us, at the moment
when they are being killed as one might only kill an animal. It is hard
to see what rhetorical end is being served here, and perhaps this adds
to the distress of reading this and the many similar accounts. They do
not fit into scientific writing, which tends to make animals seem as
different from people as possible, or into more conventional accounts
of hunting, which emphasize the large size, dangerous behavior and
cunning of the animal (most descriptions of killing polar bears, which
are very big and very fierce and hunt human beings, fit easily into this
category). One could speculatively relate Nansen's interest in
describing himself mercilessly hunting down baby bears crying for
Mummy to his anxieties about feminine softness and over-indulgence
on the *Fram*, or even to his shame about his great longing for his wife
and baby daughter, as if this caricature of Man the Hunter
compensates for the cake-guzzling bourgeois "corporations"
comfortably ensconced on sofas somewhere on the polar ice.

Nansen and Johansen built a stone hut six feet by ten, using bear
and walrus bones as tools, and passed the autumn equipping it with
lamps fueled by seal and walrus blubber and sleeping bags made of
bear skins. They had a stove and enough meat for the winter, and even
pencils and notebooks, and Nansen found that the worst problem was
dirt. The lamps smoked, and each of them had only one set of clothes
which had been soaked in blood and fat during the butchery of the
summer. Their clothes were so deeply engrained with fat and blood
that they stuck to their skin and chafed it raw, and then the open sores
were constantly rubbed by the filthy cloth. The men found that
scouring themselves with moss and sand had some effect. But when
the weather was too bad to leave the hut, "We found the next best
plan was to scrape our skin with a knife." Everything they touched,
and particularly paper, became filthy, and Nansen, in words that echo
through accounts of polar winters, almost stopped writing his journal:
" ... there was nothing to write about. The same thoughts came and
went day after day; there was no more variety in them than in our

conversation. The very emptiness of the journal really gives the best representation of our life during the nine months we lived there." Nevertheless, the talismanic power of the written word was undiminished and even intensified by the blankness all around. Any writing often seems better than no writing to those in desperate circumstances on the polar ice, where dying men spend their last minutes updating their journals ("It seems a pity but I do not think I can write more") and the lost leave messages in cairns like Hansel and Gretel scattering crumbs. Nansen was unusually fortunate in having something to read that he had not written himself:

> The little readable matter which was to be found in our navigation table and almanack I had read so many times already that I knew it almost by heart—all about the Norwegian royal family, all about persons apparently drowned, and all about self-help for fishermen. Yet it was always a comfort to see these books; the sight of the printed letters gave one a feeling that there was after all a little bit of the civilized man left.

Also like others before and since, Nansen began to find the landscape strangely futuristic:

> And everything so still, so awfully still, with the silence that shall one day reign, when the earth again becomes desolate and empty, when the fox will no more haunt these moraines, when the bear will no longer wander about on the ice out there, when even the wind will not rage—infinite silence! In the flaming aurora borealis, the spirit of space hovers over the frozen waters. The soul bows down before the majesty of night and death.

Interestingly, with food ample but limited to bear and seal meat boiled or fried, and clothes the source of hardship, the focus of fantasy changed. This is unusual; most people stuck in the Arctic spend their time imagining menus for the restaurant they will open when they get home, but then Nansen and Johansen were eating better than most people even while kayaking and sledging across partly frozen Arctic seas. (They discovered later that Nansen had gained 22 pounds and Johansen 13 pounds since leaving the *Fram*.)

> When we wanted to enjoy a really delightful hour we would set to work imagining a great, bright, clean shop, where the walls were hung with nothing but new, clean, soft woolen clothes, from which we could pick out everything we wanted. Only to think of shirts, vests, drawers, soft and warm woolen trousers, deliciously comfortable jerseys, and then clean woolen stockings and warm felt slippers— could anything more delightful be imagined? And then a Turkish bath! We would sit up side by side in our sleeping bag for hours at a time, and talk of these things.

Bears returned to the island just before the store of meat ran out in March, and preparations for the onward journey south began. By June, Nansen and Johansen had reached the southern tip of Franz Josef Land and were ready to press on towards Spitzbergen. On the 22nd, to their great astonishment, they heard dogs, and the following day a man appeared. Nansen heard him speak to the dog: "It was English, and as I drew nearer I thought I recognized Mr. Jackson, whom I remembered once to have seen. I raised my hat; we extended a hand to one another, with a hearty 'How do you do?'" The conversation went on:

> "I'm immensely glad to see you."
> "Thank you, I also."
> "Have you a ship here?"
> "No, my ship is not here."
> "How many are there of you?"
> "I have one companion at the ice-edge."
> "Aren't you Nansen?"
> "Yes, I am."
> "By Jove! I am glad to see you."

Some of this stiltedness is because English was Nansen's second language, but even so it is suspiciously reminiscent of Dr. Livingstone's fabled meeting with Stanley. The way Nansen presents the conversation in full implies that he is well aware of this, and he comments later that the accompanying "British handshake" contained a great deal of repressed emotion. The contrast with his first encounters with people back in Norway, where he is embraced, cheered and generally celebrated, brings us again to the contrast between successful Norwegian amateur enthusiasm and less successful British professional formality. It is a contrast which set the tone for the next century of polar exploration.

HABITS of the GROENLANDERS.

VI

"I Dread Getting Up": Richard Byrd Alone in the Antarctic

Richard Byrd's long dark night was more traditional than Nansen's, and his journal is an unusual and compelling example of a well-established genre. Byrd led several American interwar Antarctic expeditions in the 1930s and published accounts of each of them. They are simply written and methodical, concerned to allocate credit for the expeditions' achievements fairly. Byrd lacks Scott's romantic expectations of perfect cohesion among the men, and assumes that the tensions of communal living are naturally among the challenges of working in the Antarctic. For the most part he writes exactly as a sensible admiral might be expected to do, and this is why his account of four months spent alone in a shack on the Ross Ice Barrier, 120 miles from the expedition's Base Camp, is so intriguing. Byrd is quite clear that he undertook the period of solitude as much because he wanted to as because it was really necessary—he was no scientist and had little understanding of the implications of the meteorological data he collected—and yet he dispenses with his reasons for this choice fairly brusquely, writing of "one man's desire . . . to be by himself for a while and to taste peace and quiet and solitude long enough to find out how good they really are."

Later, Byrd suggests that the difficulties of preparing and trying to secure funding for a polar expedition during the Depression have left him in desperate need of peace and quiet, which is perfectly plausible but also entirely circular, since he would not have needed to exhaust himself with preparations if he had not been about to go anyway. In any case, Byrd, like many of those participating in interwar and post–World War II polar travel, looked for healing on the ice. In some ways, Antarctica is a strange place to look for cultural enrichment, but Byrd hoped that he would be able to read and listen to the European canon of literature and music:

> Out there on the South Polar barrier, in cold and darkness as complete as that of the Pleistocene, I should have time to catch up, to

study and think and listen to the phonograph; and, for maybe seven months, remote from all but the simplest distractions, I should be able to live exactly as I chose, obedient to no necessities but those imposed by wind and night and cold, and to no man's laws but my own.

The echo of Thoreau's *Walden*, one of the defining texts of nineteenth-century America which recounts a season spent in isolation in Massachusetts, is explicit and deliberate, but the homely image of Walden Pond is replaced by the strangeness of the Pleistocene, as if America must now look to a distant geological age as well as to the ends of the earth to find the freedom from social expectation that Thoreau could locate so conveniently close to home. Byrd presents himself almost as a modern-day anchorite, meditating alone on the sins of the world in a remote little house surrounded by spectacular natural phenomena. The exigencies of "wind and night and cold" produce their own pseudo-monastic regime, in which ice must be scraped from the instruments and observations taken every four hours, radio broadcasts must be made twice a week and the stove and lantern replenished every three days. As Byrd recognized before he began his solitude, his challenge—like that of the monk or the person making a religious retreat—was to adhere to this routine while managing his internal life without a context: "Now, against the cold the explorer has simple but ample defences. Against the accidents which are the most serious risks of isolation he has inbred resourcefulness and ingenuity. But against darkness, nothing much but his own dignity."

As he seems to want, Byrd's dignity is tested almost, if not quite, to destruction. At first he glories in his isolation, finding in his journal entry for April 7, 1933, a sequence of acute but grandiloquent images for his desolation: ". . . Even at midday the sun is only several times its diameter above the horizon. It is cold and dull. At its brightest it scarcely gives light enough to throw a shadow. A funereal gloom hangs in the twilight sky. This is the period between life and death. This is the way the world will look to the last man when it dies."

Here, Antarctic solitude seems to give Byrd the vantage-point of the last man, the sole survivor of the "death" of the planet, while allowing him to return to tell the tale. The futuristic imagery works with the references to geological time to present a place so strange that it can only be imagined as not part of the present, but it also magnifies the figure of Byrd pottering about alone on the ice: "At times I felt as if I were the last survivor of an Ice Age, striving to hold on with the flimsy tools bequeathed by an easy-going, temperate world." The cold is so intense that even the adapted impedimenta of ordinary life begin to seem more bizarre and irrelevant than anything archaeology presents. Rubber turns brittle and breaks under the slightest pressure, oil freezes hard, glass shatters spontaneously but the frozen contents remain solid for weeks on the kitchen table. Outside, "if there is the slightest breeze, you can hear your breath freeze as it floats away, making a sound like that of Chinese firecrackers." Byrd responded to this with entirely unconvincing fantasies: "To make the relatively distant reaches [of the shack] more attractive, I named one corner Palm Beach and the other corner Malibu; but with the door open I seldom felt very comfortable in either place without fur pants on."

There were more practical problems to remind Byrd of his lack of innate self-sufficiency. He had never cooked except at barbecues at home in Virginia, and the Ross Ice Shelf is not a good place for barbecues. The cookbook he expected to find in his boxes was not there, so after a few days of living on biscuits and tinned meat he realized that he was going to have to feed himself by trial and error. Byrd's relief at the opportunity for comedy is clear: "My first jelly dessert bounced like a rubber ball under my knife; the flapjacks had to be scraped from the pan with a chisel.... When I did experiment, the results filled the shack with pungent burning smells and coated the skillets with awful gummy residues." He also relates The Cornmeal Incident, in which a serious underestimate of the amount of water absorbed by cornmeal caused an eruption of bubbling cornmeal to flow over the stove and across the floor.

Nevertheless, food quickly becomes a more serious focus for dismay. As a father of four and a member of the Navy since leaving college, Byrd had never eaten alone and found the experience increasingly distressing. "A meal eaten alone and in silence is no pleasure. So

I fell into the habit of reading while I ate. In that way I can lose myself completely for a time. The days I don't read I feel like a barbarian brooding over a chunk of meat." Here as in the Thoreauvian passage earlier books appear as buttresses against "barbarity," the only thing standing between the admiral and the grunting inhabitants of the imagined Ice Age. A journal entry from the sixth week of Byrd's sojourn makes this even clearer:

> May 11 . . . 10 pm. . . . I have no manners whatsoever. If I feel like it, I eat with my fingers, or out of a can, or standing up—in other words, whichever is easiest. What's left over, I just heave into the slop pail, close to my feet. Come to think of it, no reason why I shouldn't. It's rather a convenient way to eat; I seem to remember reading in Epicurus that a man living alone lives the life of a wolf . . . now, when I laugh, I laugh inside; for I seem to have forgotten how to do it out loud. This leads me to think that audible laughter is principally a mechanism for sharing pleasure. I find, too, that the absence of conversation makes it hard for me to think in words.

> I'm getting absent minded. Last night I put sugar in the soup, and tonight I plunked a spoonful of corn-meal mush on the table where the plate should have been.

Like the bouncing jelly and erupting cornmeal, this is funny, but there is also a clear anxiety that only references to reading classical philosophy keep wolfishness at bay. The same fear is apparent in Byrd's discussion of his laughter, where the observation that he has stopped laughing, has become a less social creature, is quickly followed by a very formally phrased, analytical generalization, as though treating his own loss of humanity as a scientific experiment will make it less real. Byrd emphasizes that he still knows that sugar "does not go" in soup and there "should" be a plate between the cornmeal mush and the table. He is in fact obeying far more "necessities" than those demanded by wind and weather, because there is a tacit recognition that cutlery and crockery are the stuff of sanity (this interestingly echoes the decision of some of Franklin's men to take engraved silver cutlery with them on the final and hopeless march towards Canada). Without the ability to observe and laugh at himself, at least to notice, be amused by and *record* his failures in "civilization," it seems all too possible to Byrd that he could become a wolf or an illiterate, carnivorous barbarian. He concludes movingly, "I don't think that a man can do without sounds and smells and voices and touch, any more than he can do without phosphorous and calcium."

As the novelty of the isolation wears off, Byrd finds less to amuse him, and the need for some kind of social context, however flimsy, becomes compelling:

> This morning I had to admit to myself that I was lonely. Try as I may, I find I can't take my loneliness casually; it is too big. But I must not dwell on it. Otherwise I am undone.
>
> . . . As I dread getting up, I just lie there and listen to these sharp, clean bleats [the noise of the meteorological instruments], letting them form little conversations, little rhymes, even short stories in my mind. They have a pleasant, narcotizing effect.
>
> The silence during these first minutes of the day is always depressing. It seems real, as if a gloomy critic were brooding in the shadows, on the verge of saying something unpleasant. Sharing his mood, I merely grunt a good morning.

Here again, a terrible prospect, that of being "undone" is raised, and then quickly quashed by the self-mocking fantasy that the instruments are talking to each other. The word "narcotizing" is particularly interesting, for it makes clear that Byrd is aware that the "little conversations" and "little rhymes" are pathetic and laughable but also necessary. The fantasy of some kind of social existence offers the only anaesthetic against the dread of "being undone" by loneliness. This is why the "gloomy critic" is not much more alarming, since at first it seems that an unpleasantly inclined figure "brooding in the shadows" should be more frightening than solitude to someone in Byrd's position. But once again, it is the fleeting comedy of "grunting good morning" that—literally—saves the day. Here as elsewhere, writing about being in the Antarctic is therapy for being there.

"Great Waves of Fear"

Interestingly, as Byrd's physical state becomes more precarious he finds the solitude psychologically less threatening. Having felt increasingly tired and sometimes confused over several weeks, Byrd collapses one day while running the petrol engine that fuels the radio equipment used to communicate with the base camp at Little America. Even while crawling along the floor retching and tortured by muscle spasms, he understands what has happened and sees immediately that his underground hut is so badly ventilated that the oil-fired stove and lanterns that he depends on for heat and light are slowly poisoning him with carbon monoxide. From that day on, Byrd's life at Advance Base becomes a battle to manage his pain and illness well enough to keep adjusting the balance between light and heat and carbon monoxide. He must accept some poisoning, because without the warmth from the stove and at least enough light to find food and water while living underground in the polar night, he will freeze and starve to death. However, if he uses the stove enough to stop his skin freezing and peeling off during the night, he will die a more painful death from the gas. He becomes constantly aware that, "There are harder ways to die than freezing to death. The lush numbness and the peace that lulls the mind when the ears cease listening to the blizzard's ridiculous noise, could make death seem easy." Easy indeed, compared to carbon monoxide poisoning. Either a little too much gas or a little too much cold will exacerbate his sickness and weakness to the point where he can no longer move around to control either. After a while he becomes too ill to risk using the lantern except for light by which to eat and check the meteorological instruments but is in too much pain to sleep, so Byrd passes several weeks alone in darkness and extreme cold. There are several crises:

> Great waves of fear, a fear I had never known before, swept through
> me and settled deep within. But it wasn't the fear of suffering or even

of death itself. It was a terrible anxiety over the consequences to those at home if I failed to return. I had done a damnable thing in going to Advance Base, I told myself. . . . Much as I should have liked to, I couldn't consider myself a martyr to science.

This is the antithesis of Scott's "For God's sake look after our people." Byrd is acutely and perhaps, among polar explorers, uniquely, aware of the utter pointlessness of dying because the expedition is incompetently equipped. There is a rare honor in the admission both that he would have liked to think himself a martyr and that he couldn't, and indeed in the admission of all-consuming fear. Byrd spends a while raging with frustration and self-blame (how much more realistic, how much more convincing, than Scott's account of his own last hours which is clearly in Byrd's mind as he writes) and then the admiral collapses in tears:

> My bitterness evaporated, and the only resentment I felt was concentrated on myself. I lay there a long time, sobbing, "What a pity, what an infinite pity!" so my pride was gone as well. A Virginian, I was brought up to believe that a gentleman never gives way to his feelings. I felt no shame then, although I do now.

Byrd tried to keep up his weekly radio broadcasts because he was determined that his subordinates at Little America should not realize how ill he was and be tempted to disobey his parting order not to risk their own safety attempting to rescue him before spring came. Nevertheless, as his strength failed from week to week he began to miss many broadcasts altogether, and seemed so odd when he did communicate that, despite being limited to Morse code, the men became convinced that something had gone badly wrong and concocted a story about the scientists needing a trial run in his direction before setting off properly in the spring. Byrd was not entirely convinced by this, but thankfully allowed his judgment to be overwhelmed by his desire for survival at the critical moment and so lived to tell the tale and, braver yet, to publish it.

PART THREE

The Bitter End

It has been estimated that the death rate on polar expeditions between 1770 and 1918 was about 50 percent. Most of those who signed up for such expeditions or, as in most cases, were told that their next posting was to the far North, would have been well aware of this. For the naval crews who had no choice about where they went, the likelihood of dying in battle or from disease in the course of the Royal Navy's more conventional occupations in the late eighteenth and early nineteenth centuries was considerably higher than this. Most of them were illiterate and none of them published, so there is no way of knowing what the "hands" thought of being dispatched to the highest latitudes, but it seems likely that the work there was often more interesting and safer than the alternatives. For the officers, and for the civilian explorers and scientists who undertook their own journeys, it was quite different. They were leaving comfortable homes and reliable incomes from interesting and respected work in order to risk everything on the ice. The answer to the question of why they went is uncertain, varying from person to person and according to the historical and cultural circumstances of each voyage, but every one of them had to negotiate the distinct possibility of coming to a sticky end. Setting off for the Arctic or Antarctic during these years was accepting a significant risk of death, and men made their wills and addressed their wives accordingly.

There is clearly an extent to which joining an expedition was self-destructive behavior, and this section looks at the writing that inspired these decisions. It is here that the "polar canon," the group of texts that shape the cultural understanding of the Arctic and Antarctic, is most apparent. Interestingly, the books that sell out on publication and are still readily available in paperback decades later are not those that are particularly well written or even those whose authors achieved momentous things. Some are those that offer a digit-by-digit, mouthful-by-mouthful, breath-by-breath account of dying, and if the writer is in the unusual position of being able to recount his own dying, so much the better. The others are those that end, or sometimes begin, with disappearances, silence and footprints in the snow.

Enormous numbers of readers like the Arctic and Antarctic to be places adorned by dead bodies in dress uniform and no shoes (eaten when the sealskin, or alternatively the colleagues, ran out). These great white spaces at the top and bottom of the world are where people went to die for us, both for our edification as readers and for our greater glory as Britons or Americans or, less commonly, Norwegians or Swedes. At its height, this Anglo-American cultural investment in the poles as spaces of absence, of death and disappearance, was so great that survival was seen as positively inappropriate. Amundsen had no business reaching the South Pole and living on stolidly to tell the tale when Scott died so beautifully in failing, and Nansen's comfort on the *Fram* and competence on the ice were almost offensive. Shackleton might have saved his crew with his extraordinary bravery, perseverance and seamanship, but he was no gentleman.

Thinking about Scott's expedition in 1910, it can seem that this love of death and failure is specific to that strange English decade between the death of Queen Victoria and the beginning of the First World War. But this celebration of the (in)glorious dead was not just a phenomenon of English Edwardian decadence, for the disappearance of the mid-nineteenth-century Franklin expedition inspired plays and popular songs and over fifty American as well as English rescue attempts. The popular literature of polar exploration of our own recent *fin de siècle* is largely devoted to death and disaster. The ice continues to attract our darkest imaginings about what can happen to people and what they can do to each other, and there is still both a desire to know, to exhume the bodies and carry out forensic analysis to see exactly what happened, and a desire to go on imagining the slow descent from medal-toting Victorian bigwig to open-mouthed skin and bone in the snow. It is because of this passionate investment of the cultural imagination that this and the next section include secondary writing as well as the journals of the dead, for it seems that these urgent re-visitations of the polar lost and gone forever are as much part of the story as the initial failures to return.

The bitterest ends in polar exploration are probably those about which nothing is known, expeditions which nobody survives and from which no bodies or texts are found. Whatever their other motives, explorers risked everything in the name of expanding knowledge. The point of exploration was to leave home and return both different in oneself and bearing experience that would make "home" different. On returning one would be more powerful or better informed or perhaps just more open to the strangeness one had witnessed. Exploration is also largely about incorporating strangeness into nationhood, returning to tell a tale that then becomes part of home culture, and in this light it need not matter much whether the explorer himself returns or not, as long as his story is told. And it may even be a better story if he does not return but remains some corner of a polar waste that is forever Sweden/America/England, a national emblem in its turn incorporated by an alien land. For this reverse incorporation to work to the greater glory of the explorer and all he stands for—that is, for his death to be meaningful—it is necessary for the story of his death to go on being told. If the expedition comes to a complete end with death, if the explorer disappears and is allowed to decay silently into the howling wilderness, then he has in death become merely a private person, which is precisely not the point of exploration. If instead his death itself is fetishized and the story told and told again to the last gasp and beyond, then the body becomes a relic or a kind of cultural bookmark. *Here* lies Our Great Explorer who died heroically *here*. (See his statue outside Parliament back home.) An expedition fails not in death, which is usually more or less expected and budgeted for, but in disappearance.

It is in this context that we can best understand both the almost obsessive journal keeping of obviously doomed individuals and the almost obsessive interest in dead bodies of armchair, amateur and pro-fessional polar historians. (The ultimate examples are the detailed accounts of autopsies conducted *in situ* by Charles Francis Hall's biographer Chauncey Loomis and by Owen Beatty and John Geiger researching the Franklin expedition.) In places where it is so cold that bodies hardly decay at all, an explorer's corpse and his journal complement each other and can be interchangeable. Both tell his story, encode the narrative that readers at home are intended and eager to incorporate into our collective understanding of who we are. Even in Scott's case, we must read the body to finish the journal's last words, and so explorers are careful to die as they wish to be found.

Perhaps this self-consciousness in dying is one of the reasons that bitter ends attract such morbid fascination, for it makes death into a kind of performance, which is both repellent and commands attention. This is why the stories in this section must be less textual, less literary, than those elsewhere, for The Bitter End is necessarily a composite, much mediated tale. The point of the Explorer's Last Journal is not just the words but the faltering hand and the worn-out pencil, the uncertain, illegible marks made in the dark whose illegibility is itself telling. Most published accounts include a facsimile, but, surrounded by the learned or ghoulish speculations of the editor, it is not the same thing. The Last Journal only makes sense as part of the account of the finding of the body (the notebook is usually in his breast pocket), and so we must also have the story of the expedition that went looking for and/or found the lost expedition. The tale of the body is often unfolded by someone else, an archaeologist or forensic scientist, and may be accompanied by a photograph so that the reader can come as close as possible to seeing the man himself. By this stage we usually need at least an editor and often a historian to collate all the evidence, and if one then why not, a few years later and on the basis of new information or a different interpretation, another? And another? The episode is now a cultural myth rather than a text, a much retold story that seems to matter and is not comparable to the more straightfor-ward, "what I did on my holidays" books by those who went, did roughly what they said they were going to do, and came back.

VII
"They Are an Epic": Robert Falcon Scott and the South Pole

"What they did has become part of the history of England, perhaps of the human race, as much as Columbus or the Elizabethans, David, Hector or Ulysses. They are an epic."
—Apsley Cherry-Garrard, in *Edward Wilson of the Antarctic* by George Seaver

It is hard to write about Robert Falcon Scott because he has come to typify a kind of Englishness, and in particular a kind of English masculinity, that is historically and culturally specific. Over ninety years after his death, it is difficult to come to a serious understanding of Scott's status as a popular hero and very easy to mock the rhetoric that made a disastrous expedition into a moral triumph. Scott, whose body was found early in 1913, became an iconic figure for an England desperate to persuade the brightest and best to leave their work, their studies and their families for the near certainty of death on the battlefields of northern France. British schools were still teaching ten-year-olds in the 1980s that the deceitful foreigner Amundsen had used dishonorable means to stop the noble English Scott from reaching the South Pole first, but even then it was hard to make the leap of imagination to understand why Scott was any more than wrong and dead.

It is trite to say that the Establishment made a hero of him on purpose in order to glorify knowing self-sacrifice as a prelude to conscription in the First World War, especially as most of the military and academic establishment seem to have thought (more or less privately) that Scott got just about what he was asking for. On the other hand, the parallel between the men who could see that Scott was irresponsible but obeyed him unquestioningly as he led them to their deaths and those who knew they were being used as cannon-fodder in the trenches but followed orders anyway is interesting. Historical generalizations are misleading—particularly those relying on hindsight—but there seems to have been a cultural moment on the eve of the Great War in which it was uniquely possible for Scott's colleagues both to

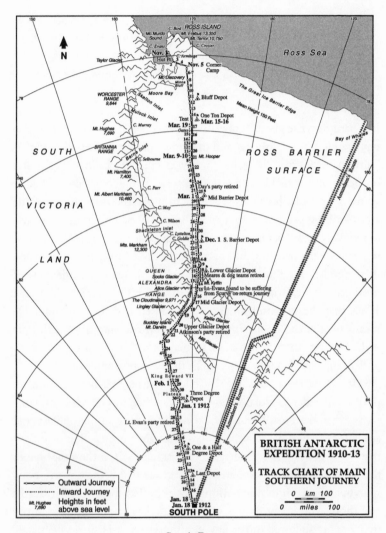

Scott's Route

recognize and articulate his manifest failings and to obey him anyway. It is perhaps this insistence on the heroic status of those who die wilfully for a specious principle that is peculiarly English. Scott certainly did his own mythmaking, but the point of mythmaking is to attract and deploy cultural energies that are already there. He could not have turned himself into a hero without the popular readiness to regard failure as heroic, and potentially more heroic than success.

Born in 1868, Robert Falcon Scott had an undistinguished naval career before developing an interest in the South Pole. Antarctica held little fascination for him, but polar exploration nearly one hundred years after Parry's voyages still offered the prospect of rapid promotion. Scott led two Antarctic expeditions, and both were controversial. Several admirals were of the view that polar exploration had nothing to do with military prowess and was a waste of naval resources, while many at the Royal Geographical Society, which had the greatest expertise in exploration, felt that naval traditions and training were not good preparations for polar expeditions. Events suggested that both were right, but the constant intriguing between the two groups meant that every aspect of publicly funded expeditions was a compromise.

Sir Clements Markham, the president of the Royal Geographical Society (RGS), liked personable young men and took Scott as his protégé, insisting against the views of Scott's superiors that he could lead an expedition. This being granted, Scott then had to accept some of the Navy's appointments of men to accompany him. It never occurred to him not to implement the Navy's tradition of housing and feeding officers and crew separately, even although there were civilian scientists and doctors on both voyages. On both journeys (the first of which was 1901–04), the conflict between exploration and science was also seen as problematic, although the difference between going somewhere in order to see what it is like and going somewhere in order to record what it is like can seem slight. Scott's voyages were culturally and socially similar, but it is the second one, ending in disaster, that seized the popular imagination and gave rise to a small polar canon of its own. The purpose here is not only to analyze what went wrong—a well-researched topic—but to look at the mythmaking that began even before the dying Scott scrawled "it seems a pity but I do not think I can write more" as he lay beside his dead or dying companions in a little tent out in the Antarctic snow.

In contrast to Amundsen's meticulous plans and careful training, Scott relied on (untested) experimental ideas and working things out as he went along. He frequently changed plans at short notice and refused to commit himself to anything until it became necessary. The results of this might have been more interesting than catastrophic if he had allowed margins for safety and error and if he had been able to plan collaboratively rather than always insisting on his own absolute authority. As it was, the 1910–12 expedition suffered from amateurishness and autocracy right from the beginning. The expedition's ship, the *Terra Nova*, leaked so much that it nearly sank on the voyage to Antarctica. The shipwrights had used bolts too small for the holes and then concealed the gaps with paint, and the pumps were not good enough to get the water out as fast as it came in. The *Terra Nova* was also badly ventilated, so as they crossed the Tropics stifling heat was added to the men's other discomforts. When the ponies and a few dogs came on board in New Zealand, they were crammed onto the open deck and tethered there, where waves swept over them and their excrement dripped through the planks onto the bunks and dining area below.

All of this was received in a spirit of larkiness which faltered only when some of the officers visited Amundsen on the *Fram* when they reached Antarctica, where they suddenly understood that these conditions were not the inevitable downside of polar exploration but unnecessary and damaging. On the voyage out they had played children's party games in between bouts of work to keep the ship afloat. Scott had planned a base camp at the Bay of Whales, but he arrived to find Amundsen already there and decided, to Amundsen's puzzlement, that it would be rude to stay. The *Terra Nova* made for McMurdo Sound instead, where one of the tractors sank during unloading and the process of transferring the cargo from the ship to the hut made it clear that, even with entirely untrained drivers and novice skiers, dogsleds and skis were far more efficient means of transport than the ponies and "man-hauling" to which Scott had committed everyone for longer journeys. ("Man-hauling," in which the men wore harnesses and pulled sledges laden with several hundred pounds of provisions, had always been the Admiralty's preferred way of doing things, and Scott was criticized then and since for refusing to take any notice of Scandinavian and American success with skis and dogs.)

After a few weeks, the expedition settled into the hut under Mount Erebus, and the *Terra Nova* left on a scientific cruise of South America. Scott was already perceived as a difficult leader even by those who were closest to him, and the conduct of the first season confirmed that view. He was secretive and insecure, inclined to change plans and then panic and change them again, and given to including and excluding people from particular duties or expeditions on the basis of how they seemed to feel about him. This time was supposed to be spent preparing for and rehearsing the journey to the Pole, but Scott's uncertainty meant that no one knew quite what to expect or how they were meant to prepare for it. He was extremely anxious about Amundsen and clearly did regard the two expeditions as racing to the Pole, whatever he said publicly about the vulgarity of such ideas and his own pure commitment to science and exploration for its own sake. The men attempted to build igloos, thinking they might be a useful backup or alternative to tents, and enjoyed arguing over the best way of doing so. If Scott had done some research before leaving, he would have already known. Tryggve Gran, the young Norwegian explorer whom Scott had brought as a ski instructor, had been requested to spend time man-hauling so the Polar Party were still incompetent on skis. Many of the ponies became useless from cold and exhaustion and had to be killed, and since ammunition was in short supply Scott told Lawrence "Titus" Oates, who cared for them, to use a pickaxe. Since Scott's opposition to dog-sledging was based on its cruelty to animals, this makes the inconsistency of his motivations clear.

In between these experiments, the expedition played soccer on the ice, wrote the *South Polar Times* (edited by Apsley Cherry-Garrard) and planned festivities for Christmas, midsummer and midwinter and the first and last sights of the sun. They had sing-songs most nights, alternating hymns with popular dance and music hall songs, and once or twice a week there were lectures, when the officers took it in turns to talk about their various areas of expertise. Herbert Ponting took his extraordinary photographs, and the scientists proceeded with their investigations. Behind the daily and weekly routines was the slow, jerky buildup of hope and expectation about the South Pole.

Scott was officially ignoring Amundsen's presence on the continent and plans for the Pole, but the occasional speculations in his journal and in other people's letters suggest that Amundsen's image stalked the soccer games and gala dinners like Banquo's ghost. The season for Antarctic exploration was alarmingly short anyway, but the presence of a competitor made the final expedition seem even more urgent and Scott became very keen to travel as lightly as possible. He wanted to use the two remaining tractors for the first part of the journey south, partly to "justify the time, money and thought which have been given to their construction" and partly because he was sure that the internal combustion engine held the future of polar travel. Neither of these, however prescient, is a good reason for using an entirely untested technology for a dangerous journey with no margin for error, and it is odd that Scott rejected the interim technologies of skis and dog-sledges for the strange conjunction of tractors and man-hauling.

There are signs of the trouble to come in Scott's prose during the final weeks of planning and preparation in autumn 1911. He writes confidently, "I think our plan will carry us through without the motors (though in that case nothing else must fail)," and a month later, "I'm afraid there is much pony trouble in store for us." By early October, with departure scheduled for the end of the month, the last few ponies are failing and Scott writes:

> Yesterday I had a good look at Jehu and became convinced that he is useless; he is much too weak to pull a load, and three weeks can make no difference. It is necessary to face the facts and I've decided to leave him behind—we must do with nine ponies. Chinaman is rather a doubtful quantity and James Pigg is not a tower of strength, but the other seven are in fine form and must bear the brunt of the work somehow.

If we suffer more loss we shall depend on the motor, and then!
. . . well, one must face the bad as well as the good.

Two weeks later, "I am secretly convinced that we shall not get much help from the motors, yet nothing has ever happened to them that was unavoidable. A little more care and foresight would make them splendid allies. The trouble is that, if they fail, no one will ever believe this."

The trouble would seem to be rather that Scott has already observed that the loss of any more horses will make the expedition dependent on the tractors, he has lost more horses and is now deciding that the tractors are no use either. This is a private journal where one would not necessarily expect absolute consistency, but such inconsistency over such a crucial issue is troubling. The start was postponed several times when the tractors broke down and had to be repaired, which involved delicate work with metal undertaken overnight in temperatures 20 and 30 degrees below freezing. This notebook ends hubristically, "The future is in the lap of the gods; I can think of nothing left undone to deserve success." This sense of entitlement characterizes Scott, but polar success—like other kinds— is not determined by what one deserves.

The tractors broke down within a few days, having moved only slightly faster than the men and horses (seven miles a day). The plan was to work the horses until they collapsed with exhaustion, and their fitness levels were so different that start times each morning had to be staggered by two hours so that everyone reached the next camp at the same time. Conditions were already much worse than Scott expected, and he wrote petulantly, "Our marches are uniformly horrid just at present. . . . The weather was horrid, overcast, gloomy, snowy. One's spirits became very low." The following day, "I am anxious about these beasts—very anxious, they are not the ponies they ought to have been, and if they pull through well, all the thanks will be due to Oates. I trust the weather and surface conditions will improve; both are rank bad at present." Here again is the sense that Scott thinks he deserves better than he is getting, that he is entitled to good weather and ponies that will somehow remain healthy when marched across Antarctica pulling immense loads on minimal food.

By November 21 the pony party caught up with the men who had started in tractors and gone on man-hauling and Scott was intrigued—but seemingly nothing more—to learn that the man-hauling party were short of food:

> They all look very fit, but declare themselves to be very hungry. This is interesting as showing conclusively that a ration amply sufficient for the needs of men leading ponies is quite insufficient for men doing hard pulling work; it therefore fully justifies the provision which we have made for the summit work. Even on that I have little doubt we shall soon get hungry.

It is hard to read this blithe prediction of hunger as anything better than smug, and at worst it seems like the terrifying prioritization of self-image over the physical welfare of others. Scott seems to anticipate hunger almost gleefully, as if it will mean that things are being done properly at last. Even on this outward trip, the men and animals were beginning to suffer from Scott's relentless assumption that everything would go exactly as he wanted it to, since in allocating provisions he had not allowed for any rest days or even days when less than thirteen miles were covered. This put the group under an absolute obligation to cover the distance whatever the weather and terrain and however sick or tired they were. The ponies were shot as they became too tired to pull the loads, and at first their meat was fed to the dogs, but by early December all the men were eating it as well. Then the first of the blizzards began and Scott panicked:

> The storm continues and the situation is now serious. One small feed remains for the ponies after today, so that we must either march tomorrow or sacrifice the animals. That is not the worst; with the help of the dogs we could get on, without doubt. The serious part is that we have this morning started our Summit Rations. . . . The first

supporting party can only go on a fortnight from this date and so forth. The storm shows no sign of abatement and its character is as unpleasant as ever.... I can find no sign of an end, and all of us agree that it is utterly impossible to move. Resignation to misfortune is the only attitude, but not an easy one to adopt. It seems undeserved where plans were well laid and so nearly crowned with a first success. ... It is very evil to lie here in a wet sleeping-bag and think of the pity of it, whilst with no break in the overcast sky things go steadily from bad to worse.... Surely few situations could be more exasperating than this forced inactivity when every day and indeed every hour counts. To be here watching the mottled wet green walls of our tent, the glistening wet bamboos, the bedraggled sopping socks and loose articles dangling in the middle, the saddened countenances of my companions—to hear the everlasting patter of the falling snow and the ceaseless rattle of the fluttering canvas—to feel the wet clinging dampness of clothes and everything touched, and to know that without there is but a blank wall of white on every side—these are the physical surroundings. Add the stress of sighted failure of our whole plan, and anyone must find the circumstances unenviable.

Scott is clearly letting off steam here, but the petulant tone and the continuing emphasis on his conviction that he deserves to succeed, that the Antarctic owes him good weather, are constant themes. He depicts a very personal battle between himself and the elements, as if he were fighting a dragon or a giant rather than trying to cross difficult terrain in bad weather. The storm has an "unpleasant character" which "forces" inactivity and the situation is not inconvenient or even alarming but "very evil," as if there is a definite moral agency in the terrain and the weather. The almost onomatopoeic cadences of the "mottled wet green walls," "sopping socks," "everlasting patter" and "ceaseless rattle" court sympathy for Scott's annoyance, but they also suggest a mind that does not withdraw or turn away from these repetitive irritations. The physical discomfort must have been significant, but it is Antarctica's success in thwarting his intention that Scott finds unbearable. Already, we have the sense of someone who has moved beyond the mundane concerns of daily welfare to devote himself to a cosmic quest. This is of course in some ways a merely accurate perception of the attempt to reach the South Pole, but it was also a dangerous way of thinking. This perception is born out when, a few days later, having shot the remaining ponies, Scott was simply cross to find that the doctor, Atkinson, thought that two of the men were also failing: "It is a very serious business if the men are going to crock up. As for myself, I never felt fitter and my party can easily hold its own." On December 10 Scott sent the dogs back and continued on foot, and a week later, finding the weather improved and the Beardmore Glacier easier to climb than he expected ("certainly dogs could have come up as far as this"), Scott returns to the old theme: "Our luck may be on the turn—certainly we deserve it."

A Wearisome Return

As they came to the summit, Scott made his much criticized decision to take four men with him to the South Pole rather than the three for whom the original plans had been made. This was his most obvious misjudgment (assuming that he wanted everyone to survive), since rations of food, the size of the tents and the quantities of clothes were all arranged—and barely adequate—for four men and would now have to be spread more thinly. The reasons, as ever with Scott, are obscure, but seem to relate to a reluctance to disappoint those he liked. It was not a kind or responsible decision, and this was freely acknowledged by everyone at the time, but by this stage Scott was in no state to cope with anything resembling dissent or criticism. The others ate what they were given, and went hungry, and marched when they were told to and were disabled by exhaustion. Tellingly, on Boxing Day 1911 Scott recorded, "We have all slept splendidly and feel thoroughly warm—such is the effect of full feeding." It is hard to imagine why he thought "full feeding" for men spending up to twelve hours a day dragging loads weighing several hundred pounds uphill on ice and snow was only appropriate on Christmas Day, but his journal gives the clear impression that suffering is both necessary and sufficient for success. The point is not just to reach the South Pole first but to explore the limits of the human capacity for hunger, exertion and sleeplessness as well. If Scott did not want to die—or at least did not want to die any more than most polar explorers, since a self-destructive impulse is something of an occupational hazard—he did perceive Antarctica as a dimension in which the battle with mortality was not to be conducted with the mundane arsenal of good food, deep sleep and sufficient warmth. One might add that his fame vindicates this strange view.

"About 74 miles from the Pole—can we keep this up for seven days? It takes it out of us like anything. None of us ever had such hard work before" (Thursday, January 11, 1912). A week later, Henry Bowers spotted a cairn in the snow, and then a black flag marking the remains of a camp. They knew immediately that, "The Norwegians have forestalled us and are first at the Pole." Scott was already losing confidence in their ability to get back, and the disappointment exacerbated this. He remained determined that nothing but luck separated Amundsen's success from his failure, and this entry concludes, "To-morrow we must march on to the Pole and then hasten home with all the speed we can compass. All the day dreams must go; it will be a wearisome return. Certainly we are descending in altitude—certainly also the Norwegians found an easy way up." They reached the Pole the next day, Wednesday, January 17, and over the following week Scott, now oddly matter-of-fact, charts their disintegration:

> The Pole. Yes, but under very different circumstances from those expected. We have had a horrible day—add to our disappointment a head wind 4 to 5, with a temperature -22, and companions labouring on with cold feet and hands.
>
> . . . We have been descending again, I think, but there looks to be a rise ahead; otherwise there is very little that is different from the awful monotony of past days. Great God! this is an awful place and terrible enough for us to have laboured to it without the reward of priority. Well, it is something to have got here, and the wind may be our friend to-morrow. We have had a fat Polar hoosh in spite of our chagrin, and feel comfortable inside—added a small stick of chocolate

and the queer taste of a cigarette brought by Wilson. Now for the run home and a desperate struggle. I wonder if we can do it.

Wednesday January 24—Things beginning to look a little serious. A strong wind at the start has developed into a full blizzard at lunch, and we have had to get into our sleeping bags. . . . At 12.30 the sun coming ahead made it impossible to see the tracks further, and we had to stop. By this time the gale was at its height and we had the dickens of a time getting up the tent, cold fingers all round. We are only 7 miles from our depot, but I made sure we should be there tonight. This is the second full gale since we left the Pole. I don't like the look of it. Is the weather breaking up? If so, God help us, with the tremendous summit journey and scant food. Wilson and Bowers are my standby. I don't like the easy way in which Oates and Evans get frostbitten.

Sat 27 . . . Our sleeping bags are slowly but surely getting wetter and I'm afraid it will take a lot of this weather to put them right. However, we all sleep well enough in them, the hours allowed being now on the short side. We are slowly getting more hungry, and it would be an advantage to have more food, especially for lunch.

Tues 30 [Wilson strains a tendon in his leg] To add to the trouble Evans has dislodged two finger-nails tonight; his hands are really bad and to my surprise he shows signs of losing heart over it. He hasn't been cheerful since the accident.

Thurs 1 . . . Evans fingers now very bad, two nails coming off, blisters burst.

On February 4 Evans and Scott fell through a crevasse. Evans seemed to have injured his head and became "dull and incapable." Everyone was suffering more and more from hunger, and on February 6 Scott wrote, "Food is low and weather uncertain, so that many hours of the day were anxious; but this evening, though we are not as far advanced as I expected, the outlook is far more promising. Evans is the chief anxiety now; his cuts and wounds suppurate, his nose looks very bad, and altogether he shows considerable signs of being played out." It is almost possible to see a kind of satisfaction in the brevity of this summary of the situation, a minuting of the expected misfortune. On February 12, after two days stumbling blindly around difficult terrain laced with crevasses, they ran out of food entirely. Wilson spotted the next depot just in time, but the shock made Scott belatedly recognize the absolute importance of ample food supplies: "Yesterday was the worst experience of the trip and gave a horrid feeling of insecurity. Now we are right, but we must march. In future food must be worked so that we do not run so short if the weather fails us. We mustn't get into a hole like this again." The entry ends, "Evans has no power to assist with camping work."

Food ran low again over the next two days, and Evans became "absolutely changed from his normal self-reliant self." The following day they set out as usual, but Evans had trouble with his ski-shoes and fell behind. Scott cautioned him to follow as fast as possible, but when they stopped for lunch they could see him far behind and making no progress. They went back for him, and found him, "on his knees with clothing disarranged, hands uncovered and frostbitten, and a wild look in his eyes. Asked what was the matter, he replied with slow speech that he didn't know, but thought he must have fainted." Evans was unable to stand up, and by the time they got him into the tent he was unconscious. He died shortly after midnight, and by 1am the others set off again for another depot. Everyone was shocked, but they also knew that he had been slowing the journey dangerously and that no one would survive unless they could reach each depot before the food from the last one (intended anyway for four rather than five) ran out.

"The Poor Soldier Has Become a Terrible Hindrance"
After this, they made more progress and by late February were picking up notes from the relief parties at the cairns. Even so, they were desperately hungry and increasingly weak, and the stored paraffin had leaked through faulty seals so fuel was "woefully short," which affected the melting of snow for drinking water as well as cooking and light. At the end of the month the temperature fell below -40°F, and Oates

admitted to severely frostbitten feet. They would have needed to cover ten miles a day to avoid running out of food and fuel, and were actually managing about five. As Scott remarked, "We are in a very queer street since there is no doubt we cannot do the extra marches and feel the cold horribly." Given his outpourings of frustration and dismay over bad weather on the way out, this seems again oddly laconic, as if Scott's remaining work is that of narrator more than explorer, relating rather than deciding the course of events.

Saturday, March 3 ... God help us, we can't keep up this pulling, that is certain. Amongst ourselves we are unendingly cheerful, but what each man feels in his heart I can only guess.

Monday, March 5 ... We cannot help each other, each has enough to do to take care of himself. We get cold on the march when the trudging is heavy, and the wind pierces our warm garments. The others, all of them, are unendingly cheerful when in the tent. We mean to see the game through with a proper spirit, but it's tough work to be pulling harder than we ever pulled in our lives for long hours, and to feel that progress is so slow. One can only say, "God help us!" and plod on our weary way, cold and very miserable, though outwardly cheerful. We talk of all sorts of subjects in the tent, not much of food now, since we decided to take the risk of running a full ration. We simply couldn't go hungry at this time.

This decision to "run a full ration," i.e. to eat whole portions even though that meant they would certainly run out of food before they could hope to reach any new supplies, is crucial, for it is a decision to prioritize ability to function in the short term over the possibility of survival in the longer term. The point is now to cope for as long as possible rather than to get home, although Scott's rhetoric takes longer to acknowledge this than his decision making would suggest. By the next day, Scott is becoming frustrated by Oates' survival: "If we were all fit I should have hopes of getting through, but the poor Soldier has become a terrible hindrance, though he does his utmost and suffers much I fear." Hints continue, and by March 10 are explicit: "Oates' foot worse. He has rare pluck and must know that he can never get through. . . . Of course poor Titus is the greatest handicap." The next day, "Titus Oates is very near the end, one feels. What we or he will do, God only knows. . . . He is a fine brave fellow and understands the situation, but he practically asked for advice. Nothing could be said but to urge him to march as long as he could." In the context of this discussion, Scott commanded Wilson to hand over to each man a fatal dose of morphine, confirming the idea that he preferred Oates to commit suicide. Nevertheless, it was another five days before Oates, having slept through the night "hoping not to wake," woke to a blizzard and—according to Scott—said to his companions, "I am just going outside and may be some time." Scott writes, "though we tried to dissuade him we knew it was the act of a brave man and an English gentleman. We all hope to meet the end in a similar spirit, and assuredly the end is not far."

The manner of Oates' death is still the stuff of sermons and school assemblies in England, but it has also received more critical attention. The revisionist historian Roland Huntford is deeply suspicious, pointing out that Wilson, who wrote to Oates' mother describing her son's death, tells no such story, although if it had happened she would surely be the person who would most want to know. "I may be some time" has become a catchphrase of Englishness, so widely known as to be the title of Francis Spufford's book, subtitled *Ice and the English Imagination*. This iconic status naturally attracts skepticism, but it requires no cultural or political agenda to feel uncomfortable with Scott's account of Oates' death. We cannot know what was said to Oates or anyone else on the subject, but it is clear that Scott had Oates' suicide in mind at least ten days before it happened. Despite all the rhetoric about Oates' nobility, Scott sees him as "a terrible hindrance" and "the greatest handicap" over a week before his death. The five days between Scott reluctantly advising Oates to keep going for as long as possible, while at the same time issuing him the overdose of morphine, and Oates' disappearance seem to give the lie to Scott's insistence that this death was freely and nobly chosen.

Whatever happened and whatever was said, Scott's text claims the credit for Oates' self-sacrifice, as if saying that "he has rare pluck" and "must know he will never get through" obliges Oates to demonstrate his pluck by dying before he jeopardizes anyone else's safety. Whether Oates behaved as Scott describes or not, by describing the act before it was carried out, Scott makes Oates' death his own. Scott defines the only honorable course before Oates takes it, making the lapse of time between the description and the event deeply problematic. Oates knows what he must do, and therefore the delay in doing it seems to indicate a reluctance to give up his life according to Scott's mythology of English masculinity. On the other hand, the longer Oates survives Scott's decision that everyone would be better off if he were dead, the more it seems that Scott is pushing a companion towards suicide, which is not particularly gentlemanly either. It is equally important to Scott's story both that dying alone is entirely Oates' own spontaneous idea and also that it is the creation of Scott's own text. For this particular myth to work, to seem suitably *mythical*, preordained and meaningful, it must also seem like history, composed of the ragged and random acts of more and less autonomous individuals. In the days between Scott's writing of Oates' end and Oates' enactment of it, we must imagine these conflicting tensions working themselves out, and Oates perhaps caught between Scott's need to make myth out of him and his own natural desire to stay alive for as long as possible, however inauspicious the surroundings.

It would not, in the end, have made much difference if Oates had waited for a natural death. Two days later, on March 19, Scott's right foot was badly frostbitten. They had two days' food left but only enough fuel to melt drinking water for one, and then the temperature fell to -40°F again. On March 21 Scott lay in the tent and Wilson and Bowers tried to walk the remaining eleven miles to the large depot. The weather was too much for them, and the three men lay in their sleeping bags in the tent and waited for death. For Scott at least, it seems to have been a long time coming. His last journal entry is a week after the penultimate one, and in between he wrote twelve letters and a Message to the Public. The other two wrote notes to their closest relatives, trying to offer consolation for their own deaths (though even amid his prayers and absolute confidence that "all is well" Wilson could not help thinking that "All the things I had hoped to do with you after this Expedition are as nothing now").

Scott, meanwhile, wrote on, a surprisingly elegant handwriting given the extreme cold, heavy clothes, unreliable light and worn-down pencil. He wrote to patrons, friends and colleagues as well as his wife, mother and brother-in-law. He left instructions for his baby son's upbringing ("Make the boy interested in natural history if you can.... Make him a strenuous man."). He wrote sincere and perhaps less sincere accounts of what went wrong and why ("I hope no attempt will be made to suggest that we have lacked support"), eulogies on Wilson and Bowers in which the tenses swerve alarmingly from the present to the past, making it unclear whether his companions are breathing beside him or not as he writes ("His eyes have a comfortable blue look of hope . . . he died as he lived, a brave, true man.") Roland Huntford sees these words as evidence of remaining energy that should rather have been spent trying to reach the depot, or at least encouraging the other two, who were healthier, to do so. Francis Spufford sees Scott the mythmaker trying to control even the publicity of his own death, and most historians are troubled by this sudden, sustained prolixity. Perhaps we should be more worried about the other two, as Scott lies there scribbling, setting his house in order and ensuring his own fulfilment in death, both of which seem concerns relatively sensible under the circumstances. One may as well go on *making sense* for as long as possible, but what of Bowers and Wilson, seemingly making nothing at all but waiting day and night for death? Scott's confidence that his body will be found and his writings read and published is even stronger that the evangelical Wilson's belief in the afterlife. Scott seems to be coming into his own even as he returns to his journal to scrawl on Thursday, March 29:

I do not think we can hope for any better things now. We shall stick it out to the end, but we are getting weaker, of course, and the end cannot be far. It seems a pity, but I do not think I can write more.

R Scott

Last Entry

For Gods sake look after our people

When Apsley Cherry-Garrard found the bodies the following spring, Bowers and Wilson lay fastened into their bags as if asleep, their letters neatly folded and tucked away. Scott had put his papers away, but had opened his bag and his clothes before he died, and flung one arm across Wilson. Perhaps the other two died first or perhaps they lay down quietly and turned inward as if for sleep while Scott wrote, but certainly even his last entry sounds as if they are all still alive, in his book if nowhere else.

"We Will Not at This Moment Raise the Question"

Most of the polar party's apotheosis happened after the 1914–18 war, making it tempting to speculate that without the cultural needs and anxieties engendered by the loss of so much of the young male population of Europe, Scott's South Polar expedition might have been remembered for no longer than the Greely Expedition or the death of Charles Francis Hall. However, since most of Scott's survivors joined up as soon as they got back to England and were in no position to write anything until the war was over anyway, the Great War may have done nothing more than heighten the national affection for Scott. The London *Times* of February 11, 1913, provides evidence both ways. The paper was entirely devoted to the story, but the editorial's praise is distinctly tempered, invoking the race with Amundsen and the possible wastefulness of polar exploration even as it claims to dismiss them:

Thus ends a great and truly heroic adventure, undertaken quite voluntarily by these officers and their followers, with the object of settling some unsolved problems of geography, natural history and other sciences. In judging Captain Scott and his friends, let us put out of our minds all the gossip which from time to time has been circulated about "a race" between him and his Danish rival Captain Amundsen. . . .

We will not at this moment raise the question whether the scientific results of these arduous polar expeditions are, or are henceforth likely to be, adequate to the cost—to the cost of valuable lives which may always have to be paid. It is more consonant with the universal feeling of the moment simply to add our tribute to the courage, the perseverance in the face of enormous difficulties, which every member of the expedition has shown since the beginning. . . .

By the time Apsley Cherry-Garrard came to write his own excellent account of his winter journey with Oates and Wilson in search of penguin embryos, on which they all nearly died (and which produced no useful data whatsoever), he was able to be explicit about the nostalgia that made the myth of Scott so attractive:

This post-war business is inartistic, for it is seldom that any one does anything well for the sake of doing it well; and it is un-Christian, if you value Christianity, for men are out to hurt and not to help. . . . It is all very interesting and uncomfortable, and it has been a great relief to wander back in one's thoughts and correspondence and personal dealings to an age in geological time, so many hundred years ago, when we were artistic Christians, doing our jobs as well as we were able just because we wished to do them well, helping one another with all our strength, and (I speak with personal humility) living a life of co-operation, in the face of hardships and dangers, which has seldom been surpassed.

Perhaps, finally, this offers a key to the British treasuring of Robert Falcon Scott, and explains why other nations find it both typical and incomprehensible. The era that Cherry-Garrard describes as "artistic and Christian" was no more of a Golden Age than any of the other periods so called. A substantial minority of the population were starving, and the majority cared so little that this only came to light when most of the poorer young men proved unfit for active service in the war. Maternal and infant mortality rates were higher than they had been since the seventeenth century and most people had little access to healthcare and education, while the elite passed lives of leisure with unrivaled opportunities for conspicuous consumption. But because the First World War forced the government to depend on women (to keep the country running while the men were at war) and the working classes (cannon fodder), and left an urgent need for capital, which made taxing the rich inevitable, the pace of political change between 1918 and 1922 was greatly accelerated. Women voted, the great country houses began to close, the empire started to slip away. War marked the "end of an era" in a way that nothing else could, and made a space for yearning. There was so much grief for so many men that perhaps Scott, dying far from the bloody brutality of war and dying in innocence of the wholesale slaughter of an entire European generation, became an emblem of all that was lost. If he died partly because he insisted on regarding polar exploration as a mythic quest rather than a matter of warm shoes and good engineering, perhaps he is mourned because of rather than despite this romanticism. Others of his generation also thought of themselves as capable of things that mattered, and their ambitions and personal achievements counted for nothing in front of the bayonets and guns in the trenches. Scott's death is not an obliteration, and so he can stand for those who had no chance of an idiosyncratic end.

VIII
Ballooning to the North Pole: The Andrée Expedition

The idea of attempting to reach the North Pole in a nineteenth-century hot air balloon with no backup of any kind might seem like almost suicidal Edwardian eccentricity, but it is only so from the vantage-point of our own easy reliance on air travel, which is the fruit of precisely such endeavors. From the medieval Norse use of a compass to navigate the North Atlantic to the Byrd Expedition's experiments with tractors and the routine use of satellite navigation systems by contemporary polar travelers, new technologies have always been of great interest to explorers. Conventional and established technologies had failed to reach the Pole (and killed a great many people along the way), so it was not obvious that newer ones would be any less reliable. Like Nansen's equally radical plans, Salomon August Andrée's ideas developed in conscious opposition to the Anglo-American naval hierarchy's exclusive attitude to polar exploration.

Andrée, who grew up in Sweden, first became interested in aeronautics and ballooning when as a young man he went to the World's Exposition in Philadelphia in 1876. He began to theorize about a system of transatlantic balloons, using the trade winds to carry passengers and freight. His companion Nils Strindberg had likewise spent his youth learning about ballooning and photography, and was so confident about the safe return of the expedition that he became engaged immediately before setting off. The third member of the expeditions, Knut Fraenkel, was much younger than the other two, a railway engineer with a passionate interest in new technologies. They left Danes Island, off Spitzbergen, on July 11, 1897, and never returned.

Ballooning was an attractive way of trying to reach the Pole because it avoided both the great perils of trying to navigate a boat through the polar ice cap and the dangerous and grueling process of trying to walk or pull sledges across the ice. The theory was that, if a sufficiently dirigible balloon could be designed, it would be possible to reach the Pole in about ten hours from Spitzbergen, although forty-eight hours was more likely. Skeptical writers suggested problems ranging from birds pecking holes in the balloon to a lack of oxygen high over the Arctic, but Andrée was determined and eventually raised the necessary funding. Since, if all went according to plan, the men would be safe from exhaustion, malnutrition and falling through the ice or down crevasses, the greatest problems were keeping warm and being as sure as possible that the balloon was utterly reliable. Andrée devoted great ingenuity to the packing and equipment. To quote the editor of his journals:

> The danger of fire made the preparation of the food on board a balloon filled with hydrogen gas a very difficult problem, but a friend of Andrée's, Ernst Goransson, CE, succeeded in solving it in a most ingenious way. The cooking apparatus, constructed by him, hung at 26 ft below the car, and was heated by a spirit-lamp, which by means of special devices, could be lit and extinguished where it hung by the persons in the car. A mirror, placed at an angle of 45° in front of a hole in the apparatus lying level with the flame, allowed the cook to see if the lighting had been successfully carried out or not.

The first year Andrée attempted the expedition, 1896, he arrived in Spitzbergen late in the season and the wind did not come into the right quarter before autumn closed in. The following year, all went well, and on July 11 the *Eagle* was launched. Problems began almost immediately. As the balloon left the shore, it was noticed that the steering ropes were still lying on the beach. The innovative screw fastenings had come undone during takeoff, and Fraenkel, Strindberg and Andrée were adrift in the Arctic in a balloon with no steering mechanism. Before the *Eagle* left the bay, it was seen to dip briefly into the water. It rose again and continued out of sight into the low cloud.

The detailed information about its subsequent movements is available because the men threw out written accounts in buoys which eventually washed up on the coasts of Iceland and Norway, and because they dispatched a couple of carrier pigeons. A public information campaign meant that these manuscripts, picked up by old

The launch of the Eagle *in 1897*

and young beachcombers across the Arctic archipelago, were returned to Stockholm and eventually published. For the first forty-eight hours, the balloon rose well in the sun but fell alarmingly in cloud. The ballast was being used up very quickly, and soon the balloon began to bounce and drag across the ice floes and freezing dark sea. This dragging and crashing continued for two days, during which it was impossible to sleep and difficult to eat. The men threw out more and more ballast in trying to lighten the balloon so it would take off again, eventually disposing of all the medical supplies and much of the food in their desperation. None of them was adequately clothed to survive much time on the ice, a point which clearly preyed on their minds as they made lists of what they were wearing. A freezing fog came down and settled on the ropes, making things even worse as the balloon became less and less buoyant. On July 14 they abandoned the grounded *Eagle*.

The terrain on which the three men found themselves was the most treacherous and difficult the Arctic can offer. The ice that often covers the Arctic Ocean in winter had partly melted and begun to break up, leaving gaps (leads) of the coldest possible water between the shifting and cracking ice floes. There is no practical or efficient way of traveling under such conditions. Sledges, skiers and walkers are in constant danger of falling through or being washed off the ice floes, which are in any case constantly moving in relation to each other and following the drift of underlying ocean currents. Even the largest boats, moreover, may be crushed by the ice and, even if they do not sink, will almost inevitably get trapped and end up carried by the slow ice drift. To this day, it is only submarines that are able to navigate these waters with any degree of control.

Andrée, Fraenkel and Strindberg had to decide whether to try to walk across the ice floes, badly equipped and inadequately clad, or stay still and hope that they would drift towards somewhere where they might survive. It was not much of a choice, and they decided to set off towards Franz Josef Land, where Nansen had survived a winter on the ice. If they sustained much hope, they were not allowing for the immense superiority of Nansen's equipment and training.

The three men spent the first week after landing preparing as well as they could for a long trek. They had left with food sufficient for six months, two sledges, a small makeshift boat, three sleeping bags and some survival equipment. Much of this had been thrown out of the balloon as ballast, but at this stage they were still able to prepare a daily hot meal and were all hopeful about their chances of getting home. Strindberg wrote to his fiancée Anna every day, although they all now knew that they would have to survive a winter in the Arctic before they could hope to communicate with anyone else. Once they set off, it quickly became clear that the sledges were too heavy for one person to pull up and down the hummocks of ice, and all three moved one sledge as far as they could and then went back for the other. The navigational instruments had survived and they had some idea of where they were, but in dense fog there would have been neither sun nor horizon and it was hard to make calculations with any accuracy. The leads in the ice became so wide that they had to use the boat to ferry the sledges precariously across, making progress even slower and more arduous, and by late July they were managing at most a mile or two each day.

Strindberg wrote to his fiancée on her birthday, "One has plenty of time to think, and it is sweet to have such pleasant memories and such happy prospects for the future to occupy my thoughts." He told her he was healthy and hopeful, and the following day, having fallen through the ice twice, added, "The most delightful hour of the day is when one has gone to rest and allows one's thoughts to fly back to better and happier times. But their immediate goal now is our wintering place. We hope to have things better in the future." The next day, they could no longer pull the sledges and decided to abandon more provisions, keeping enough for a further forty-five days. The killing of a bear encouraged them to leave even more food in hopes of replacing it by hunting, and they ate as much as they could and continued on their way. The snow covering the ice became wetter, and they were constantly soaked as they struggled through the knee-high slush. When at last the sun appeared on August 1 Fraenkel's observations showed that they had been drifting west faster than they had walked east. Strindberg stopped writing to Anna, and they ran out of bear's meat. Shooting a new one the following day was some consolation, but it was so tough that they damaged their forks trying to eat it.

Raw Brain and Algae Soup

On August 4 the party admitted that they were simply not progressing eastwards and decided to aim for a smaller depot island to the north of Spitzbergen. A week later, they were again low on food and often had to crawl across the rough ice. By the middle of August they were all suffering from colds, Fraenkel had gastric problems, and they had begun to be grateful when they could shoot and eat seagulls. Andrée's diary entry for August 20 shows just how grim the trek was:

> The sledges must often be pulled at great speed at one part of the crossing, and slowly during another part. They must often be swung round on the middle of a point, or in the middle of a pass. The axe and the spade must often be employed in order to make a road. Tracks for one or both of the runners must be hewn. Perhaps the sledges have to be entirely unloaded, or else they are balanced across the boat. . . . The quays break just when the weight of the sledge rests on them. The sledge, with its valuable cargo, is in a position of the greatest danger.

Even so, humor and curiosity were still there, and the next day Andrée wrote, "This evening, on my proposal, we tasted what raw meat was like. Raw bear, with salt, tastes like oysters, and we hardly wanted to fry it. Raw brain, too, is very good, and the bear's meat was easily eaten raw." They made algae soup, which Andrée liked very much and the other two considered edible in an emergency, and kept detailed accounts of the birds they saw and their calls. All had diarrhea, for which they took opium, and Fraenkel began to suffer severe gastric pain. The summer was ending, and the darkness began to return at night. Nevertheless, on September 1 they had a rest day to repair damaged clothing and sleeping bags, and Andrée wrote, "Everyone sewed, and we chatted, ate and drank. We were in the best of humours, especially when Strindberg announced that we were in 81° 16" N, and thus that we had been drifted rapidly southwards by the prevailing strong NW wind. We even took sandwiches and coffee with our bear's-meat dish at dinner." Strindberg's birthday, three days later, was also as good as they could make it:

I awakened him, giving him letters from his sweetheart and relations. It was a real pleasure to see how glad he was. To-day we have had some extra food on account of the day. The breakfast consists of bear's-meat beef with bread, and Stauffer's pea soup with bear's-meat and bear's-fat. At dinner, fried bear's-meat kept warm inside our waistcoats. Supper, bear's-meat, bread and goose liver paste, Stauffer cake with syrup sauce, syrup and water, speech from Nils, lactoserin chocolate. Strindberg kept his birthday by falling in very thoroughly, sledge and all, into the soup. We had to pitch our tent after three hours' march, and then had a very troublesome and time-wasting business to dry him and his things. Much of the bread and biscuits and all the sugar damaged, but we had to keep it in any case, and that was done by drying a part of the bread slowly and using it as before. The remainder was fried along with the bear's-meat and the sauce. The sugar was poured into the chocolate and coffee in its liquid form. The biscuit-mud was mixed with cold water, and then boiled together with the chocolate . . . . The accident to Strindberg did not lessen our festal mood, but we were jolly and friendly as usual . . . .

Over the next week ammunition became a concern, and Fraenkel developed a painful and badly blistered foot, which worsened until he could no longer pull a sledge. Then Strindberg's health also began to give out, and all the while they were still working against the drift and making very little real progress. On September 17 they resigned themselves to wintering on the open pack ice, and must have known that this meant probable death. They built a kind of igloo on a big ice floe and with a net tried to catch plankton to eat. Two days later they caught several seals, enough to give them hope of surviving into February, and began to drift past White Island, which seemed to comprise a huge glacier and some cliffs. Landing looked both impossible and undesirable, but they were drifting towards Spitzbergen and wintering there would be relatively easy. The building of the ice-house continued apace, and by the time the floe they were living on broke up suddenly one night, Strindberg was working on a vaulted roof. But on October 3 the ice on which their stocks of meat lay drifted away from the small piece on which the three men stood. The remaining four pages of Andrée's diary are almost illegible, but the men managed to reach White Island, where Andrée seems to have written something about the beauty of the glacier and the northern lights. There is a brief note about "moving" in Strindberg's hand, on October 17, and after that, silence.

In October 1930 a sealing ship stopped at White Island. The crew of the *Braatvag* found a piece of cooking equipment lying on the beach, which led them to investigate further. Amidst the remnants of what seemed to have been a makeshift tent made from oiled balloon cloth, they found Fraenkel's skeleton, while nearby lay Andrée's clothes, pulled off by animals. His scattered bones lay where bears had dragged them from the tent. Undisturbed by animals were the stove full of paraffin, the expedition's supply of money, and some plates with food still on them.

Strindberg's body was laid out and buried in a shallow grave nearby, his engagement ring lying where his left hand would have been, and between that and the tent much of the expedition's equipment was strewn. This included rolls of exposed but undeveloped film, which scientists in Stockholm were later able to print. All the guns were there and there was plenty of ammunition, and in a rock larder by the shore an impressive supply of carefully butchered meat. They had matches and dry driftwood, and the stove was in such good order that when found it could still boil a litre of water in six minutes. The sledges were still drawn up high on the beach with the boat. The main weakness, as all along, seems to have been that all three were quite inadequately clothed for a polar winter, and the best guess is that first Strindberg and then the other two died in their sleep of cold. As polar deaths go, it was perhaps not so bad.

IX

Eating Each Other: Adolphus Greely's *Three Years of Arctic Service*

The Greely Expedition, officially the Lady Franklin Bay Expedition, was one of several late-nineteenth-century American attempts to reach the North Pole. Lieutenant Adolphus Washington Greely, a Civil War veteran, commanded a small group of U.S. Army soldiers, two of whom, an astronomer and a photographer, enlisted in order to join the expedition. Twenty-two men left St. John's, Newfoundland, aboard the *Proteus* on July 4, 1881. Three years later, six returned.

The *Proteus* stopped in Greenland to pick up dog teams and two Inuit men, Thorlip Christiansen and Jens Edward, to drive them. When the ship dropped the expedition in Lady Franklin Bay in mid-August, one man asked to return home, "saying that he thought such a course calculated to promote the harmony and interests of the expedition," and two more were sent back as physically unfit for Arctic service. Another man, Lieutenant Kislingbury, asked to be discharged, "dissatisfied with the expeditionary regulations," but the *Proteus* departed as he collected his bags and Kislingbury was left with the expedition but relieved from duty, an unfortunate position in which to begin.

They began by building a double-layered, single-story house, with separate quarters for men and officers: "It will be observed that the bathroom abutted against the chimneys, so that this indispensable adjunct of an Arctic house was always comfortable for the persons using it." Winter came early, and they passed the time exploring locally, hunting and making some scientific observations, although this was not a primary purpose of the expedition. Greely wrote:

> At 5 am I was awoken by the calling of a ptarmigan, which seemed to be challenging another bird which answered within a few feet of me. I called to Whisler, who had the revolver, to shoot the bird. He reported that it was perched on the ridge pole about two feet above my head. As he was a good marksman, I told him to take very careful

aim and shoot it; but Connell, who was in the [sleeping] bag with me, displayed such a marked lack of confidence in Whisler's marksmanship, that in deference to his doubts I directed Whisler not to fire, and so the bird escaped.

When spring came, a party was sent to reach a new furthest north, which, in extreme discomfort, they did, attaining 83° 23.8" N on Lockwood Island on May 13. Greely led groups who mapped much of northern Greenland over the short summer, but by late August the engineer had been caught stealing fuel alcohol to drink and there was increasing anxiety about the failure of the expected relief boat. By September, with the days shortening fast, Greely acknowledged that they would have to get through the winter on the remaining supplies from the previous year. It was not an impossible task, but neither would it be easy.

"A Stern and Frightful Reality"
Spring of 1883 found all the men in good physical health, but there had been problems of discipline throughout the winter and there was growing resentment of Greely's authority. Greely decided to set up depots so that the expedition could head south by boat if no relief ship appeared in the second year. This was opposed by Dr. Pavy, the first time Greeley's account makes detailed reference to dissent: "Dr. Pavy was an excellent physician, but his previous Bohemian life made any restraint irksome and subordination to military authority particularly obnoxious. A man of active mind and quick parts, his lack of any order or system proved most injurious to the natural history interests, which were in his charge. His unfortunate death causes me to refrain from any further comment than is absolutely essential." Pavy's two-year contract expired in July, and he declined to renew it or to hand over his journal as part of the expedition's official papers: "As Dr. Pavy insisted that he was out of service, and refused positively to obey my orders, it became necessary to place him in arrest, with permission to take such exercise as was necessary within a mile of the station. Every consideration was shown him, notwithstanding which he broke his

parole. I was unwilling, however, even then, to resort to any extreme measures, and so did not place him in close arrest, trusting that leniency with him would have no demoralizing effect on the party."

Greely then decided to abandon the station and head south if no relief party appeared by August 8, but the bay remained frozen and the weather was bad: "Time pressed, our fresh meat and vegetables were gone, our fuel nearly exhausted, and everything in an unsettled condition." On August 9 they set off, a 27-foot steam launch pulling a string of smaller craft, despite the adverse weather and dangerous ice conditions. The engineer, on whose competence their survival depended, continued to get drunk on stolen fuel alcohol. By early September they were hopelessly beset by ice and had food for a miserable two months left. At this point Greely decided to try to reach land—and, he still hoped, a relief ship—by sledging across the sea ice. At length they made a makeshift camp near Cape Sabine, from which Greely tried to send small groups to look for the relief ship or any depot it might have left. Conditions were too bad for them to reach any of the places from which this might have been possible. In early October they built three huts and, with ammunition running low, began to work on making Greely's ceremonial sword into a harpoon for walruses and seal. They had about a month's short rations left, and were becoming so weak that building the huts was a slow and debilitating process. Fuel for cooking was also running low.

On October 8 Sgt. Rice returned from a trek towards Cape Sabine with the news that the relief ship had sunk but left some rations in a depot there. Greely, knowing that they were too weak to move the rations to the new camp, decided to abandon the camp and head for the depot, although he knew there would not be enough food to get all of them through the winter: "I, however, am fully aware of the very dangerous situation we are now in, and foresee a winter of starvation, suffering, and probably death for some." All the relief ship's crew had taken refuge with another U.S. Navy vessel, and the captain had left a note at the depot assuring Greely that "everything within the power of man will be done" to rescue his expedition. It was not.

In late October the party reached a resting place near the depot and began to build another hut. Through lack of energy and materials, this structure was barely tall enough to kneel in and could only just hold all twenty-four men lying down: "The men, though wretched from cold, hard work and hunger, yet retain their spirits wonderfully. I broached today the question as to what should be our winter ration, but leave the point undecided until the [abandoned] English cache reported damaged by Lieutenant Garlington is visited by us. God knows what we shall do if it is spoiled, this hut will be our grave; but, until the worst comes, we shall never cease to hope for the best."

It was then that they learned from a scrap of newspaper wrapped around a lemon from the cache that the second relief ship had been lost as well. The consequences were clear. "It was frequently said that those who were near and dear to us at home were more to be pitied than ourselves. We were facing a stern and frightful reality, but they could not fail to be mentally tortured by doubts and fears of every kind." The men pounced ravenously on a cask of moldy dog biscuits found at the English cache, even though they were green. Greely estimated that they might have enough food for everyone to eat something every day until early March, although others objected that they had no chance of surviving on such rations. Dr. Pavy was particularly vociferous. Greely writes:

> The first days of November gave us a realizing sense of the horrors and miseries to be expected from a sunless winter of nearly four months' duration under existing conditions. Nearly half of the party were unfit for duty, by reason of frostbite or injuries received during our arduous autumn work. Our sleeping bags and clothing were already frozen to the ground, and their interiors were thawed only by the heat of our bodies, and froze solidly on quitting them. The roofs and walls speedily gathered frost and ice, as did every other article in our wretched hut.

By mid-November, with the men on starvation rations, food was being stolen from the stores. In early December Greely became sure that Dr. Pavy was stealing food from the sickest men who were under his constant care. He felt unable to discuss this because of the expedition's increasing dependence on medical treatment:

> Jan 2nd—The doctor severed the fragment of skin which held Elison's right foot to his ankle unknown to the patient.
>
> Jan 12th—Elison is thirty-four years old today. He is cheerful and doing wonderfully well, although both feet and the greater part of his hands are gone. I gave him half a gill of rum to celebrate the day. The doctor reports that Cross', Schneider's, Lynn's and Ellis' mouths are looking as though they might have a touch of scurvy. . . .
>
> Jan 13th—Lieutenant Lockwood gave me much anxiety all night through, as at times he seemed to be decidedly out of his head. It appears that he has been saving up small amounts from each day's food; and, from his own account, he ate today twenty-four ounces of solid food; an imprudence which has tended to break him down. He sees everything double, and is very weak.

On January 18, 1884, Cross died. The real cause of death was starvation and scurvy, but the doctor reported it as "heart failure" in order to avoid depressing everyone else. Elison complained frequently of pains in his feet—which had been amputated weeks earlier without his knowledge—and others showed signs of severe malnutrition. Cross was buried in a shallow grave with what ceremony the expedition could muster, and Greely decided against using up ammunition by firing a salute. Lockwood spent the rest of the month showing signs of increasing insanity and physical weakness. On February 2 Greely sent Jens and Rice off on a trek to find another, distant promised cache, with instructions to cross Smith Sound and try to raise help from the Etah Inuit if, as was expected, the cache was not there. They returned four days later with nothing, having found no cache and been unable to cross the Sound. Brainard developed breathing and kidney problems.

By mid-February the men had run out of water and fuel with which to melt ice. Dr. Pavy argued with most of the others, and refused to treat anyone with whom he was at odds. By the end of the month the food was almost finished and they planned, in desperation, to leave the winter quarters and to cross Smith Sound in the hope of finding help and food from somewhere. But the ice had broken and they had no boat, so gave up. On March 21 Greely writes, "It is surprising with what calmness we view death, which, strongly as we may hope, now seems inevitable. Only game can save us. We have talked over the matter very calmly and quietly, and I have always exhorted the men to die as men and not as dogs. There is little danger of these men failing in the dire extremity, for the manly fortitude and strength of the many compel respect and imitation from the few."

On March 24 everyone was overcome by fumes from the alcohol stove, and in the scramble to leave the hut Henry was seen to steal a lump of bacon and eat it raw. This was confirmed when he vomited it up later, and Henry was consequently forbidden to leave his sleeping bag. They began to catch a few birds and shrimps, but all the men were getting rapidly weaker and sicker, and on April 4 the Inuit Christiansen died of starvation. Lynn died on April 6, but Rice had to sleep with the body in his sleeping bag for the night because they could not bury it without eating something first. Lynn had been popular, and Greely was upset by his death:

> He asked for water just before dying; we had none to give. It was noticeable, in after cases, that almost invariably from six to twelve hours before consciousness ceased thirst began, and a request for water was repeatedly made. Lynn's death affected us all deeply. He was a strong, vigorous man of even temper, simple in his manners and tastes, a kind comrade, a faithful soldier, whom all liked and respected. In three years' service I had but one occasion to criticise his conduct. ... During the winter, he had repeated almost daily, in season and out of season, the motto of Kentucky, "United we stand, divided we fall." I had strenuously inculcated that idea, and I doubt not that its pathetic reiteration by Lynn most impressively stamped it on the mind of even the dullest, to the advantage of discipline and unity.

This repetition of a military slogan by a man slowly starving to death in the care of the Navy high in the Arctic has a pathos to which Greely seems immune. Discipline and unity had nothing to offer Lynn; united he fell. Rice and Frederick set out the next day to try to reach some beef which had been abandoned on an earlier trip, but Rice died in Frederick's arms after a few miles.

> Frederick's condition may be more readily imagined than described. Starved by slow degrees for months, weakened by his severe and exhausting labours, chilled nearly to numbness, he was alone on an extended ice-field with his dead comrade. His sleeping bag was miles from him, and to reach it he must struggle against a cutting blast filled with drifting snow. Such a march might well daunt the strong and hearty, but to that weak, starving man it must have seemed torture and destruction.

But he did return, so that more lives would not be risked looking for him. While Frederick was burying Rice and completing his journey, Lockwood raved for twelve hours and then became unconscious and died. Jewel died two days later, and then Long and Jens shot a bear, which hugely improved rations for everyone. Nevertheless, Kislingbury, who had tried to join the bear hunt but had been unable to walk 200 yards, began to "show a very decided mental derangement," while Greely himself developed heart problems. He feared for the leadership of the expedition if he died, as several men had now openly accused Dr. Pavy of stealing food. While he and others were ill, Henry stole much of the remaining precious alcohol and got very drunk. The Inuit Edward drowned while hunting at the end of April.

In early May Greely became so ill that he expected to die at any time, and furious accusations and counter-accusations of stealing raged among the men, culminating in what Greely believed to be a serious threat of mutiny by Pavy. Greely threatened, and intended, to kill him but was too weak to fetch his gun. By the middle of May, with two days of meager rations left, everyone made wills and arranged their remaining possessions: "Spent nearly all day in getting my personal effects in order, so as to ensure their preservation in case of my death. I have pinned to most of the few little articles which I have, a paper setting forth that they are my property, and what has been their history. Others of the party are engaged in a similar manner, although they are all in good spirits."

Anarchy seemed to threaten on an almost daily basis, and a week after this Greely wrote, "Discovered today that about five ounces of Elison's bacon has been taken by some unknown person. A couple of days since an ounce of Long's lunch was stolen. Extremity is demoralizing some of the party, but I have urged on them that we should die like men and not as brutes." Again, humanity is threatened by extremity; there is a real fear that the Arctic will turn people into animals. Ellis died on May 20, and Pavy began to show a surprising surge of health and energy, which Greely may have found strange even at the time: "Dr. Pavy is working wonderfully hard getting ice for water, and, strange to say, is making a collection of stones covered with lichens. His strength and energy lately are quite surprising, I am glad to write something good of him." Three days later Ralston died while sharing a sleeping bag with Greely, who stayed in it until morning. The survivors were unable to take the body to "the cemetery." The six strongest left were still living and, alarmingly in the light of later investigations, often eating apart from the weakest, one of whom, Whisler, died a few days later, followed by Israel: "I am compelled to raise him and feed him, which is a tremendous drain on my physical strength. He talks much of his home and younger days, and seems thoroughly reconciled to go. I gave him a spoonful of rum this morning; he begged for it so exceedingly hard. It was perhaps not fair to the rest to have given it to him, as it was evident it could not benefit him, as he was so near his end. However it was a great comfort and relief to him, and I did by him as I should like to have been done by in such a time."

While Greely tried to adapt the burial service to accommodate Israel's Judaism, Kislingbury died at the beginning of June, followed by Salor. "We had not strength enough to bury Salor, so he was put out of sight in the ice-foot." Evidence and accusations of stealing again abounded: "Our condition grows more horrible every day. No man knows when death is coming, and each has long since faced it unmoved. Each man who has died has passed into the preliminary stages of mental, but never violent, wandering without a suspicion that death has marked him. Only those who lived knew, and at the first wanderings we looked at each other, conscious that still another was about to pass away."

Henry now confessed to Greely that he had been stealing food and could not stop. Greely told him that if he did not stop, they would all die, and gave written orders that Henry should be shot if caught stealing again. On June 6 he was found pilfering food again, and, since Henry was now clearly stronger than any other pair of men together, three men were given three guns and told to shoot him. The rest of the men were told about it later. Bender and Pavy died the same day, followed a week later by Gardiner. The survivors were by now eating seal-skin sleeping bags when they could eat anything, and spending their waking hours writing the stories they did not expect to be able to tell:

> Long weak and very sick, unable to hunt last night. It is his thirty-second birthday. Gave him a spoonful of the gill of brandy remaining. Schneider this evening appeared to wander a little. Had nothing but tripe de Roche, tea and seal-skin gloves for dinner. Without fresh bait we can do little in shrimping, and so live on lichens and moss alone. Elison expressed a desire that his arms and legs should go to the Army Medical Museum in the interests of science. His case is most singular; he is in the best health of any of us. Schneider is doing no outside work but wrote up yesterday an account of Elison's November trip at his dictation. Bierderbeck is engaged in writing up the medical case; his term of service expires in five days and he promises faithfully to complete it, but cannot believe that he will last much longer.

A storm began, and soon no one could eat or move. Brainard tied a spoon to the stump of Elison's hand so that he might be able to eat wet sealskin after the others, who usually fed him, were dead, and then they lay down in their bags and waited dumbly for the end. After three days of this, a ship's whistle was heard. Brainard tried to crawl out of the tent to raise a distress flag, and a few minutes later the seven survivors were rescued. Elison died during an attempt to tidy up his badly amputated limbs on board the rescue ship.

The aftermath of the expedition was dogged by rumors of cannibalism. Greely would say only that no crime against the laws of God or man had been committed, and the official naval inquiry discreetly decided to content itself with this. Others were less easily silenced, especially following reports from the rescuers that they had found some of the coffins strangely light and, on opening them to investigate, had found flesh removed in neat chunks from the limbs of most of the dead. Even Greely's diary seems to offer some circumstantial evidence for this conclusion, since those who were strong enough to go on "hunting" trips away from the hut remained a great deal healthier than those who were too weak to move far, even though they caught almost nothing. Under the circumstances—in the last days the survivors tried to eat a lemming's skull so old it crumbled in the hands of those who still had hands—it seems neither unlikely nor entirely unforgivable that they might have taken advantage of a better source of energy.

PART FOUR

Visiting the Dead

From the earliest Norse journeys in the Arctic to the work of modern forensic archaeologists, the exhumation of earlier travelers has been a distinctive feature of Arctic travel. This book's preface begins with Bjorn Jonsson's account of "Lik-Lodin, who lived about the middle of the eleventh century" and was "in the habit of sailing to the northern ubygder or waste places in the summer, and bringing back the bodies of those who had been wrecked in the drift-ice." Lik-Lodin was motivated by the monetary expressions of gratitude from those whose relatives were thus saved from the perdition that might result from not being buried in hallowed ground, but his descendants have less clear-cut reasons for uncovering the dead. Sometimes, as in the case of the Andrée expedition, people who are hoping to find survivors of a lost expedition are saddened to find graves or bodies instead. On other occasions—like Apsley Cherry-Garrard's return to Scott's tent—the surviving members of an expedition seek out dead companions in order to collect the letters and diaries and carry out a proper burial, although even this assumes that both the dying and the surviving groups understand and follow certain conventions. It is necessary to write as you die at the Poles because someone will come to read what you write, and it is necessary to find the bodies of the dead in order to read what they wrote. Writing, in this account, works to legitimate both death and exhumation. As we saw with Scott, a fully written death is not absolute; to write one's own dying is to extend one's power as an interpreter beyond death, to deny the pointlessness of death. A traveler who writes as he dies assumes that someone will care enough to contend with the conditions that killed him to find his writing—and it also, of course, constitutes an invitation to searchers and readers to burrow in a corpse's pockets, send his letters and read his diaries. The interaction between the explorer and his public continues even as his body begins to decay.

This strangely literal relationship between bodies and manuscripts is one of the oddest and most distinctive characteristics of polar writing, and interestingly it seems to apply predominantly (if not exclusively) to the Arctic. Antarctic graves are more likely to be treated as shrines than mines of information, and a third and more disturbing way of visiting the dead occurs only at the North: from at least the eighteenth century onwards, there has been a steady procession of men heading north for the primary purpose of exhuming their predecessors. Nearly all of these have been interested in one expedition: the last journey of Sir John Franklin.

X

"A Fate as Terrible as the Imagination Can Conceive": Sir John Franklin's Last Expedition

Franklin, who died in 1847, is often seen as the Victorian equivalent of Scott. Revisionists would say that both men (and their subordinates) died of arrogance, because they refused to learn Inuit survival skills and insisted on venturing to the ends of the earth equipped as if for an aristocratic shooting expedition in Scotland. That is a convincing and increasingly uncontroversial account of why Englishmen died at the Poles, but does not address the more interesting questions of what they were doing there in the first place and why they became heroes after death. In these respects, the two men are very different.

Franklin, much more than Scott, was securely part of the Establishment before he undertook his last expedition. Already fifty-nine when the expedition left in 1845, he had been in the Arctic twice before, looking for the Northwest Passage, and had (briefly and unsuccessfully) served as governor of Tasmania. He was already knighted and should, in many people's view, have been settling down to enjoy retirement, telling travelers' tales and patronizing his juniors in the Royal Navy. But both Franklin and his wife, Lady Jane, were desperate for him to have one more attempt at the Passage, to redeem the failure in Tasmania or vindicate the appalling suffering of his second expedition, or perhaps just to end a well-known but variable career on a triumphant note. Admiral Sir John Haddington allowed himself to be convinced of the benefits of experience over those of youth and strength, and on May 19, 1845, Franklin commanded the *Erebus* and *Terror* as they left Greenwich and headed north, first to Stromness on the mainland of Orkney, then to Greenland and at last to Baffin Bay, north of Hudson Bay on Canada's Arctic coast. None of the men on board was ever seen again.

Unlike Scott's Antarctic expedition, which was the object of such intense public excitement that each pony was officially named after the school that sponsored it, it seems unlikely that anyone outside the

Navy and the Hudson's Bay Company would have known or cared much about Franklin if he had either succeeded or failed less spectacularly. Navigating the Northwest Passage would have been an interesting achievement, but the eighteenth-century view that the passage would revolutionize world trade by allowing the fast transport of goods from the Atlantic to the North Pacific had long been abandoned. Samuel Hearne and George Back had both mapped much of Canada's northern coast, and it was quite obvious that sailing large ships along it would be a remarkable feat, and only occasionally possible in very mild years with the right winds and great good luck (nuclear submarines are the only vessels that do this regularly now, and even this is not always possible or safe).

The establishment of the British Empire made fast trading routes less of an issue anyway, since the colonies provided guaranteed markets for British goods and guaranteed sources of cheap raw materials without resorting to the vagaries of international competition. Before Franklin's loss, the newspapers of the day were so full of the mass slaughter of British young men in the Crimea that there was little space left for polar exploration (domestic news focused on bread riots among starving laborers, while there were pages of advertisements for emigrant ships bound for Australia, New Zealand and South Africa). Understandably, there was none of the fanfare that accompanied Scott's or Nansen's departure; at first, the Franklin expedition was not an emblem of national identity, but just another of dozens of teams gradually mapping the Arctic archipelago and northern Canada.

In the nine years between Franklin's departure and the first news of the expedition's fate, all this had changed. There were popular ballads about Lady Franklin's widowhood, spiritualist mediums all over Britain and America were falling over each other to claim supernatural information about the two ships, and the London *Times* referred to the lost men as "The Arctic Expedition" as if there were no others. As stories began to trickle back from the Arctic, there were poems (good, bad and indifferent, but mostly bad), Sunday school tracts, plays, "panoramas" and magic lantern shows devoted to the exemplary nobility of the men on the expedition. Charles Dickens, already a figure of national importance, took a public interest, and Wilkie Collins wrote a play about the expedition.

From the earliest accounts, Lady Jane Franklin is credited (or blamed) for fueling and manipulating her lost husband's celebrity. She relentlessly commanded and pleaded with the Admiralty to send out search party after rescue expedition after search party, rejecting those who brought unwelcome news and petting those who told her what she hoped to hear. When the Admiralty's patience and resources ran out and the men were officially declared to have died in service, she turned to fundraising and organized her own search parties, continuing the quest for the whole story for years after it became clear, even to her, that her husband and all his colleagues were dead.

This search for narrative, one might say, offers the key to Franklin's apotheosis. Franklin's most important difference from Scott in terms of the polar pantheon is that he was never found. Neither his grave nor his journal has been discovered in 150 years of searching, and it is this persistent absence that gives his story its immediacy. For all the academic research and popular speculation poured into the expedition's dissolution and disappearance, no conclusive story has emerged. Some of the men had scurvy when they died. Some of them probably died of starvation. Some of the bodies seem to have been eaten—or at least butchered—by people. Some of them died in places that suggest they gave up hope and waited for the end, and others seem to have fallen and died as they walked towards hunting grounds. Their canned food was probably substandard, contaminated with lead and infected by botulism, but they left ample supplies of other provisions heaped on the beach. No journals and only one legible paper have been found, and the bodies alone tell a partial and ambiguous tale. The narrative remains fragmented where Scott's is excessively polished.

The *Erebus* and *Terror* had been provisioned for three years, so, when nothing had been heard of Franklin by 1848, a ship left for the Bering Strait (taking the conventional route via Cape Horn) to search the western end of the Northwest Passage, and Dr. John Rae and Sir John Richardson made an overland survey of the central part of the route between the Mackenzie and Coppermine rivers. A few months later, the Arctic veteran James Clark Ross set off for Lancaster Sound, but when no one found any sign of the lost men there was no great alarm at the Admiralty. Several Arctic crews had survived four years on provisions intended for three, and the Canadian Arctic was so vast, such complex terrain and so little known that it was entirely possible that the *Erebus* and *Terror* were either making unimagined discoveries or frozen in for an extra season.

By 1850, however, the situation looked more serious, and the Navy sent eight ships, the Hudson's Bay Company sent two and the U.S. Navy sent two to look for Franklin. They were joined by one ship financed by Lady Jane herself, and the thirteen ships cooperated to find signs that the Franklin expedition had spent its first winter on Beechey Island, where they had had a house, a forge and an observatory, and where they had left three graves marked by engraved headstones. None of these gave any clues about a subsequent disaster. At the beginning of 1854 nothing else had been found, and the Admiralty advised Lady Jane that the officers and crew of the *Erebus* and *Terror* would be considered dead as of March 31. Since the men had to be declared dead before their families could receive naval pensions, this was reasonable, but Lady Jane refused her pension and promptly abandoned her widow's mourning dress, worn to advertise grief, for the bright colours worn only by those who were not bereaved. It was not a position that could be sustained for long. On October 23, 1854, the London *Times* published Dr. John Rae's report to the Admiralty on his return from the Arctic:

> I met with Esquimaux in Pelly Bay, from one of whom I learnt that a party of white men (Kabloonans) had perished from want of food some distance to the westward, and not far beyond a large river containing many falls and rapids. Subsequently, further particulars were received and a number of articles purchased, which places the fate of a portion, if not of all, of the then survivors of Sir John Franklin's long-lost party beyond doubt—a fate as terrible as the imagination can conceive.

The substance of the information obtained at various times and from various sources was as follows:

In the spring, four winters past (spring, 1850), a party of "white men," amounting to about 40, were seen travelling southward over the ice and dragging a boat with them by some Esquimaux, who were killing seals near the north shore of King William's Land, which is a large island. None of the party could speak the Esquimaux language intelligibly, but by signs the natives were made to understand that their ship, or ships, had been crushed by ice, and that they were now going to where they expected to find deer to shoot. From the appearance of the men, all of whom except one officer looked thin, they were then supposed to be getting short of provisions, and they purchased a small seal from the natives. At a later date the same season, but previously to the breaking up of the ice, the bodies of some 30 persons were discovered on the continent, and five on an island near it, about a long day's journey to the NW of a large stream, which can be no other than Back's Great Fish River (named by the Esquimaux Oot-ko-hi-ca-lik) as its description and that of the low shore in the neighbourhood of Point Ogie and Montreal Island agree exactly with that of Sir George Back. Some of the bodies had been buried (probably those of the first victims of famine); some were in a tent or tents; others under the boat, which had been turned over to form a shelter, and several lay scattered about in different directions. Of those found on the island one was supposed to have been an officer, as he had a telescope strapped over his shoulders and his double-barrelled gun lay underneath him.

From the mutilated state of many of the corpses and the contents of the kettles, it is evident that our wretched countrymen had been driven to the last resource—cannibalism—as a means of prolonging existence.

There appeared to have been an abundant stock of ammunition, as the powder was emptied in a heap on the ground by the natives. ... There must have been a number of watches, compasses, telescopes, guns (several double-barrelled) &c., all of which appear to have been broken up, as I saw pieces of these different articles with the

Esquimaux, and, together with some silver spoons and forks, purchased as many as I could get. . . .

None of the Esquimaux with whom I conversed had seen the "whites," nor had they ever been at the place where the bodies were found, but had their information from those who had been there and who had seen the party when travelling. . . .

I may add that, by means of our guns and nets, we obtained an ample supply of provisions last autumn, and my small party passed the winter in snowhouses in comparative comfort, the skins of the deer shot affording abundant warm clothing and bedding. . . .

The last paragraph makes Rae's (justifiable) sense of superiority clear, the implication being that if he and his party could survive an overland trek of hundreds of miles by living off the land in "comparative comfort," then there can have been no need for the well-provisioned Franklin expedition to die of starvation. Rae was attacked by everyone from Lady Franklin herself to Dickens for failing to authenticate this story before publishing it. This was not entirely fair, since the letter itself is emphatic that the testimony is third-hand and since this report was intended for the Admiralty and was leaked to the *Times*. It is interesting that the traditional account of the outraged Victorian Establishment rising up to defend its son against the unspeakable charge of cannibalism seems to be a telescopic view of the contemporary reaction. The *Times'* editorial the following day commented sagely, "We dare not trust ourselves to dwell upon the horrors which obscured the dying hours of so many noble-hearted men. There is no agony, bodily or mental, which they must not have endured in their icy prison before they sank to their last long rest. All honour to their memory!"

And that, for a few days, was that. Bread riots at home and the Crimea abroad took over again. Cannibalism, it seems, was an occasional and regrettable necessity which ought not to be mentioned, more akin to menstruation and childbirth than anything criminal. If Franklin's men had had the misfortune to be reduced to it, then the least that could be expected of his Arctic colleague was to keep it quiet. A few days later, doubt, almost certainly prompted by Lady Franklin, set in:

> Is the story told by the Esquimaux the true one? Like all savages, they are liars, and certainly would not scruple at the utterance of any falsehood which might, in their opinion, shield them from the vengeance of the white man. . . . Their constitutional timidity might have been overcome when they found the white men enfeebled and emaciated by disease and starvation. . . . It cannot but remain a violent improbability that a party so strong as they are represented to have been should have suffered the savages to depart from their hands without securing or compelling the services of a sufficient number of guides. If the Esquimaux could live through the starving time, it is strange indeed that the white men should not have been able to accomplish the same feat.

It seems here that the idea of cannibalism and the idea of Inuit testimony are beginning to collapse into each other. It is unspeakable that the British Navy should have resorted to eating each other and unbearable that "savages" *who will not write things down* should be the ones to tell the *Times* about it. "All savages lie" (the Cretan paradox comes to mind), and no gentleman eats a colleague; these things are simply not admissible and will not be admitted. There is an absolute imperial need for everything that happens to be collated and to make sense in the metropolis, and the idea that Franklin's story might exist only in Inuktitut, only in places that the British have not yet mapped, is as intolerable as the idea that 135 of the Navy's finest men might have been so changed by their experience of a foreign land that they ate each other.

All the evidence, filtering back to London throughout the following decades as more of the Inuit learned English, suggests that Rae's information was right, but at the time accepting this story was partly an act of faith, even on his part, *not* because "savages are liars" but because, particularly so very far north, most of the Inuit had no exposure at all to the English language and none of the Europeans spoke more than very basic pidgin Inuktitut. In many cases, the very idea of communication between officers of the British Navy and Inuit hunters is a convenient fiction. Rae was right—Rae's informants were right—but readers in London were torn between the need to believe that the Empire understands every word "savages" say and the need to believe that an Englishman's values are utterly incorruptible no matter where he may find himself. The only way around this was to construct a Boy's Own Story which conformed to the genre of didactic imperial fiction, and this was the version written by the dozen and given by the thousand as a Sunday school prize and a gift to the school library.

"A Mere Accumulation of Dead Weight"

The next report came from Leopold M'Clintock, who was commissioned by Lady Jane Franklin to command an expedition that returned in 1858. On the western shores of the Boothia Peninsula, they encountered an Inuit hunter who had a Navy button on his coat. The ship's Inuit interpreter told him that it came from "some white people who were starved upon an island where there are salmon" (the description suggests either a rocky translation or Inuit incomprehension of Franklin's approach to Arctic survival, but in either instance an immense cultural gulf) and M'Clintock eagerly offered to buy any other objects from the same source. The objects produced by the local community set the tone for the rest of M'Clintock's discoveries: "First of all we purchased all the relics of the lost expedition, consisting of silver spoons and forks, a silver medal . . . part of a gold chain, several buttons, and knives made of the iron and wood of the wreck, also bows and arrows constructed of materials obtained from the same source."

The same people told M'Clintock that the inhabitants of King William Island had seen two abandoned ships, one of which sank through the ice before they could board it, but that the other had been an excellent resource to them for years. He crossed to King William Island, where he was able to buy "six pieces of silver plate, bearing the crests or initials of Franklin, Crozier, Fairholme, and McDonald; they also sold us bows and arrows of English woods, uniform and other buttons. . . ." It was in late May, walking along the shores of King William Island towards the Back River, where it was assumed Franklin's men had gone in search of good hunting and a land route south, that M'Clintock and his colleague Hobson began to make real discoveries. M'Clintock found a body later identified by records as that of Harry Peglar of the *Terror*.

> Shortly after midnight of the 25th of May, when slowly walking along a gravel ridge near the beach, I came upon a human skeleton, partly exposed, with here and there a few fragments of clothing appearing through the snow. . . . A pocket book afforded strong grounds for hope that some information might be subsequently obtained respecting the unfortunate owner and the calamitous march of the lost crews, but at that time it was frozen hard. The substance of that information which we gleaned upon the spot may thus be summed up:
>
> This victim was a young man, slightly built, and perhaps above the common height; the dress appeared to be that of a steward or officer's servant, the loose bow-knot in which his neck-handkerchief was tied not being used by sea-men or officers. In every particular the dress confirmed our conjectures as to his rank or office in the late expedition,—the blue jacket with slashed sleeves and braided edging, and the pilot-cloth great-coat with plain covered buttons. We found, also, a clothes-brush near, and a horn pocket-comb. This poor man seems to have selected the bare ridge top, as affording the least tiresome walking, and to have fallen upon his face in the position in which we found him.
>
> It was a melancholy truth that the old woman spoke when she said, "they fell down and died as they walked along."

The dead body, at last, tells its class and occupation as no Inuit account could. Three days later, Hobson dismantled a cairn surrounded by clothes and cutlery to find two notes on one of the Admiralty's printed forms for discovery ships to record information. The first, written on May 28, 1847, told that the expedition had

wintered at Beechey Island, sailed up the Wellington Channel to 77°
and returned, "Sir John Franklin commanding the expedition. All
well." The additional note of April 25, 1848, said that the *Erebus* and
Terror had been beset in the ice and abandoned, Franklin had died on
June 11, 1847, and so far nine officers and fifteen men had also died.
It was signed by Crozier (now commanding the expedition) and
Fitzjames (the captain of the *Erebus*). This explained the initial
problem, but gave no information about what the survivors had done
or where they might have gone. A few days later, Hobson found a 28-
foot boat mounted on a sledge. It appeared to be full of clothes and
strange oddments, but there were also two bodies:

> One was that of a slight young person; the other of a large, strongly-
> made, middle-aged man . . . large and powerful animals, probably
> wolves, had destroyed much of this skeleton, which may have been
> that of an officer. Near it we found the fragment of a pair of worked
> [embroidered] slippers, of which I give the pattern, as they may
> possibly be identified. . . . They had originally been 11 inches long,
> lined with calf-skin with the hair left on, and the edges bound with
> red silk ribbon. . . . The other skeleton was in a somewhat more
> perfect state. . . . Close beside it were found five watches. . . . Five or
> six small books were found, all of them scriptural or devotional works,
> except the "Vicar of Wakefield."
>
> Amongst an amazing quantity of clothing there were seven or
> eight pairs of boots of various kinds—cloth winter boots, sea boots,
> heavy ankle boots, and strong shoes. I noted that there were silk hand-
> kerchiefs—black, white and figured—towels, soap, sponge, toothbrush
> and hair-combs . . . in short, a quantity of articles of one description
> and another truly astonishing in variety, and such as, for the most part,
> modern sledge-travelers in these regions would consider a mere accu-
> mulation of dead weight, but slightly useful and very likely to break
> down the strength of the sledge-crews.

There was also some chocolate and 40 pounds of tea; and "in the
after part of the boat we discovered eleven large spoons, eleven forks,

and four teaspoons, all of silver; of these twenty-six pieces of plate, eight bore Sir John Franklin's crest, the remainder had the crests or initials of nine different officers.... I do not know to whom the three articles with an owl engraved on them belonged, nor who was the owner of the unmarked fork." Nearby were "about four feet of a copper lightning conductor" and "long pieces of hollow brass curtain rods." M'Clintock, who was after all in the pay of Franklin's wife, and who had seen John Rae's career destroyed for publishing what she disliked, refrains from much comment on this extraordinary array of bric-a-brac trailing along a beach in the High Arctic, but it would not be hard to read the po-faced ignorance of "to whom the three articles with an owl engraved on them belonged" as a quiet and horrified snigger. Similarly, the precision of "about four feet of a copper lightning conductor" sounds like someone parodying rampant insanity by quantifying it exactly, as if three or five feet might have made perfect sense.

This bizarre collection of objects is as much responsible for the ongoing fascination with the Franklin expedition as the cannibalism. If these relics must stand in place of the bodies and journals to which we usually look for narratives of polar death, then the tale they tell is perhaps worse than that offered by the local people. The conjunction of these trappings of Victorian domesticity with the bare gravel beaches and barren snow of King William Island spells out how hopelessly far these men were from home. It is hard to imagine a better emblem of alienation than the curtain rods dragged for miles across the snow in a boat, only to lie beside the skeleton of an exhausted officer, along with three different kinds of silk handkerchief.

There have been various attempts to make some sense of this baggage; perhaps Crozier's men were insane from lead poisoning from the solder on their faulty tins or maddened by scurvy, or perhaps the Victorians were so different from us that engraved cutlery was a fetish of personal identity that had to be taken everywhere with its owner, but it seems so far from any pragmatic realm that the best interpretation is probably textual. A few more human bones have been found since M'Clintock's and Hobson's discoveries, all of which indicate that cannibalism did take place, and even that this retreating party were carrying the severed limbs of their dead companions as provisions for the journey, raising the alarming possibility that they used the engraved silver cutlery to eat each other. After all, if one must eat people, then perhaps the engraved silver helps to represent the eaten as food and the eater as a diner.

To this day no one has found Franklin's grave or the "cement vault" containing his papers, which some interpretations of the Inuit testimony suggest should be on King William Island somewhere. And except for the three bodies found by M'Clintock and Hobson on King William Island, and the three men exhumed by Owen Beattie in the 1980s on Beechey Island (see Chapter XI), nobody has found any other graves or complete skeletons despite ample evidence that some must be there. What we have instead is this catalogue of mid-nineteenth-century men's fashions and upper-class domestic impedimenta marking Crozier's footsteps but leading nowhere. It is as if, finally, the goods of the imperialists have come to replace the men themselves, for the objects spread along that coast were only briefly British. Chocolate made with beans from West Africa or perhaps South America, tea from India, silk from China, brass and copper from India, sponge from the Mediterranean, toothbrushes and perhaps combs of ivory from African elephants, clothes of American cotton, and silver from almost anywhere but probably not Britain—the resources of empire serve as epitaphs for those whose unbearable deaths are also unspeakable.

XI
Interrupting His Cold Sleep: John Torrington

In the autumn of 1984, a photograph of John Torrington appeared in newspapers across the world. Aged twenty, Torrington had light brown hair and blue eyes. He was a small man, about five feet four, and very thin. He was wearing grey linen trousers and a high-collared blue and white striped shirt. He had been dead since 1846. The picture was greeted with fascination, distress and outrage. Torrington was so long dead that all attempts to locate any of his descendants before the exhumation had failed, but many of those who had never heard of him until they saw his photograph felt strongly that his grave should never have been disturbed and certainly that the picture should not have been published. For those of us unused to medical and forensic photographs, it is an innately disturbing picture. Owen Beattie and John Geiger, who were responsible for the exhumation, remark in their book *Frozen in Time* that "Torrington looked anything but grotesque," but to many others—he looks much worse. The pulled-back lips, cloudy eyes and blackened face recall horror films and subsequent imaginary presences in dark corners, while his pallor, his bound limbs and bare feet make the long-dead Torrington seem terribly vulnerable. To gaze on this image is to feel oneself both voyeur and victim, staring

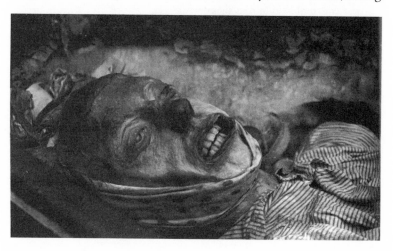

at a body prepared for burial that no one was meant to see again and stared at by a ghoul. *Frozen in Time* has inspired (or provoked) several major Canadian writers, notably Margaret Atwood, in "Age of Lead" in *Wilderness Tips* as well as her introduction to the 2004 edition of Beattie and Geiger's book, and Mordecai Richler in *Solomon Gursky Was Here*. The Canadian poet Jennifer Footman's poem, "For John Torrington," spoken as if by Torrington's mother, encapsulates the horror as well as some of the alarming contradictions in the twentieth century's view of Torrington's picture:

> The scientists unearthed my son
> for scientific reasons. In science,
> they say, ends justify means.
>
> John, they found you and Hartnell and Braine
> 140 years dead and fresh as today.
> I formed you well, preserved choice flesh.
>
> They claim lead solder in the cans
> killed you and the rest of Sir John's men.
> But we know better, you and I.
>
> A strange northern lethargy flooded
> over you, took you into its sticky white fog,
> drowned you in its pincer.
>
> Your open eyes accuse me, John,
> Your lips curl back in a comic grin,
> expose your perfect teeth.
>
> I hear the words you'd say if your jaw wasn't
> tied shut like a mumpish child.
>
>> I am cold, mother,
>> my tongue is glued to my palate with fear
>> of the voices possessing my head.
>> This haunting shreds my mind

furrows my soul
even my thoughts are brittle.
These new wisdoms
eat a man alive
eat a man dead.

John, I see through the shadow
of your half-shut eyes. You peer as if amazed
at being freed from your grave of ice.

I see a world sour and sick, Mother,
would dearly shut these tired balls of ice,
keep my hell to myself, watch nothing of yours.

I feel the signs you'd make
if your hands were free of the thongs
binding you like a man ready for execution.

My signs would burn the living white hot.
I have been on the rack and back
have had my fill of Eliot's
'frigid purgatorial fires'.
I dance the sign of the cross, Mother,
etch it deep into the heart of hell,
lick the world with the devil's tongue.
I dance Dervish dances, mother, dances
learned from echoes vibrating in ice.

Go back to your frozen grave, leave me to mine.
Time is done, incense bells rung.
No more son, no more mother.

We are ashes and dust,
Perhaps in our next resurrection we'll find
dead scientists and dig them up to conclude
our story
justify our own ends.

This poem is stunning because it presents Torrington as neither quite dead nor quite alive. The speaking mother is shocked by her child's exhumation and yet has things to say, can still interpret his dead and bound body as a mother must interpret that of a baby. Footman dwells on the physical relationship between the mother and son, the reappearance of the body which is Torrington but was made in his mother's womb, but also explores the way Torrington has become part of the ice, metaphorically as well as literally frozen. At first, he still inhabits his body almost as the living inhabit theirs; he would speak if his tongue were not frozen and his jaw tied shut and would sign if his hands were not bound and then—Torrington now clearly speaking for himself rather than intuited by his mother—it becomes clear that the Arctic itself has absorbed him into a cold hell. At this point the interaction is over, but there is no consolation. The mother recalls her own deadness, and the point is that all this is long gone, that the dead may not properly be recalled or revisited. The poem works so well because it replicates the discontinuity of time that the exhumation seems to create. Torrington's mother was— would have been—alive when he died and alive when he first looked as he does in the photograph splashed across the weekend papers in 1984. Because of his preservation, Torrington looks as if it is far too soon to dig him up, as if exhuming him is an act of traumatic sacrilege. Those who look at him return to a recent death and on-going grief, although in fact he had been dead for 140 years and, since all attempts to find any of his descendants failed, had in that time become almost as anonymous as a medieval or ancient Egyptian burial. But the picture seems to deny that anonymity and in doing so to invoke Torrington's consciousness as well as his forensic identity. He looks as if he might wake up. The "haunting" that "shreds his mind" is both the scientists' haunting of him, their refusal to let him rest in peace, and his haunting of us, his re-creation as the monster under the stairs in a thousand households that his picture entered in 1984. Footman's Torrington is stuck between death and life, still closely identified with his strangely preserved body and yet part of a polar hell.

The book that the anthropologist Owen Beattie co-wrote with the historian John Geiger obliquely acknowledges this dismay, although the descriptions themselves of the exhumations and autopsies of three members of the Franklin expedition are characterized by a combination of justification in the name of science and an uneasy deployment of the Gothic. The Foreword concludes by remarking that *Frozen in Time* is meant to show "how the work of a Canadian scientist and his associates is helping to explain one of the great mysteries of British and world exploration" and that "most of all," "it is an attempt to put the famous photograph of the Victorian seaman John Torrington . . . into some kind of context, and to show that there were reasons for the interruption of his cold sleep." The question the book does not address is the one with which Footman's poem implicitly begins and ends: why is it necessary to "explain" the "mystery" of the Franklin expedition? *Frozen in Time* presents "science" as a self-evident end in itself, for which codes which might usually govern curiosity may be suspended. In some ways this insistence sits oddly with Beattie and Geiger's respect for each of the three sailors', but particularly Torrington's, individuality. Partly, perhaps, because these three dead men still look like themselves, as if the connections between identity and physical appearance that characterize the living are unbroken, Torrington, Braine and Hartnell appear both as individuals requiring dignity and as archaeological raw material. *Frozen in Time* replicates, but can neither acknowledge nor resolve, the Arctic dilemma of human remains old enough to qualify for archaeology but human enough to seem personal.

In 1981, Owen Beattie, an anthropologist at the University of Alberta, decided to apply some methodologies of forensic physical anthropology to whatever remained of the Franklin expedition. Unable to find any significant material evidence of the last months of the expedition—Rae's boat, scattered bodies and bizarre collection of objects were long gone—Beattie planned instead to exhume the three men who died during Franklin's first Arctic winter, whose engraved headstones had become an eery landmark. *Frozen in Time*'s introduction to Beattie's project exemplifies the discursive difficulties that are to follow, for we learn that Beattie "believed that the Franklin disaster warranted at least one last pilgrimage in the interests of science" and that King William Island might "hold secrets that could be exposed by the use of the latest equipment and methods employed in physical anthropology." Despite this reference to "science" as a kind of final truth whose interests are best served by "pilgrimage," Beattie wonders "if the ghosts of the 105 men who died on the island, and at nearby Starvation Cove, still watched over their frozen ground." This is a book which is torn between the scientific imperative and the Arctic Gothic as its primary mode, an unsettling uncertainty which mirrors the difficulties of visiting the dead.

Beattie and his team reached the site of three graves in August 1984. These burials dated from the first weeks of 1846, when Franklin was still alive and whatever disaster struck later was months in the future. They represent illness or accident rather than anything endemically wrong with the entire project, but Beattie hoped that, in the absence of any material evidence about what happened later, detailed forensic analysis of these burials might provide some useful information. Once landed on the tiny Beechey Island where the Franklin expedition passed its first winter, 1845/46, Beattie surveyed and began to excavate the graves. A pause followed while he awaited final permission to proceed with the exhumation of these relatively recent Christian burials, but at last the Polar Shelf radio operator read out letters of permission "to proceed with the exhumation, autopsy and reburial of John Torrington." They now began to clear off the last layer of ice and gravel still covering Torrington's coffin:

> As they neared the coffin lid, the wind picked up dramatically and a massive black thunder cloud moved over the site. The walls of the tent covering the excavation began to flap loudly, and as the weather continued to worsen the five researchers finally stopped their work and looked at one another. The conditions had suddenly become so strange that Kowal observed, "This is like something out of a horror film." Some of the crew were visibly nervous and Beattie decided to

call a halt to work for the day. That night the wind howled continu-
ously, rattling the sides of Beattie's tent all night and sometimes
smacking its folds against his face, making sleep difficult.

Beattie himself seems set apart from the psychological vulnerabilities
of "some of the crew." By making the comparison to a horror film
through direct speech, Beattie and Geiger make the suggestion
without lending it authorial weight. The statement that Beattie's sleep
was disrupted by the tent blowing against his face (rather than, for
example, any fear that his project was turning into a horror film)
similarly asserts his rational pragmatism while providing the reader
with reason to feel very differently about it.

Having resumed work after this incident, the next problem was
that the coffin was filled with a solid block of ice on top of the body.
Beattie's team began to thaw it by pouring water over it. Torrington's
shirt and "perfectly preserved" toes began to show through, but "the
face remained shielded, covered by a fold of the same blue wool that
had lain over the outside of the coffin." Beattie and Geiger write, again
collapsing science and the Gothic, that "this created an eerie feeling
among the researchers; it was almost as if Torrington was somehow aware
of what was happening around him." At last this wool is defrosted:

> Using a pair of large surgical tweezers he pulled the material up
> carefully as it was freed by the melting ice. This was a very difficult
> and meticulous task as he tried to prevent any tearing of the material
> and had to work hunched closely to it. Then suddenly, as he pulled
> gently upward on the right edge of the material, the last curtain of ice
> gave way, freeing the material and revealing the face of John
> Torrington. Carlson gasped and sprang to his feet, allowing the fabric
> to fall back on Torrington's face. Pointing with the tweezers, Carlson
> said in a strangely calm voice: "He's there, he's right there!" The others
> quickly gathered at the graveside and while everyone peered at the
> fabric covering, Beattie seized its edge and pulled it back.
>
> All stood numbed and silent. Nothing could have prepared them
> for the face of John Torrington, framed and cradled in his ice-coffin.

Despite all the intervening years, the young man's life did not seem far away; in many ways it was as if Torrington had just died.

It was a shattering moment for Beattie, who felt an empathy for this man and a sadness for his passing, and who also felt as if he were standing at a precipice looking across a terrifying gulf at a very different world from our own.

What is striking here is the real sense of Torrington as a person and not just a body, and this is both *Frozen in Time*'s strength and its weakness. The insistence on Torrington's humanity, the reiteration of the sense that he might wake up, cannot but seem ghoulish in the context of his exhumation, while the description of the corpse as a "man" for whom the leading scientist feels "empathy" works against the gestures towards scientific objectivity or dispassion. There is a sense that Torrington is not quite dead enough for archaeology and not quite recent enough for grief. This is particularly clear in Beattie and Geiger's extraordinary account of removing Torrington's body from his coffin:

By far the strongest and most vivid memory Beattie has of that summer centres around the final thawing of Torrington's body in the coffin and lifting him out of the grave in preparation for an autopsy.

It was a remarkable and highly emotional experience, with Carlson holding and supporting his legs, Beattie his shoulders and head. He was very light, weighing less than 40 kilograms (6 stone) and as they moved him his head rolled onto Beattie's left shoulder; Beattie looked directly into Torrington's half-opened eyes, only a few centimetres from his own. He was not stiff like a dead man, and though his arms and legs were bound, he was limp. "It's as if he's just unconscious," Beattie said.

And then *Frozen in Time* returns to a clinical register and Torrington turns back into archaeological evidence. Torrington's clothes are removed and his body opened up so samples can be taken. The top of his skull is sawn off so part of his brain can be removed and Beattie sees that, beneath the oddly lifelike exterior, Torrington's cells have been destroyed by their own enzymes and his organs have shrunk to two-thirds of the expected size. Long dead, then. Archaeological evidence. And yet, "Beattie kept Torrington's face covered throughout the autopsy; somehow, this gave the reassurance that his privacy was maintained and illustrated how strongly the face is perceived as the window of our soul and the reflection of our identity." What it also illustrates is Beattie and Geiger's own sense that Torrington's soul was in some way still there, still behind his eyes even as they sawed through his skull.

The field season was coming to end by the time Torrington had been reburied with muted ceremony, and Beattie's group were drained by working days which had sometimes stretched through the 24-hour Arctic light. Beattie had hoped to excavate all three graves but decided that the other two would have to be left for the following year. However, he was troubled by indications that Hartnell's grave had been disturbed and chose to investigate this, without attempting another autopsy, before returning to Edmonton to analyze Torrington's samples. The team found Hartnell's coffin in a surprisingly shallow grave, smashed through with a pickaxe in several places and with the lid ajar. This coffin was also full of ice, and on melting it they saw "a ghostly image taking shape through the ice—a frightening, shimmering face of death." Many find the photographs of Torrington and Hartnell equally alarming and the two men, or bodies, look similarly undead. But *Frozen in Time* works by constructing individual identities, personalities as well as biographies, for the three men and, most importantly, by finding these personalities still writ large on the faces of the dead. So Torrington "embodied a youthful, tragic innocence" while Hartnell is "a sea-hardened nineteenth-century sailor" "shouting his rage."

"A Curious and Solemn Scene"

Back in Edmonton, Beattie's research led him to an old, unpublished letter from Commander Edward Inglefield which explained the disturbance of Hartnell's grave. Leading a privately funded expedition searching for Franklin in 1852, Inglefield had decided (to quote from the transcript of a speech later given to the RGS) "to ascertain the condition in which the men had been interred." Inglefield's description of the process mirrors Beattie's in conflating scientific and cultural expectations:

> My doctor assisted me, and I have had my hand on the arm and face of poor Hartnell. He was decently clad in a cotton shirt, and though the dark night precluded our seeing, still our touch detected that a wasting illness was the cause of dissolution. It was a curious and solemn scene on the silent snow-covered sides of the famed Beechey Island, where the two of us stood at midnight. The pale moon looking down upon us as we silently worked with pickaxe and shovel at the hard-frozen tomb, each blow sending a spur of red sparks from the grave where rested the messmate of our lost countrymen.

This image of two Victorian gentlemen standing beside an open coffin on an Arctic beach in the dark, feeling a corpse they cannot see in order to determine the cause of death is perhaps one of the strangest in polar writing. There are internal discrepancies that point up the literary rather than factual nature of this account, for Inglefield moves from a night so dark that it "precluded our seeing" to the view of a "curious and solemn scene" seemingly illuminated by moonlight on snow. This passage aspires to be both a first-person account of an encounter with an emaciated corpse in the dark and a classic Gothic vignette seen from a suitably striking distance. It is hard, it seems, to visit the dead without self-consciousness.

Beattie's analysis indicated that Torrington had a history of lung disease and had probably died of pneumonia. But Beattie also found extremely high levels of lead in Torrington's bones and hair, which had also been the case with bone fragments thought to come from other Franklin sailors. A cache of tins found on Beechey Island had been so badly soldered with lead that contamination of the food inside seemed inevitable. An explanation for the scale of the Franklin disaster began to emerge. Back at Beechey Island in 1986, Beattie reexhumed Hartnell and, working past the damage done by the 1852 exhumation, discovered to his astonishment that surgeons on board the *Erebus* had carried out an autopsy shortly after Hartnell's death. Beattie's team were excited about this, since it constituted a unique opportunity to learn about nineteenth-century medical practice, but for the amateur reader it also illustrates the strangeness of death, and the compulsion to revisit the dead, in the Arctic. A man dies. His doctors are, presumably, not completely sure why, or fear that there may be a connection with another death a few days earlier, and so carry out an autopsy. They conclude that he died from tuberculosis and the man is buried, attended by his friends and by his brother, who is on the same expedition. Five years later, when the rest of the expedition has disappeared, a searcher exhumes him, incidentally using a pickaxe to drive shards of the coffin into the man's chest and arm. This searcher unbinds one of his arms and slashes his shroud and shirt with a knife, feels him in the dark, takes his coffin plate and reburies him carelessly and in haste. A hundred and thirty years after that, a group of scientists dig him up again, this time with great care, unwrap his grave-clothes to discover that he is naked from the waist down and cut the stitches over the incisions of the first autopsy in order to study both the man's body and the processes to which it has been subjected. Hartnell's body 150 years on seems not so much the house of his soul as a book by many hands. *Frozen in Time* engages at least as much with Hartnell's interim visitants as with the man himself, turning him into a palimpsest that offers a contrast to the very personal understanding of Torrington.

The final autopsy, of William Braine, is described with the readerly teasing one has come to expect. The coffin lid is lifted and, "'I see some bright red,' Carlson said, as all the researchers peered at an area of blood-red ice covering Braine's face." "Blood-red" naturally conjures images of blood pouring from Braine's head and freezing around his face, but no—"When the thawing was started, the red colour over Braine's face quickly took on texture and shape. It was a kerchief of Asian design with a pattern of leaves printed in black and white." Nevertheless, to continue the quote from *Frozen in Time*:

The vivid colour seemed so out of place deep within the grave, and
the filmy nature of the material caused it to cling tightly to the face
it covered, accentuating the outlines of Braine's brow, his nose, chin
and cheeks; and in the centre, behind small tears in the kerchief, the
black oval of his partly opened mouth was visible. Poking through the
tears were some incisor teeth, producing a frightening, scarlet grin
which left every one of the crew transfixed.

Although they refer to Braine as "nearly alive" and "this frail and
lifeless man" rather than as a corpse or body, Beattie and Geiger
portray Braine as far more dead than Torrington. The body had
decomposed so far as to turn green before burial, and there were
"lesions . . . on the left and right shoulders, in the groin area and along
the left chest wall. . . . Close inspection revealed teethmarks." Braine's
body had begun to rot and had been gnawed by rats before being
hastily bundled into the grave.

Torrington stands out in cultural and artistic responses to Beattie's
work, and there are several reasons for this. The most obvious is that
it was a photo of Torrington that appeared in the news in 1984 and
many writers and artists responded to this image before, or instead of,
reading *Frozen in Time*. But the book itself reflects this bias, devoting
more space to Torrington and presenting him in more detail as more
human, even though one of Hartnell's descendants chose, improbably,
to be present at his exhumation. Perhaps Hartnell seems thoroughly
dead because of his procession of post-mortem visitors, all of whom
confirm his deadness by cutting his flesh and rearranging his body,
while Braine is gnawed, a bit green and—probably because of this—
has not been so carefully or lovingly prepared for burial as Torrington.
It is John Torrington, the first to die, who is disclosed to Geiger and
Beattie and then to the world washed and dressed for the grave like
someone who matters, interred with affection and then left for dead.
This sense of Torrington as uniquely precious underlies both Beattie
and Geiger and Jennifer Footman's accounts of him. In her introduction to the 2004 edition of *Frozen in Time* Margaret Atwood
comments, "Here is some-one who has defied the general ashes-to-

ashes, dust-to-dust rule, and who has remained recognizable as an individual human being long after most have turned to bone and earth." Ashes and dust have in some way marked each of the other two, and in the light of this perception Torrington seems comparable to Scott in resisting the anonymous deaths of most of their generations. The intact body seems to constitute some kind of parallel to the autobiography of dying; in both cases, we are left with the impression of a personality, a subjectivity, which remains present among us after the heart's last beat.

XII

Arctic Arsenic: Charles Francis Hall and the Search for Franklin

Charles Francis Hall was an unsuccessful small-time entrepreneur from Cincinnati who became fascinated by polar exploration and particularly by Franklin's disappearance. Partly because M'Clintock returned as Hall was starting to raise support for an expedition, but mostly because he was obviously an amateur, all of Hall's expeditions were run on a shoestring and without any official support. This pushed him into a dependence on sailors on American whaling ships and the Inuit, sources of expertise scorned by the British and U.S. navies, which was largely responsible for the successes he achieved. Nevertheless, Hall was a very difficult man to work with and, without the strict protocols and engrained traditions of the military, his expeditions frequently teetered on the brink of anarchy. In the American Arctic in July 1866, he shot an unarmed sailor, Patrick Coleman, claiming that the man had been speaking mutinously and that he had had no choice about summary justice. Hall's journal is blank for this time, but in a text published by the government after Hall's death in 1871 and believed by his biographer to be authentic, Hall says that he shot him because Coleman was big and strong and unarmed and he, Hall, thought he was unlikely to win a fight. When he returned to the States, England and Canada both declined jurisdiction over the shooting because it had taken place north of Dominion territory, and the United States seemed to want to ignore it. Hall was never held to account, and no verdict was ever available for Patrick Coleman.

This account of Hall's career is brief because Hall's published writing concentrates on popular, dismayingly racist and pseudo-anthropological accounts of the Inuit. Nevertheless, subsequent explorers (and particularly Nansen) were very mindful of Hall's life and death, and to this extent he is an important part of the culture and mythology of polar exploration. More pertinently, he devoted his life to trying—and failing—to visit Franklin's dead and was himself exhumed by his biographer Chancey C. Loomis in 1968. What follows is drawn partly from Hall's *My Life with the Esquimaux*, published in London in 1864 (before he left for the final journey during which he heard about the end of the Franklin expedition), and partly from Loomis' meticulously researched biography, *Weird and Tragic Shores,* published in 1971.

Hall's main contribution to the explanation of Franklin's disappearance was a great deal of Inuit testimony that no one else had had the patience or the linguistic skills to collect. Hall depended on an Inuit couple, Tookoolito and Ebierbung, to act as guides and interpreters, and was unusual among nineteenth-century explorers in accepting the presence of Inuit women and children on his treks. Like Nansen, Hall was an eccentric amateur who was convinced that the Establishment had made a mistake, but unlike Nansen he was wrong and also, by all accounts and by his own writing, deeply unpleasant. Hall insisted, "Supposition alone has induced the world to believe them all dead . . . the truth could now so easily be obtained, and the ground to explore so small and comparatively so easy of access!" His research was flawed by this passionate desire to conclude that some of Franklin's men were still alive and awaiting rescue, which made him convinced that any Inuit account of unexpected foreigners in odd places was a sighting of Franklin survivors (most of them seem to have been sightings of Franklin searchers). It is clear that he learned that Francis Crozier, Franklin's second-in-command, had survived for some time after the loss of most of the expedition, and had led a diminishing party around the King William archipelago in a fruitless search for food and help until they died of starvation. What he also discovered, however, was not what he, the British public and particularly Lady Jane Franklin wanted to hear.

In March 1867 Hall reached the shores of the Polar Sea opposite the King William archipelago where M'Clintock had reported finding remains. He spent days talking to the leader of the Inuit village there, and was given sketch maps and told of a ship sinking suddenly, many tracks in the snow and, fifty miles away, a large tent. Hall recorded in his journal:

> Three men first saw the tent. It had blankets, bedding & a great many
> skeleton bones—the flesh all off, nothing except sinews attached to
> them—the appearance as though foxes and wolves had gnawed the
> flesh off the bones. Some bones had been severed with a saw. Some
> skulls with holes in them. Besides the blankets, were tin cups, spoons,
> forks, knives, two double-barrel guns, pistols, lead balls, a great many
> powder flasks, and both books and papers written upon.

On another island, the Inuit had found the bodies of five
Europeans. Four had had their limbs sawn off and the flesh removed,
but the fifth lay peacefully wrapped in a blanket with an unopened
tin of meat at his side. Hall was very keen to find these and other
relics, but when he crossed the strait the snow lay so thick that there
was nothing to be seen. Careful searching revealed only a few bones,
so Hall erected memorials and held ceremonies where the Inuit told
him they had found bodies. When he realized that the Inuit villagers
had met Crozier and a few other survivors and left them to starve,
he became disillusioned with the whole endeavor and headed
home as soon as possible. Hall's interest in the Inuit was founded in
the stereotype of "happy, childlike natives," and when oral history
finally convinced him that some Inuit moralities were not the same
as his own he was disgusted. It is a clear example of the symbiosis
between the idea of the Noble Savage and the perception of
barbarity; Hall could not conceive of Inuit who conformed to
neither image.

Death on the *Polaris*

Hall's third expedition, this time in search of the Pole rather than
Franklin, was a much more professional affair, funded by Congress and
supplied by the Navy. Such expeditions are almost invariably well-
documented even in collapse—even, as we have seen, in death—but
Hall's is one of very few to lapse into silence. His journals were burnt
by his colleagues, who may also have been his murderers, and despite
huge public interest at the time there seems to be no remotely reliable
published first-hand account of the expedition. Loomis' biography

relies on manuscript material in the Smithsonian Institution, which has minimal impact on cultures of exploration.

From the outset in 1871, Hall was uncomfortable with the involvement of authorities other than himself, and spent the first few weeks trying to assert superiority over men who were better educated and of higher social standing than himself. The problem was that a condition of Hall's congressional funding was that the expedition should carry out scientific work, and the undereducated and insecure Hall felt very threatened by the presence of professional scholars. The scientists soon became impatient with Hall's petty tyrannies, fueling discontent on both sides. Hall began to forbid the scientists to do any science, and the situation became untenable before the ship left Greenland. Hall told the scientists, particularly Dr. Bessels, that he was keeping accounts of misdemeanors that he would report to the authorities when the expedition was over. Meanwhile, the crew had gained illicit access to the *Polaris'* supply of alcohol and were regularly drunk.

There was little ice that year, and Hall made his furthest north in a matter of days after leaving Greenland. Then, at the beginning of September, the ice closed in and the ship was trapped. They drifted for a week before anchoring to a huge grounded iceberg near the shore, from which it was possible to transfer stores and scientific equipment to land in case the ship was crushed. A few daylong hikes took place, and returning from one of these Hall complained of feeling sick. He took to his bed, vomiting, and soon became partly paralysed and occasionally demented. Left to rest in his cabin, Hall seemed to be recovering and after two weeks got up and returned to the decks. But almost immediately he became ill again and died within forty-eight hours. The crew buried him with what ceremony they could muster in a shallow grave.

A few days later, terrible storms came up. Although the ship survived, its position for the rest of the winter was so precarious that the Inuit moved out onto the ice where they felt safer. On board, relations between the scientists and the remaining sailors and explorers worsened. The carpenter, named Nathaniel Coffin, began to believe that people were trying to kill him, which might have been plausible if he had not thought that they were drilling through the wall beside his bunk to spray carbonic acid on him as he slept. It was not until the following summer, when expedition members were able to get away from each other in a series of half-hearted attempts to seek the North Pole in small boats, that the tensions eased at all, and then only as long as the warring factions were apart.

When at last the ice melted and the ship came free, it was clear that the ice had seriously damaged the hull. The Inuit Hans Hendrick's wife gave birth to a baby boy in August. The pumps were kept going for weeks as the sailors struggled to get away from the ice before the brief summer ended, but they burned unsustainable quantities of coal, and on October 12 the ship was crushed by huge floes of sea ice in a severe gale. Some of the crew jumped out onto the ice while others tried to salvage food and equipment. The Inuit men got their children onto the ice and returned, with their wives, to save what they could from the ship. The ships' ropes then broke, leaving nineteen men, women and children on the ice and the rest of the crew still aboard the *Polaris*. The ice floe was nearly four miles around but constantly breaking up, and they quickly drifted into the open Arctic Ocean. The following morning, those on the floe saw the *Polaris* making good speed away from them under steam and sail. There seemed to be no attempt at rescue.

The Inuit built iglus on the floe and the Americans built wooden huts, but food supplies quickly ran low and the Inuit were able to catch seal and bears just often enough to stave off death from starvation for everyone. The first floe broke up and they moved to a second one and then a third and fourth, but as the months passed the ice began to melt and floes were smaller and further apart. Several times equipment and supplies were washed away as waves swept over the pieces of ice, but they were far too far from land to hope for safety. The German-speaking scientists, who were armed, began to refuse to speak except to each other and in German. There was pilfering from the frequently exhausted stores, and some of the American sailors and the Inuit began to fear that the Inuit children might be killed and eaten. Those with guns began to abuse those without, making it uncomfortably clear that power no longer rested on anything but the capacity to kill. It was at this point that they were rescued by the astonished crew of a whaler, the *Tigris*, and eventually taken home to face huge publicity and the inquiries of the authorities about Hall's death and the collapse of the expedition.

These inquiries found that the *Polaris* had run aground and those on board had wintered ashore, helped and fed by the local Etah Inuit, before trying to set out again in small boats, from which they were rescued by a Dundee whaler and taken to Scotland. When questioned, the men said they had not seen the people on the floe and that the ship was too badly damaged for them to have been able to attempt rescue even if they had. When it came to Hall's death, the naval Board of Inquiry heard that he had accused nearly everyone of trying to murder him during the final delirious weeks, but also that Hall's letters and papers had been burned after his death. This aroused suspicions whereas the murder allegation alone could simply have been a symptom of Hall's illness. Closer investigation revealed that he had drunk a cup of coffee, which some witnesses said had been specially prepared for him, immediately before falling sick. It emerged that Hall had continued to be dangerously ill as long as Dr. Bessels was treating him but recovered when he refused treatment. Bessels had diagnosed a stroke probably caused by going from extreme cold outside to extreme heat in the cabin, and had injected Hall with quinine over several days; several witnesses said that Bessels had treated Hall with kindness and patience and showed no umbrage at being accused of poisoning. Since Hall had also told anyone who would listen that Bessels was surrounded by blue vapors which sometimes also appeared on other people, his other allegations became less plausible and the Board eventually concluded that Hall had died of apoplexy and that Bessels had treated him as well as possible.

When Loomis' archival research was complete, he had read all existing primary and secondary sources on Hall's life. This is usually the point at which biographers sit down and write, whatever the gaps in knowledge and unanswered questions. But Loomis, feeling "not that Hall certainly had been murdered, not even that he probably had been murdered, but only that murder was at least possible and plausible" wanted more information than the written sources were able to provide. He writes, eliding the reasons for wanting to exhume Hall with the official justification for doing so,

> I had applied to Denmark's Ministry for Greenland for a permit to travel to Polaris Promontory; arguing that if the case were recent, a court presented with the evidence would order an autopsy, I requested permission to disinter Hall's body and have Frank Paddock perform an autopsy on it. Given the high latitude of its burial, there was a good chance that the body would be well preserved.

The point that both *Weird and Tragic Shores* and *Frozen in Time* gloss over is that the cases are *not* recent. Autopsies are, and were in the nineteenth century, carried out if and when there is a possibility of taking action in response to any findings, be it the institution of criminal proceedings or the containment of a public health problem. Unexplained deaths need explaining in case something needs to be done and not because all lives need a properly concluded narrative. Anyone who might have murdered Hall was long dead by 1968 and, whatever the consequences of another cause of death, they were long over. The cases are not recent, there is nothing to be done, and no one argues that all historical as well as modern unexplained deaths require forensic investigation. There are reasons for exhuming nineteenth-century Arctic burials, but they are not the same as those for modern autopsies. Like Geiger, Loomis had difficulty getting permission for his project—it was not immediately obvious to those charged with the daily administration of the area that this was a necessary thing to do.

Eventually permission was given, however, and Loomis and his colleagues flew out to Hall's Rest, in the far north of the Arctic archipelago. Like Beattie and Geiger, Loomis has a clear and literary sense that he is involved in a cosmic endeavor. He writes of the first night, "During the night, under the unsetting sun, the weather changed. When we set out early in the morning to do the job for which we had come, the sky was suitably lowering, the land suitably bleak. The day before had been too bright for the work for which we had come." The euphemistic ellipsis of "the work for which we had come" establishes Loomis' own sense of the transgressive nature of the exhumation, while the louring skies—a less dramatic version of Beattie and Geiger's Gothic thunderstorm—gesture towards the conventions of fiction rather than biography. Loomis continues:

> For a year I had wondered how I would feel when the coffin was opened. Hall might well have become a skeleton—but in the Arctic air, lying on the permanent frost that had prevented his grave diggers from digging deep, he might have been perfectly preserved. It was impossible to know what was in the coffin, and much as I dreaded finding a skeleton from which nothing could be proved, I also dreaded finding the man himself, just as he had been. Having spent three years violating his mind by reading his private journals, now I was going to violate his body. I had been haunted by a vision of a rather offended face peering out of the coffin, a face asking, "Is there no limit to what a biographer will do?"

In this confessional and slightly whimsical account, there is again a sense that the Arctic dead, preserved by permafrost, might not be entirely dead, might still be "the man himself." The dead Hall speaks in Loomis' imagination, or at least his face asks, and the question does not seem unreasonable. Exhumation and autopsy are not so much the limit of what a biographer will do as the limit of what a biographer can do, where biography has changed from an intellectual exercise to a viscerally physical one. Loomis' account of the relationship between the exhumer and the exhumed offers an interestingly personal contrast to Beattie and Geiger's self-consciously scientific writing—the interest in visiting for its own sake is explicit in *Weird and Tragic Shores*.

The digging begins: "All of us wanted to be properly solemn, but our nerves short-circuited our sense of awe and we found ourselves making absurd jokes." The jokes end when there is "a whiff of decay" and then part of the coffin lid breaks, revealing part of an American flag inside. Loomis removes the lid to find a body "completely shrouded in a flag":

> Frank carefully peeled back the flag from the face. It was not the face of an individual, but neither was it yet a skull. There were still flesh, a beard, hair on the head, but the eye sockets were empty, the nose almost gone, and the mouth was pulled into a smile that a few years hence will become the grin of a death's head. The skin, tanned by time and stained by the flag, was tightening on the skull. He was in a strangely beautiful phase in the process of dust returning to dust. The brown skin, mottled by blue stain and textured by the flag that had pressed against it for almost a hundred years, made him somehow abstract—an icon, or a Rouault portrait.

Because Loomis did not publish a photograph of the dead Hall, this gentle and self-consciously artistic portrait of the dead face relieves and absolves the reader as well as Loomis himself. Despite the ominous skies and dread of a specter, here is nothing worse than art by decomposition. The abstraction to which Loomis refers is emphasized by his discussion of *the* mouth, *the* nose, *the* skin rather than Hall's or *his* features. The oddly inverted phrasing, "There were still flesh, a beard, hair on the head" makes Hall's decaying face into an interesting set of components rather than the expression of his former or present identity.

The autopsy revealed that most of Hall's internal organs had almost disappeared, and so it was difficult to take samples on which to base a full analysis. Loomis took a fingernail and some hair, and, back in Toronto, the analysts found that Hall had ingested large and increasing quantities of arsenic in the last two weeks of his life. As Loomis points out, there are several possible interpretations of this phenomenon, not all of which are entirely sinister; many nineteenth-century patent medicines contained arsenic in fairly high concentrations, and Hall may have dosed himself through the final, delirious weeks of his illness. Nevertheless, immediately before being taken ill he had complained of the strange, sweetish taste of the coffee he had drunk, and arsenic does have such a taste. It is probable that Hall was gradually poisoned by a member of the expedition who was close to him as he lay in his tiny cabin through the six-month night of Arctic winter.

PART FIVE
Women at the Ends of the Earth

There have, of course, been women in the Arctic for thousands of years, though little distinctive women's history survives. Inuit women had their own boats, bigger, heavier and more stable than the small hunting kayaks used mainly by men. Different groups and communities had and have different traditions, but women usually took responsibility for curing, preserving and sewing furs, making embroidered boots and winter clothing that is beautiful as well as more practical than anything European explorers were able to devise. When the Europeans began to record Inuit customs in the seventeenth and eighteenth centuries, the women in most communities tended to organize childcare communally so that more adults were available for subsistence projects like hunting and tent-making.

The idea that Inuit men encouraged guests to have sex with their hosts' wives is likely to be a European misinterpretation of the custom of the whole family sleeping naked in a row under furs, which kept everyone warm by sharing body heat. Guests were of course expected to sleep with the family, but not necessarily to have intercourse with the women who lay beside them. The European men's lack of interest in Native women's stories means that the experiences of these women are largely inaccessible in published English-language sources.

The first European women to go to the Arctic went with the Hudson's Bay Company. Although the HBC did not allow its employees to take their wives with them until the end of the eighteenth century, it is clear that some women, escaping difficult home lives or determined not to be parted from much-loved partners, bound their breasts flat, cut their hair, cross-dressed and set off for a new life in the Far North. The most famous of these is Isobel Gunn. Isobel grew up in the Orkney Islands off the north coast of Scotland. These islands were always the last stopping-off point for ships heading into the North Atlantic (several of Franklin's men were recruited in Orkney), and when times were hard during the Highland Clearances at the end of the eighteenth century, many men who could no longer make a living fishing and subsistence farming signed up to the HBC.

Isobel's lover was among them. Isobel disguised herself and signed up under the name of John Fubbister in the summer of 1806. Her disguise seems to have been entirely convincing—although the reasons for her urgency became apparent later—and she was posted to Fort Albany, far away from her lover. She performed hard physical work uncomplainingly and well through the Arctic winter, and went with her colleagues to the HBC's trading post for a few days of celebration over Christmas. On December 29 the others returned to work loading supplies for the inland posts, and Fubbister, saying "he" was ill, asked to stay behind until he felt well enough to travel. To quote from Alexander Henry, who was in charge of the post at the time:

> I was surprised at the fellow's demand; however, I told him to sit down and warm himself. I returned to my own room, where I had not been long before he sent one of my people, requesting the favour of speaking with me. Accordingly I stepped down to him, and was much surprised to find him extended on the hearth, uttering dreadful lamentations; he stretched out his hands towards me, and in piteous tones begged me to be kind to a poor, helpless, abandoned wretch, who was not of the sex I had supposed, but an unfortunate Orkney girl, pregnant, and actually in childbirth. In saying this she opened her jacket, and displayed a pair of beautiful, round, white breasts . . . . In about an hour she was safely delivered of a fine boy, and that same day she was conveyed home in my cariole, where she soon recovered.

Isobel Gunn continued to work as a domestic servant in Canada for a few years, but eventually seems to have returned to Orkney, presumably with her son. It is not clear whether she was ever reunited with her lover.

More usually, Hudson's Bay and North West Company men took Native American "wives" for the duration of their residence in the North. Native American women supplied HBC employees with mocassins (absolutely necessary for any travel in the region) and produced all of the food used on journeys and much of what was eaten daily at the forts. They also served as guides to the early mapmakers, and kept boats and snowshoes in good repair. It is not surprising that many of the disoriented British men formed close attachments to Native women. With no priests, these unions could not be formalized, and many women were deserted when their "husbands" finished their contracts and returned to Britain. The social structure of the relevant Native American communities was such that "abandoned" women could re-assimilate and re-marry fairly easily. The children of these partnerships, however, were ambivalently regarded; some, usually the offspring of wealthy men, were taken back to England to inherit estates and seem to have "passed" successfully in late eighteenth- and early nineteenth-century society, while others, deprived of both Native American and European educational traditions, found that the world of the HBC was the only one in which they could function and lived out their lives as servants at trading posts.

From the beginning of the nineteenth century, an informal marriage according to "the custom of the country" developed. This involved a written contract between an HBC employee and the father of the woman he wanted to marry, and was regarded by nearly all participants as being just as binding and serious as a religious ceremony. In the wake of this development, the HBC began to establish schools for the children of such marriages, and with the teachers came priests. In 1824 Miss Mary Allen went out from Guernsey to start a girls' boarding school in Rupert's Land (we can only speculate what a nicely brought-up girl from the Channel Islands made of northern Canada). She married, and was followed by a succession of English Victorians determined to teach the mixed-race girls "the ornamental branches of education." The skills which were always useful and sometimes essential for survival, such as curing skins, making winter clothing and processing meat into pemmican and other calorie-dense foods that would keep throughout the winter, were displaced by macrame, embroidery, a little polite piano playing for hymns and perhaps—at a stretch—a smattering of French or Italian.

This education could have resulted in some Native American women being treated with the same respect as merchants' wives in Britain, but instead the presence of the Anglican Church was judged to make northern Canada a fit place for European women. The status of Native American and mixed-race women fell quickly when newly married British women in crinolines began to come off the yearly supply ships.

XIII
Babies on Hudson Bay: The Letters of Letitia Hargrave

James Hargrave took leave from his Chief Tradership with the HBC in 1837 in order to return to Scotland and find a wife. He was 39, and had always been a vociferous critic of marriages between HBC traders and Native American women. In January 1838 he was introduced to Letitia Mactavish, the 25-year-old daughter of a wealthy and well-respected Sheriff of Kilchrist House in Argyllshire. Letitia had had a standard early-nineteenth-century upper-class woman's education, including some time at a finishing school, and had not been further from home than Edinburgh. They married during Hargrave's leave the following year, and he took her to London before setting off for Fort York. Letitia's family preserved her letters, which are of interest partly because they provide a rare and unusually frank account of domestic and personal life in the HBC, and partly because her prose is both pragmatic and charming. There are not enough women writing about polar travel before the year 2000 for generalizations to be possible, but a similarity of style can certainly be seen among the three travelers of this section. They share an unassuming and amused readiness to write about the challenges of daily life at the top and bottom of the world—a topic most of the men cannot approach without celebrating hardship—and an unreflecting interest in the picturesque. Both are evident from the beginning of Letitia Hargrave's letters.

She and her husband went to Liverpool to catch the new train down to London, and Letitia wrote home describing the experience to her mother and sisters: "We paid £5 for our 2 tickets, and our luggage being weighed except my dressing case carpet bag and hams as we were allowed lbs 100 each and had to pay 2d per lb above that, which amounted to thirty shillings—You had as well remember this as people often take more than is needful." The hams seem a particularly good addition to their 380 pounds of luggage, and it is clear that trains were still very much a novelty to be celebrated, for "The railroad engines are all tastefully decorated with green branches and ribbons to represent flowers . . . and the authorities strut about with huge bunches of lilac and red tulips in their button holes."(A lovely thought for anyone with more recent experience of British trains.) Letitia's gleeful enthusiasm for anything new and potentially interesting is entirely typical of her writing.

The couple enjoyed a brief residence in London, staying at a hotel where Dickens often dined. Letitia was taken to see the new Houses of Parliament being built ("they are to intrude a long way into the river"), and began to shop for the clothes she was told she would need in place of the standard trousseau. James gave the shoemaker detailed instructions about the kind of walking boots he required for his wife, and Letitia astonished the London dressmakers with her demands for multi-layered fur coats and the warmest possible underwear. It all came in useful; she was to write home a year later:

> While the stove rages I am clothed in flannel from the neck down to the wrists and ankle, wearing a man's flannel jacket (knitted) drawers to my feet made of bath coating duffle socks and English stockings under mocassins & a merino gown the body lined with the said bath coating . . . a pair of dark blue cloth leggins which the women here tie round their waists as we used to have our stockings when little, but I button mine to my drawers which they don't wear. Mine are embroidered with crimson pink white and black ribbons but theirs have beads which look much better & don't fade as mine do.

The detail here shows Letitia's eagerness to familiarize her family with every step of her new life, but it also works to keep herself a little distant from the ways of life she describes. As long as her clothes are strange enough to be anatomized, she is not taking them for granted and thus differentiates herself from "the women here" at the same time as adopting their very practical customs. The reference to "our stockings when little" both reasserts her real sisterhood and serves to make a continuum between childhood memories shared with her sisters and the new life far away. It is typical that, as she negotiates these old and new identities, Letitia is not shocked, and does not expect her family to be shocked, by the casual observation that the costume of

"the women here" does not include drawers. She repeatedly
undermines the expectations she raises of stereotyped Victorian
womanhood.

Letitia's wardrobe was by no means complete when the
Hargraves moved on to Gravesend as guests of James' boss while they
waited for the ship to Canada. Letitia would far rather have enjoyed
the shops and sights of London for as long as possible before setting
off for the remote trading post in the Far North, but it was the first of
many occasions on which she had to put up with whatever the HBC
ordained. She wrote home in frustration, "this place is only remarkable
for quiet and shrimps" and the shrimps were no compensation for the
quiet. Some signs of regency splendor remained but Letitia was,
understandably, not much impressed. "There are baths close to us very
gay as far as architecture goes—but they say extremely muddy and
only better than the river itself in as much as dead cats and dogs are
excluded by some sort of draw bridge. They call them salt water but
I don't suppose that ever was, or ever will be attested as I can imagine
no one with courage to taste." The humor and the readiness to cast a
skeptical eye on those who sought to entertain her with the conventional sights would stand Letitia in good stead as she came to terms
with the HBC's expectations of wives.

When, eventually, they were allowed to go on board, things did
not improve. Letitia remains matter of fact and wry no matter what
the cause for complaint, but she knew that she would be thousands of
miles from home for many years, communication limited to biennial
letters even in the worst emergencies, and seasickness must have been
the last straw. The captain did his best to accommodate the handful of
HBC wives and daughters traveling on the boat, but facilities were
limited and Letitia found herself sharing a small cabin with three
other distressed—and subsequently seasick—women. She sent a final
letter home from Orkney, where they docked to take on the last fresh
supplies and the Orcadian HBC men whose leave was over:

> My berth is next to the Stewards pantry and the smell of old cheese
> &c. is insupportable. . . . We are all getting alive. The day is shockingly

bad, wind cold and rain but we are all up and writing, dressed to death and the ship pitching till I don't know where I sit.... Mrs Finlayson was dreadfully ill.... She is so very thin and her nose has got literally transparent.... I did not thank you for the curry recipe which both the Dr and I perfectly understood. We can get every ingredient except the middle sized onion.

After that she resorted to a diary, although it was so rough that she could not often write:

June 25th 1840: In bed all yesterday and great part of today. Ship pitching so that we cd. not dress—the most provoking part is that we have been beating about waiting till the Prince of Wales came out of Stornoway. Mr Hargrave and the Capt went on board of her lest any letters might have been forwarded there from Stromness, but only got a parcel of shortbread from Capn. Royal for the ladies here—Nice food for 4 sea sick women. Never knew what sailing was before.

The voyage was relatively short, but Letitia had had enough. Weakened by seasickness and chronic cystitis, about which she did not dare consult the ship's doctor, she broke down when the sailors' response to the sight of land was to drink themselves into oblivion: "My 1st exploit on being lowered into the yawl, was to turn my back on the company and cry myself sick." (James' response to this is not recorded.) But within a few days, Letitia was feeling much better, and becoming fascinated by her new life. She soon found herself "in the family way" and took a particular interest in the babies she saw around Fort York. Her attitude to the Native Americans was not enlightened, but she was intrigued by difference, and this itself can be seen as an achievement for the product of a Victorian finishing school in Edinburgh:

I have not been near enough to inspect closely but I shall make Margaret fetch a child over without the mother that I may examine it. The moment it is born they get the bag stuffed with soft moss which has been in readiness & stuff the wretch in it up to the neck, bind it tightly round like a mummy, so as to make it as firm & flat as a deal board, then fasten it around their own back & work away about what they have to do. . . . The Indians all walk with their feet turned in from this discipline & their arms are as stiff as if there was not a joint in them. While the whites gentle and simple are running about perspiring with haste the Indians stalk along the platforms with their backs bent as if it were entirely for pleasure that they were wheeling barrows. They march so slowly and look so stately that they remind me of people on the stage. . . . When I want flowers or berries I show them a specimen & give them a shove and off they go. It never happens that they fail.

It is obvious that Letitia sees herself writing from a position of superiority, particularly in the casual intention of taking a baby away from its mother so that she can "examine" it, the clear implication being that she wants to treat the baby in a way that its mother would not allow. Combined with the description of the "Indians" bent double pushing barrows as if for pleasure and the suggestion that "shoving" is the best way of requesting botanical specimens, this shows Letitia at her most unattractive and insensitive. It is, however, interesting because it is as she adopts the vocabulary of the scientist on a field trip that Letitia's enthusiasm runs dry. The "examination" of the baby, the anthropological observations of childcare and the plant "specimens" all come from the discourse of nineteenth-century science. The contrast with her detailed and excited interest in Native American women's fashions makes the point very clear, and one might speculate that the sudden assumption of a haughty scientific vocabulary in relation to babies can be related to her own ambivalence about motherhood and particularly about undertaking motherhood surrounded by alien traditions and assumptions. Dressing up is playful, but babies are "wretches" to be "stuffed" into bags of moss and kept there.

Even so, a few weeks later, she writes enchantingly: "I have a little more paper so will finish by saying that I don't think my crisis will be before the end of March. I have been sensible for the last fortnight of a sensation as if there were a goose ducking itself. It may have been before that but I did not observe it." When Letitia wrote to tell her mother about the birth of her son, he was already nearly two months old and the letter had little chance of reaching Scotland:

> I am sure you will be glad to know that the Baby was born on Thursday 1st April [1841] and has been with the exception of a cough which does not reduce him at all perfectly well ever since. I soon got well as I was up in a week & quite recovered in 3.... They all say he is a very strong child as he fights well & can perch himself up quite stiff. He is very knowing at any rate as he knows well when he is attended to & shouts if I speak to anyone but himself.... He took a fancy to walking up and down the room so that we are kept marching all the time that he is not asleep or drinking.... I much fear his name will be Joseph as it is the name of Hargrave's father.

The affectionate boastfulness here is familiar to anyone who has asked a parent how the baby is doing. The baby continued to thrive, despite being badly bitten by mosquitoes. Letitia worried about weaning Joseph onto the HBC diet of game and fish, and sent home for some porridge oats for him. As he grew, she tried to find vegetables and became increasingly annoyed with her cook:

> There is no where any appearance of vegetation. I have cresses & radishes in a box in the house, & have also planted French beans to try if they will come to any good. There seems to be no parsley in the country. We have spinage in August but they maltreat it, cut the whole stock boil it bodily, mash fibre seeds and all with butter and pepper. You may believe it is a pleasant dish. I really think the cookery here will end me. It is fearful. I cant go into the kitchen & bully a great fat Orkney brute.

This is the beginning of a frustration with the Far North which grew as the years passed and more children were born. No longer eager to observe native plants or to learn about local cuisine, Letitia begins to behave like a colonist, like a settler rather than a visitor, cultivating familiar plants against all the odds and finding difference more annoying than intriguing.

The social life at Fort York in the 1840s was limited by rigid distinctions of caste and anxiety about too much association between young girls who had been taught, either in Scotland or in the mission school, that virginity was a girl's most precious commodity and the mixed-race women who had grown up without this sexual double standard. Despite her own careful upbringing, there was an extent to which Letitia valued common sense over propriety, and she never seems convinced that the presence of the established church at Fort York is much of a blessing. Missions to Native American communities who had minimal contact with Europeans irritated her, since she could see no point in attempting to convince people who had been devastated by disease brought from Europe and frequently starved that they had much for which to thank a European god: "I think that wretches who don't know six times in a year what it is to have a full meal, are not likely to have a keen sense of the goodness of God." It did not help their case that the missionaries expected to stay with her and ate too much of her carefully hoarded carbohydrates. Even the vicar's wife did not escape, for Letitia wrote, summing up vicars' wives for years to come, "She kills people with kindness & spunge cake in the forenoon & tea & psalm tunes in the evening."

Troubles came to the Hargraves in the following years. Their next son—born, Letitia thought, earlier than expected—was dead when she went to congratulate him on first sleeping through the night. She grieved alone, for James was busy from before breakfast until bedtime when the boats came in, and did not even eat at home. An unnamed but serious illness followed her bereavement and lasted many months. Meanwhile, as Joseph got older, the issue of his education became pressing. The mission school was open when a teacher could be found and closed the rest of the time, and the Hargraves never considered it for their son. When he was old enough, he would have to be sent back to Scotland, where he would receive letters from his parents twice a year and might hope to see them again when his father retired from business. Letitia had always known this was waiting, but she postponed it as long as possible. After the death of her second son, she did not even take for granted that Joseph would survive so long:

> It is full two years since we came here & all that time I have not been
> 4 miles away from the Fort. How much longer we are to remain I
> have no idea & except for hearing from home I don't care but if he
> [Joseph] lives he must go home in 5 years & if I live, I hope I will have
> the courage to send him if I can't go myself.

Joseph was still at home with his parents when a third child, a daughter also named Letitia but always called Tash, was born, and in later years Letitia was pleased and surprised to find that Tash, who was not two when Joseph left, could remember her big brother. Letitia wrote resignedly during this third pregnancy:

> I am as well pleased with York as at first, but I am only so from never
> thinking. You may believe that the eternal barreness of white water &
> black pines are not very enlivening to the spirits. The sky is always
> beautiful night or day, the Aurora being magnificent & the stars very
> bright. I sew from morning till night except standing on the platforms
> while Beppo [Joseph] is playing about with a host of husky dogs or
> digging up the snow and going out every morning with him in the
> carriole. I do nothing else.

The emphasis on the unchanging starkness of the Arctic landscape here contrasts with Letitia's sense of her own and her family's dynamism and productivity. The scenery is "barren" and "eternal," while she has a poignant awareness of both fertility and mortality. Her industrious sewing and her son's playing and digging seem pointlessly repetitive in this remote and minimalist setting.

A further two daughters were born, but either Letitia wrote fewer letters in later years or a smaller proportion survive. She and James campaigned ceaselessly to be posted somewhere more suitable for a young and growing family, and eventually James was ordered to Red River where there was a small colony as well as an HBC post. While he dealt with the move, Letitia took her daughters home to leave the older two at school and introduce the baby to her family. Everyone enjoyed the visit, and Letitia took the opportunity to stock up on clothes and wallpaper and furniture to ship back to the new house. The girls were fascinated by London, and apparently happy to be left in this brave new world. James missed his wife painfully, and consoled himself by lovingly preparing the first home they were to own, rather than rent from the HBC. He was particularly pleased with a rocking chair made especially for his wife, but when Letitia eventually returned to Canada they had only a few weeks together before she was taken ill. Typhoid moves fast, and when the end came Letitia had not even gone to bed. She died in the hand–made rocking chair.

XIV

My Antarctic Honeymoon: **Jennie Darlington in Antarctica**

Jennie Darlington thought she was the first woman in Antarctica, and she may well have been right, although any captain who either found a disguised woman on board or took one from a Pacific island on the way would have tended to keep quiet about it. Jennie Darlington was a young society woman in New York in the 1940s, spending her time as she had been trained to do: dressing herself, meeting marriageable young men, going to parties and occasionally doing some polite charity work to pass the afternoons. She was planning to go to Europe to study art, although one has the strong impression that her interest in art was not well developed. A suitably feminine equivalent of the Grand Tour was in the cards when, at a party given for some carefully selected naval officers, she met Harry Darlington. In *My Antarctic Honeymoon*, he is tall, dark and handsome, but frankly rather rude, and—like many women before and since—she has to decide that his strong and silent behavior is sexy rather than socially inadequate before she can fit him into the American Way and categorize him as marriageable. The difference between Harry's behavior at these parties and the pre-departure socializing of British naval expeditions underlines the growing cultural divergence of post–World War II British and American expeditions. No one's motives for going to the poles are pure, but Jennie is explicit about Harry's need to escape his inability to function in post-war America, a much less likeable version of Admiral Byrd's longing for retreat. British expeditions of the same date were in general still going where they were told to go because they were told to do so, and keeping their upper lips stiff at all times. This approach has its disadvantages but does at least require everyone to be polite, a constraint from which Harry Darlington might have profited.

Jennie's glass, at this first party, is empty, but Harry is too absorbed in the needs of the enormous dog he has brought to the cocktail party to do the gentlemanly thing, and he wanders into his host's kitchen to find something to feed the dog while she is talking to him. Jennie, surprised, follows, and, being ever eager to please, finds herself offering to make dinner for the dog. Harry accepts, and we can immediately see what is going to happen: "As he spoke, the last, rounded portion of the sun dropped into the ocean behind him. Simultaneously the light that died with it was replaced by his sudden smile." The planets, presumably, realign themselves around the man's teeth and Jennie is lost to upper-class New York and unmixed metaphors for the rest of time.

> I looked up at Harry inquiringly. The intensity in his eyes was so much like that in the dog's gaze I was disconcerted. Then, with an abrupt gesture that ended the strangeness of the moment, he pointed to the plate. "O.K., Chinook."
>
> The husky responded instantly. As he grabbed the bone, his long white fangs made a fierce crunching noise. . . . Something about the way he stood and the dog's quick obedience indicated a togetherness that went beyond the average relationship between a man and a dog. At the same time there was an untamed quality. They looked out of place in the small kitchen, as though close confines made them uncomfortable.

A togetherness beyond the average relationship between a man and his dog does not seem the most attractive attribute of a potential boyfriend, even without the untamed quality, but Jennie is undeterred, even when Harry, having been told that she dislikes seafood, promptly takes her to a fish restaurant. This too is just another sign of his general superiority, for "Just as he found himself unable to sit comfortably in average-sized chairs, he found it difficult to fit into contemporary civilization." Most wives of polar explorers concur that the men's fascination for far-flung places is part of their appeal, but Jennie Darlington is unusual in romanticizing someone's obvious inability to socialize. Two weeks later, we come breathlessly to the proposal scene. Jennie's plans to leave for Europe are still progressing and Harry is preparing for the first post-war American Antarctic expedition. On her last evening in New York, he takes her out to dinner and is as taciturn as usual. Making a final check on her passport and tickets before she goes to bed, Jennie finds that her passport is missing. As she frantically begins to unpack, Harry telephones and breaks the good news:

> "Jen, your passport is in a place where you'll never find it."
>
> "Harry," I cried desperately, "the bo-boat s-sails in the morning."
>
> Quietly, undramatically, Harry said, "Jen, there's one way to get your passport back. That's to marry me."
>
> I didn't trust myself to speak. He's not serious, I thought. This is carrying a joke too far.
>
> "Harry p-please, you've go-got to—"
>
> "Jen," he cut in abruptly, "you've got to marry me."
>
> In the silence that followed, I knew suddenly that he was serious, more serious than I had ever known him to be before.

Marrying him proves ineffective, since even after she has given up her lifelong dreams of a big white dress and a robed church choir, and accepted Harry's ideal of an unadorned registry office at eight in the morning with two of his colleagues as witnesses and her parents told after the event, her passport is still not forthcoming. There is no honeymoon because Harry is so busy with the Antarctic plans, though at this stage he is assuming that she will live with her parents for the two or three years of his absence. If Jennie despaired, or longed for Europe, she keeps it out of her unremittingly perky prose. It was only when the wife of Captain Ronne, who was leading the expedition, expressed a desire to go that there was any suggestion of Jennie going to the Antarctic, too. Her husband was deeply opposed to the idea, arguing that women on board would only destabilize male bonding and that there was no place for them away from homes and kitchens. His dog was all the company he required (there was no question of leaving Chinook behind). The rest of the expedition threatened to desert in South America if they were not given written assurance that no woman would set foot on Antarctica, but Commander and Mrs. Ronne prevailed. Particularly given the men's subsequent entirely friendly relationship with Jennie, this shared conviction that her company would be absolutely catastrophic seems odd, but there was clearly a sense that the Antarctic Way of Life would be destroyed by a woman's presence, however malleable and subservient. Modern female workers at Antarctic research stations sometimes complain of a similar ethos.

Anyway, Jennie found that, having thought she was accompanying her new husband as far as Chile to say goodbye and get what use she could out of her silk trousseau, she was bound for Antarctica. With the trousseau. She is typically philosophical: "Hastily I dabbed my nose with the last bit of powder it was to wear until my return to civilization. For protection against the polar wind I applied lipstick."

A Dog's Life

Further complications awaited the Ronne Expedition. A British base had been established only a few yards from the old American hut, which Ronne was planning to reoccupy. Rights to territory in Antarctica are notoriously hard to define, and in 1946 there was no way of establishing who had the right to be where. Even Ronne admitted that the British had an unaccountable idea that the two groups might cooperate to the extent of sharing resources as well as conversation, but for reasons that are never made clear Ronne was determined that there should be no fraternizing, especially when he found that the British had cleared up the American hut and stayed in it while they built their own base. One of the strangest episodes in Anglo-American relations followed. The two groups spent over a year living within sight of each other on the Antarctic ice, and members of the American expedition used to creep out and work their way around the entire circumference of the island in order to approach the British base from the other side, so that they could take afternoon tea with the Brits—who had, on this occasion, better food as well as a better social life—without Ronne accusing them of treason and threatening disciplinary action. Using a form of telegraph, Ronne tried to persuade the American Navy to declare war on Britain because the British expedition was flying a Union Jack within sight of the American base, which he took as an act of aggression against U.S. citizens going about their lawful business on U.S. territory. Then the Brits added insult to injury:

> Hard on the heels of the flag incident came the squabble over what Harry called "squatters' rights" to the two-hole privy.
>
> Although the British had set up their own hutments they still maintained a territorial toehold on the American-built plumbing at the American-built camp. The Anglo-American toilet became a major issue. Following a meeting of what we termed the island's "privy council" Major Butler admitted that his party had yet to fully abandon the privy, built by the United States Government on United States territory.

The British built their own toilets (or did without—history does not record) and Ronne forbade further communication, even when a British ship called to bring supplies. Jennie was forbidden to send a letter to her mother on the relief ship in case it bore a British postmark. The first time she sneaked over to the British base to see what it was like, she encountered one of the men half way across. He stared at her in horror and then ran away, explaining, when she arrived at the hut and introduced herself, "Like a man encountering an orange trail marker after being lost, he said, 'Thank God!' In heartfelt tones he concluded, 'I thought I'd gone round the bend. I do apologize. After mucking about on the glacier for several months I mistook you for a mirage.'"

This surreal episode set the tone for Jennie Darlington's "Antarctic honeymoon." Despite sleeping in a cubicle divided from the rest of the hut by a curtain, after a few months Jennie found herself pregnant. Afraid of her husband's furious reaction to this piece of feminine inadequacy, she concealed it from everyone, and struggled across the ice to the American Toilets while seven and eight months pregnant without a word of dismay: "Our plumbing facilities were primitive. During the winter night it was a major operation to reach them. Hanging onto the guide rope to keep from being lost or blown away, you made the journey from bunkhouse to outhouse largely on hands and knees. . . . Queuing up in a raging blizzard and a fifty-mile-an-hour gale in the middle of the Antarctic night is an indescribable experience." Especially, one would think, with a seven-month fetus bouncing on one's bladder all night. Jennie took the chance of spending more time alone in their cubicle to read her husband's diary of a previous expedition, hoping to discover the smoldering emotion that must underlie his persistent strength and silence:

> Then I saw Harry's diary, its leather as worn and stained as an old shirt. Here, I thought, is a chance to learn about my husband's past. Opening the diary at random, I read, "Cold as hell. Dogs sick." I turned to another entry. "Cold as hell. Dogs great."

Harry's passion for dogs offers two more rather startling pictures of married life in the Antarctic: "'Butt the husky' was a game Harry played with Chinook. It entailed getting down on all fours in front of the dog and trying to shove him backward with the top of your head while the dog did the same to you." Better yet: "Usually, unable to arouse him, I left the job to Chinook, who, after howls, face lickings and pawings, did the trick."

The expedition was not a success from any point of view. Because the U.S. Navy had not been convinced that the Ronne Expedition was likely to achieve anything useful, it was seriously underfunded and very badly managed. On the voyage down to Chile, most of the huskies had sickened and died, and only then was it realized that they had not been immunized against distemper. Harry was very keen for dog sledding to be an important part of proceedings, so ". . . they were so desperate to keep the expedition's trail programme from collapsing, they were willing to try anything once—alpacas, poodles, sheep dogs, a whippet and several overgrown cocker spaniels—even a goat, had the commander permitted Harry to bring it along." This did nothing to convince the unexpected audience that the Ronne Expedition was conceived along entirely sensible lines: "When the hardy Britishers, dog lovers all, caught sight of our motley collection of undernourished Chilean canines, including a Spanish spaniel Corgi, an unknown variety of sheep dog and the joyless 'nude' whippet, tethered out on the Antarctic waste, they were convinced that the American expedition was a new variety of traveling polar side-show." One imagines that the Brits had a more entertaining year than they had hoped for.

Jennie's Antarctic honeymoon—and her book—ended with the providential arrival of the American relief ship a couple of weeks before she expected to give birth. Ronne had still not been told of the expected event, and it had been thought likely that the expedition would spend another year on the ice until a few days before the ship appeared. The apparent prospect of giving birth unattended in the expedition's hut seems to have caused Jennie little dismay, but perhaps, considering whom she had married, this was as well.

XV
The Fairyland of the Arctic: Isobel Wylie Hutchison in Greenland

Isobel Hutchison was a botanist at Kew Gardens outside London who spent much of the 1920s and 1930s traveling alone around Greenland and the North American Arctic. Her passion for Greenland developed after bringing home a cypress cone from the garden of Gethsemane. The seeds ripened in her trunk on the way home to Scotland, so she planted them. The resulting trees were given as official gifts from Scotland to Iceland and Greenland, and Hutchison met officials of the Danish colonial service in Greenland, whose stories of rare flowers and berries inspired her to seek, and eventually obtain, permission to visit the colony, which was usually closed to all outsiders. It was the beginning of a passion which led to several remarkable journeys.

Hutchison did not identify herself as an explorer, since she traveled primarily as a botanist, and made no particular record of whether other Europeans had been there before her or not, but her methods of transport, her accommodation and the unusual situations she cheerfully accepted put her among the hardier travelers of her day. Her unremitting romanticism about the Arctic deserves serious attention because she knew what she was talking about; this is not someone celebrating the beauty of the polar night from the comfort of a good armchair by a warm fire, nor indeed someone discussing Noble Savages while ensconced in an orderly and well-policed metropolis. Her attitude to the Inuit is certainly patronizing and offensive to modern tastes and her descriptions of land and seascapes often verge on the twee, but it is the juxtaposition of this polite writing with her extraordinary courage and endurance that makes Hutchison's writing so intriguing.

> We are setting sail . . . for Fairyland, the Green Isle on which the ever-venturous spirit of the Gael has set his ever-receding paradise, the land wreathed in mists beyond which the sun is always shining, "where there is no sin, no discord, naught but sweet song to be heard," a land

of laughter and light and flowers which is reached in a crystal boat into which nothing evil may enter unseen.

This conflation of the Arctic and the biblical Promised Land sounds quite mad at first reading, but it is part of the long tradition of Arctic romanticism going back at least to Frobisher and perhaps as far as the Vinland and Greenland sagas. Hutchison's prose is remarkable, but she is right that the "ever venturous spirit of the Gael" (the culture of the Highlands and Islands) had for centuries been fascinated by the strange, ice-bound lands glimpsed on the routine journeys of fishermen and traders. Hutchison makes much of her Scottish identity, describing Scotland as part of a North Atlantic community with Greenland, Scandinavia and the archipelagos of Orkney, the Shetlands, the Faroes and Spitzbergen. In the 1930s this was an eccentric view, but between about 1000 and 1550, when travel was easier by sea than on land, and since the Celtic renaissance of the late twentieth century, it was and is widely held. Hutchison's sense of herself as a woman and a Scot is central to her narrative, but it is frequently hard to find behind the voice of metropolitan hauteur: "The Danish monopoly has kept the natives very free from the vices of modern civilisation . . . there are no gaols, and crime of a serious nature among the merry little men and women is practically unknown; nor are there any lunatic asylums."

Hutchison knew the story of Hans Egede and was delighted to find that the ship from Copenhagen to Greenland was named after his wife, Gertrud Rask. There were two other female passengers, an Inuit midwife who had been training at the Royal Hospital in Copenhagen and the bride of a Danish colonial administrator. The voyage passed in a haze of cherry brandy and good cheer, interspersed by spectacular sunsets, and Hutchison was delighted to set foot in Angmagsalik, where "civilization" had first appeared at the turn of the century. Again, Hutchison combines a war-weary appreciation of Inuit pragmatism with a surprising lack of respect, commenting that,

> The Eskimo race was probably the first to conceive the notion of settling men's differences by arbitration. If the League of Nations could revive the idea of the "Drum Dance," in which the antagonists

competed by mockery alone, and the palm was to the man who, by the vote of the majority, could make the greatest laughing-stock of his enemy, there would be no further need of navies or armies.

Nevertheless, on the same page we learn that, "the native of Angmagsalik . . . is only now emerging from the cloud of heathen superstition which so recently enveloped him." It seems that there should be something to be said for a cloud of heathen superstition which renders armies and navies unnecessary, but Hutchison is determined that traditional Inuit beliefs and observances are morally bankrupt and the church is Greenland's best hope of law and order:

> One must remember that it is within recent years that the last heathen were baptised in East Greenland. On my return from Sangmissok in October there was among the passengers a strange-looking, sad-faced old fellow, an old European topcoat flapping incongruously over his kamiker. He was pointed out to me as an East Greenlander who, before his conversion to Christianity, had murdered nine persons, including two wives and that old enemy of man—his mother-in-law. On being baptised, he interviewed the pastor, and inquired in much trouble what he was to do about this little matter.
>
> "For," said he, "I did not know it was wrong to kill them. They were no good to me any more."
>
> The pastor, faced with this ticklish problem, rose to the occasion.
>
> "Since you did not know that you were doing wrong," he said, "the matter need not trouble you now, so long as you never do it again."
>
> The man promised, and has so far kept his word. He has even found a third woman brave enough to marry him, though not without some slight trepidation.

This is not the only occasion on which Hutchison is duped by criminals claiming that their crimes and misdemeanors are culturally sanctioned. Believing unmodified Inuit culture to be debased, she simply accepts that thieves and murderers know no better. Of course, this is nonsense; while many Inuit societies practiced euthanasia, particularly in the depths of bad winters when it became clear that there was not enough food for everyone to live until spring, such tiny communities could ill afford to tolerate violence or theft. It sometimes seems that Hutchison's investment in the Arctic as the place where fantasies are realized extends even to this perceived lawlessness. She offers us the possibility of a place where, at least until very recently, one could not only play with the fairies in a crystal boat but kill one's mother-in-law without a second thought.

It is not surprising, with these expectations, that Hutchison remains acutely and constantly aware of her own strangeness in Greenland. Like Letitia Hargrave seventy years earlier, she is happy to trade some of her clothes for the Inuit women's kamiker, sealskin trousers and boots, after discovering that the mosquitoes could get through "even Scottish hosiery." Both women are much more cheerful about abandoning conventional Scottish clothes than most of their male contemporaries, although Hutchison resumes wearing her skirt and hat for church where she sits beside the similarly attired midwife. She realizes halfway through the service that "the only place left for such anachronisms as ourselves was the front bench of the men's side." The tone is jocular but she is clearly aware of the serious cultural implications of the presence of European fashions in this remote Greenlandic community. She and the midwife are "anachronisms," out of time but also, sitting on the men's side, out of place, beyond available classifications and therefore inevitably disruptive of those classifications.

There is a strong sense that, far from being daunted by this role, Hutchison immensely enjoys her own strangeness. The intoxicating realization that she is already so alien to the expectations of those around her that she can do anything she can think of without being thought any odder has its own momentum. She puts together an expedition to explore some of the northernmost fjords once inhabited by the medieval Norse Greenlanders, hoping to find a fabled birch forest. (Greenland, like Iceland and most of the North Atlantic archipelago, has very few tall trees.) Her incantatory glee spills over into scorn of those who take pleasure in more conventional excursions:

> A pound a day to hire seven servants and a house-boat, for a journey up one of the loveliest fjords in the world—a fjord into which no modern Briton has yet penetrated! A fairy journey in search of the birchen trees of Greenland: the birchen tree, the outlaw's tree—the tree of Erik the Red and Robin Hood (. . .) A pound a day to purchase such an adventure! Yet there are persons who spend a pound a day (and more) to dine on oysters and ice-cream with a distant view of trams.

This celebration of cheapness and low pay sits oddly with the reappearance of the fairies. Hutchison's delight in having servants is reiterated throughout her travels, from the announcement that, "'Kivfak' is probably the first word of Greenlandic the stranger learns, and means a servant," to her account of her servant's tears when she eventually returns to Scotland. To some extent, this is part of Hutchison's pleasure in playing at domesticity in this strange land, for, like the eighteenth-century missionaries whom she is often consciously imitating, she hopes and believes that homemaking in the Far North partakes in the creation of a new and better life. Having servants both confirms her status in the community of which she longs to be a part (a much higher status than a single female botanist could aspire to at home) and makes a public statement about the importance of her own domesticity. In Greenland if nowhere else Hutchison can be lady of the manor, and it is a manor encompassing great wonders:

> The little colony of Umanak, in which I am to winter, is huddled on the side of an island which at first sight appears to be nothing but an immense rock culminating in a curiously tilted twin-peaked mountain as high as Ben Nevis. The mountain is of reddish colour. This, and its strange shape (like the heart torn from a freshly killed animal), have given it the name "umanak"—the heart-shaped

mountain. Nothing more stony-hearted than this awful peak could be imagined; even the snow scarcely finds foothold on its tortured ledges. The fichu of debris which the winds have stripped and draped about its naked shoulders, out of which the gaunt brows of the mountain hoist themselves imperiously, seems to cover some secret which must remain inviolate until the Crack of Doom splits the red heart of Umanak for the last time.

The kaleidoscopic mixture of metaphors here is oddly effective. The settlement is not literally a "colony," since most of the inhabitants are and always have been Inuit, so the term is also a metaphor relating to the strangeness of any attempt to settle in such a hostile landscape. This mountain of red rock then becomes "the heart torn from a freshly killed animal," a distinctly gothic image to British readers, but one that might occur readily to someone familiar with Inuit hunting practices. This very fleshy heart immediately becomes metaphorical— the peak is so "stony hearted" that it repels even snow, although the mountain is also very literally a heart of stone, a stone-shaped heart. The metaphors whirl again, and this menacing hill becomes a victim, "tortured" and "stripped." The "fichu" of debris makes it a female victim (a fichu was an ornamental little lace shawl or collar), but then the imperious gaunt brow turns the mountain back into an aggressive masculine figure. The secret and the cracking heart seem to go back to the mysterious gothic presence that we started with.

Partly, of course, this is just unpolished writing, but the outlandish images collapse into very literal descriptions in a way that conveys Arctic mysticism rather well. Here is a landscape that seems at once tortured and torturing, fragile and (metaphor collapses into literalism again) impervious. The Arctic appears a place where even geology cannot be kept away from metaphor, but also, to Hutchison's endless fascination, as a place where one might reasonably hope to keep the home fires burning. This contrast is rather charmingly encapsulated by her account of the last few days of light before darkness sets in for the winter:

The sun is now getting obviously lower in the heavens each day . . . every day he slants further and further across my bookcase, travelling slowly but steadily from Guy Mannering to the Bible, from the Bible to Bentham and Hooker's British Flora, departing with a last lingering caress on the broad red and gold back of Chamber's Twentieth Century English Dictionary, from which I would not be parted for the world, for it contains the roots of all our English words, and there is no study more fascinating than that of roots, whether they be of words, plants, or the quiet sleepers sown here under my feet in weakness to flower elsewhere.

Umanak figures here as a place holding both literal and metaphorical roots, a place of philosophical importance; as a place where a bookcase properly stocked with the Scottish canon will be caressed by the lingering sun, and also as a place where the sun deserts people for months at a time. Once again, we see the Arctic as both a canvas onto which fantasy can be projected and as a uniquely strange space with compelling properties of its own. Hutchison's final account of her experience of this contradiction is arresting, despite the flaws in her prose:

It occurred to me suddenly that, in such a place, at such an hour, with no light save the stars and the Merry Men (for the moon had not yet risen), I might well be afraid, and that I was not afraid at all—that here in the graveyard I stood not amid the dead, but amid the living. It was in the other colony, behind the lighted windows, that the dead ate and drank and slept and went about their daily toil. Here in the starlight under the aurora shook a pulse like that of Spring, the pulse of a life which had long since awakened out of sleep. I stood there for a little while in the holy silence, my hand upon the latch of eternity, and then turned back through the snow to eat and sleep yet a little longer with the slumbering earth.

PART SIX

Literature on Ice

XVI
The Loud Misrule: Arctic Imagery in English Poetry

Little has been written on the theme of Arctic and Antarctic imagery in canonical English literature, but such imagery is surprisingly pervasive. From surviving fragments of Anglo-Saxon poetry to twentieth-century Canadian women's writing, the English literatures of the northern hemisphere show a persistent fascination for polar landscape. John Donne, many of whose most famous images have to do with Elizabethan navigation and cartography, was intrigued by the theoretical possibilities of the poles as the still points of the turning world (the phrase itself is a quote from T. S. Eliot). James Thomson, an eighteenth-century poet, used the Arctic as a symbol of Earth's fallenness and alienation from the Promised Land. For Coleridge, the Arctic and Antarctic were fascinating and terrible places, fit settings for mythic events. Mary Shelley picked up the Romantic interest in these extreme landscapes and turned it to her own ends in *Frankenstein*, where the misguided polar explorer is as dangerous as the monster's creator. This, combined with Charlotte Bronte's interest in the Arctic, initiates an uneasy tradition of women writing about these historically masculine spaces, either imagining a feminized polar region, transformed into an escape zone for women, or attacking the masculine ideology of polar purity.

Male writers' interest also persisted, now often caught up with the personality cults of Franklin, about whom both Tennyson and Swinburne wrote, and Scott, who is an important presence in *Peter*

Pan. The rising interest in the sagas and Norse mythology in the later nineteenth century led to an enduring English literary interest in Iceland, exemplified by William Morris and W. H. Auden and cultivated by major twentieth-century poets including Ted Hughes and Seamus Heaney.

Melting the Ice: John Donne and James Thomson at the North Pole

John Donne (1572–1631) is often seen as a difficult poet to read, partly because his seventeenth-century English, lacking the narrative context of a play, is harder to understand than Shakespeare's, and partly because one of the things he writes about is the difficulty of language. This is of importance to a literary history of polar exploration because one of Donne's favorite examples of the difficulty of metaphor is the language used to describe the North Pole. It is both a place like any other, an ordinary if uncomfortable part of the earth's surface on which one may stand or sit in the usual way, and the almost magical point towards which compasses are drawn and upon which all forms of navigation and travel depend. We spend our lives spinning around these frozen axes, the almost unimaginable spaces which keep hours and seasons in their place and make the North cold and the South hot and the East early and the West late, and yet when we get there they are just cold ground, more of the same inhospitable ice where cold feet and empty bellies are as acute as they were yesterday and will be tomorrow.

Antarctica existed only in theory to Donne and his contemporaries (it seemed likely that there was a counterweight to the Arctic) and no one had stood at either pole, but cartography and travel were the great topics of the day and the search for the Northwest Passage was attracting men and funding at a rate that would not be reached again until the early nineteenth century. It was the age of Raleigh and Drake, in which the English began to learn about other continents and nothing was more exciting than geographical discovery.

Donne uses Arctic imagery in two ways, one of which is interesting mainly because it shows how thoroughly the English had assimilated the idea of the polar regions three hundred years before Scott. In several of the love poems, the poles are simply an image of extremity. In the *Epithalamions*, or poems in celebration of marriage, the true test of passion is whether it could melt the North Pole:

> The Passage of the West or East would thaw
> And open wide their easie liquid jawe
> To all our ships, could a Promethean art
> Either unto the Northerne Pole impart
> The fire of these inflaming eyes, or of this loving heart.

Donne is playing with the idea of sexual passion being "hot," making the bridegroom's eyes "inflaming" ("enflamed" as modern English would have it), and then extending the image until these metaphorical flames, if only the "Promethean art" could transfer them to the North Pole, would melt the ice blocking the fabled Northeast and Northwest Passages to the Pacific. It is a spectacular image which presents love (or desire—Donne does not always distinguish) going global, burning ice and melting oceans.

At the same time, Donne the court poet is politically astute, picking up on his sovereign's passionate ambition to open the great oceans to British trade and claim the luxuries of the exotic Orient. However, since the effect of this fiery love would be to open the jaws of the passages to ships, there is also a suggestion that "our ships" would be consumed. This did happen—the death and/or disappearance rate of sixteenth- and seventeenth-century Arctic expeditions was as high as in the nineteenth century—but it is also another evocation of the power and magnitude of the groom's desire. His love is so strong that it could melt the ice cap and swallow the British Navy. There is a very similar use of polar imagery in *Satire III*:

> Dar'st thou dive seas, and dungeons of the earth?
> Hast thou courageous fire to thaw the ice
> Of frozen North discoveries?

Again, the capacity to thaw the polar ice is the test of emotional strength. Is your courage hot enough to melt the frozen North? Again also, there is a more complicated and more specific point, for the reference to "frozen North discoveries" as if it is a place name (The Discoveries) suggests a more literal meaning. People do "dive seas, and dungeons of the earth" and people do also discover the frozen North, melting in the process the metaphorical ice which seals off parts of the world from human knowledge. The point here, then, is that these things are possible on one level or another. Some Englishmen do have the courage to venture into new and strange worlds, just not the "thou" of the satire.

Donne's *Divine Poems* use the Arctic in a completely different and much more theoretical way. "Upon the Annunciation and Passion Falling upon One Day" is a meditation on the year 1608, when, unusually, the days commemorating Gabriel's announcement to Mary that she will have a son and Christ's crucifixion coincided. The church simultaneously remembered Christ's conception, the moment in which, assuming human form, he started the journey towards death, and his death, the moment in which, abandoning human form, he returned to eternal life. The paradoxical aspects of this are always hard to think about, because it is difficult to remember at the same time that Christ's coming to life was also his coming to death and that his dying was also his birth. It is precisely the difficulty of this thought that interests Donne when the Annunciation and the Passion coincide, obliging believers to concentrate on two almost impossible and almost incompatible things at once:

> . . . this day hath shown,
> The Abridgement of Christ's story, which makes one
> (As in plain Maps, the furthest West is East)
> Of the Angels Ave, and Consummatum est.
> How well the Church, God's Court of faculties
> Deals, in some times, and seldom joining these!
> As by the self-fixed Pole we never do
> Direct our course, but the next star thereto,

Which shows where the other is, and which we say
(Because it strays not far) doth never stray;
So God by his Church, nearest to him, wee know . . .

These lines offer the need for navigation to substitute the Pole
Star for the Pole itself (because the star is visible and the Pole is not) as
a metaphor for a Christian's need to substitute the Church's interpretation of Christ's life for God himself (because the Church can offer
paradoxes where God, incorporating incompatible states, is simply
unthinkable). We do not "direct our course" by the unchanging Pole,
which is "self-fixed," only attached to and only defined by itself, even
though perfect navigation and mapmaking would need to do so.
Instead, we use "the next star thereto," the Dog Star Sirius, which looks
so close to the North Pole that it is good enough for all practical
purposes. In fact Sirius does move in relation to the Pole, but not
enough to derange navigation when we make the practical assumption
that it is the same thing and "doth never stray." In the same way, the
Christian knows God by his Church. They are not the same thing, but
as theoretically perfect navigation is impossible, so a full and accurate
understanding of God is impossible. Without the Church, Christians
would constantly have to think of God as embodying Christ's
conception and crucifixion in the same instant, which is a serious
challenge to the human understanding of the world. Instead, there is
the Church, which "deals well" in "some times but seldom" requiring
believers to confront this difficulty. Usually, the days are kept apart and
the events can be thought of separately, but sometimes it is necessary
to remember God's capacities for states and events beyond human
comprehension. Similarly, it is usually better to think of East and West
as opposites like North and South (or birth and death), but in fact in
"plain maps" "the furthest West is East"; clear maps show that if you
keep going West long enough, you will find yourself East of where you
started. Theoretically, East and West are not different, although it is colloquially convenient to regard them as being so, just as it is colloquially
convenient to regard Sirius as bearing a fixed relation to the North
Pole. There is a parallel circularity in the life of Christ, where the

angels' "Ave," "Hail" at the beginning of "Hail, Mary, full of grace . . .
blessed is the fruit of thy womb" means the same thing as
"consummatum est," "it is finished," spoken at Christ's death.

James Thomson, writing nearly a century later, also fantasizes the
melting of the Arctic ice. Thomson (1700–1748) was a poet and
playwright, hugely popular in his own day and for over a century
afterwards. His most famous work is *The Seasons*, a book-length poem
that relates the turning of the year to the passage of history and human
life. It was reprinted endlessly in the anthologies that made up most
of most people's reading for pleasure until novels began to take over
from poetry towards the end of the eighteenth century, and reading
The Seasons for the first time can be an odd experience as one
recognizes lines repeatedly quoted in nineteenth-century fiction.

The section on winter moves steadily north, describing the Arctic
as the fearsome source of icy weather throughout the world as if an
ice age is struggling to sweep the planet. Thomson is intrigued by
polar phenomena as signs of the Arctic's deeper strangeness. He
invokes "dancing Meteors" that "ceaseless shake/A waving blaze
refracted o'er the Heavens" and the sun "winding his spiral Course"
"for gay rejoicing Months" (a somewhat liberal account of the
midnight sun). Thomson sweeps the globe with an extraordinary
aerial view. "Should our eye/Astonish'd shoot into the Frigid Zone"
we would see the wastes of Siberia, "Desarts lost in Snow" where
"solid Floods" stretch "their icy Horrors to the frozen Main." Even
there, "Life glows" and the pleasingly named "furry Nations" live
beneath the "shining Waste" of snow "warm together press'd" while
"the branching Elk/Lies slumbering sullen in the white Abyss." This
visionary account calls to mind aerial photography and television
documentaries of natural history, an impression which intensifies as
Thomson swoops again "Wide o'er the spacious Regions of the
North" to observe "the Sons of Lapland" who conveniently "ask no
more than simple Nature gives" and whose wives are "all Day long in
useful Cares employ'd" inside reindeer-skin tents while the Sons
themselves "draw the copious Fry" from the river. "Still pressing on"
past the volcanoes of Iceland,

And farthest Greenland, to the Pole itself,
Where failing gradual Life at length goes out,
The Muse expands her solitary flight;
And, hovering o'er the wild stupendous Scene,
Beholds new Seas beneath another Sky.
Throned in his Palace of cerulean Ice,
Here WINTER holds his unrejoicing Court;
And thro' his airy Hall the loud Misrule
Of driving Tempest is for ever heard:
Here the grim Tyrant meditates his Wrath;
Here arms his Winds with all-subduing Frost;
Moulds his fierce Hail, and treasures up his Snows,
With which he now oppresses half the Globe.

In this version, the North Pole itself is another realm, where human life is extinguished and legendary beings take possession. There are new seas and a new sky, ruled by the personification of Winter in his Ice Palace. (It is perhaps not too irreverent to remark that he is the obvious forerunner of Hans Christian Andersen's Snow Queen and C. S. Lewis' White Queen, each of whom commands the winter weather and has an unearthly winter palace.) Thomson's Winter is a serious as well as picturesque figure, the source of much evil securely ensconced on earth. He starves livestock and brings famine to whole nations, and smothers landscapes until the plight of polar explorers becomes emblematic of humanity's misery:

As if old Chaos was again return'd,
Wide-rend the Deep, and shake the solid Pole.
Ocean itself no longer can resist
The binding Fury; but, in all its Rage
Of Tempest taken by the boundless Frost,
Is many a Fathom to the Bottom chain'd,
And bid to roar no more . . .
    . . . Miserable they!
Who, here entangled in the gathering Ice,

> Take their last Look of the descending Sun;
> While, full of Death, and fierce with tenfold Frost,
> The long long Night, incumbent o'er their Heads,
> Falls horrible.

Here, Thomson presents the ocean freezing as symbolic of an utterly disordered world. Even in the midst of a tempest, the sea itself is finally overwhelmed by winter's "binding Fury" and "chained" to the ocean floor. The imagery of violence and imprisonment makes this ice age seem cataclysmic and almost unnatural, while the shift from the geographical to the personal perspective brings home the horror in a disconcerting way. The idea of a silent and static ocean is strange and striking, but the image of explorers taking their last look at the vanishing sun before "the long long Night . . . falls horrible" is disturbing, particularly when Thomson follows up with a more detailed account of the fate of Sir Hugh Willoughby, who failed to find the Northeast Passage for Elizabeth I and was caught in the Arctic by another winter:

> And to the stony Deep his idle Ship
> Immediate seal'd, he with his hapless Crew,
> Each full-exerted at his several Task,
> Froze into Statues; to the Cordage glued
> The Sailor, and the Pilot to the Helm.

Thomson's Arctic is deathly, a place of invincible and dangerous immobility. Winter, creeping south, takes away human agency until the world is full of "Mortals lost to Hope." Winter "spreads his latest Glooms,/And reigns tremendous o'er the conquer'd Year." All the vegetation is dead and all the birds are silenced; "Horror wide extends/His desolate Domain." Nevertheless, having shown the final triumph of the distinctly pagan winter, Thomson turns again and produces another spring. "Virtue sole survives" the Arctic apocalypse and is appropriately rewarded by a heavenly renewal which has little to do with the earthly pleasures of the first spring. Thomson concludes hastily, "The Storms of WINTRY TIME will quickly pass,/And one unbounded SPRING encircle All." For both Thomson and Donne, then, the North Pole is a place where a different and more intense order of reality obtains. Donne's vision is far more complex and abstract, but both writers present the Pole as a source or symbol of truth by which an understanding of the world is defined.

Hell Freezes Over: The Albatross and Frankenstein

Perhaps the most famous polar poem in English is Samuel Taylor Coleridge's "Rime of the Ancient Mariner" (1797). In this strange, archaic narrative poem, the old sailor stands outside a village church, stopping people on their way into a wedding and compelling them to listen to his life story. He is an eerie and insistent figure, and, although he has to hold the guests with "his glittering eye" his story of an Antarctic voyage is certainly worth listening to. The poem has been intensively analyzed since its first publication and a great multitude of sources, polar and otherwise, have been identified, but for a literary account of polar travel it is probably most interesting to assume that Coleridge is more interested in descriptions of the Antarctic in general than in a particular account of a particular journey. In any case, it is clear that for Coleridge as for Donne and Thomson, the polar regions are unearthly places of intense significance, where great moral dramas are enacted with a purity that would be impossible in the inhabited world. For all three poets, the poles are hyper-real.

Despite its reputation, the polar parts of Coleridge's poem are fairly brief. After leaving the harbor, the ship is carried south "for days and weeks" by "a Wind and Tempest strong." They pass the equator (the sun is over the mast at noon) and keep going until,

> Listen, Stranger! Mist and Snow,
> And it grew wond'rous cauld:
> And Ice mast-high came floating by
> As green as Emerauld.

And thro' the drifts the snowy clifts,
Did send a dismal sheen;
Ne shapes of men ne beasts we ken——
The Ice was all between.

The Ice was here, the Ice was there,
The ice was all around:
It crack'd and growl'd and roar'd and howl'd——
Like noises of a swound.

At length did cross an Albatross,
Thorough the Fog it came;
And an it were a Christian Soul,
We hail'd it in God's name.

The Marineres gave it biscuit-worms,
And round and round it flew:
The Ice did split with a Thunder-fit;
The Helmsman steer'd us thro'.

After this, a "good south wind" bears the ship rapidly north and as long as the albatross is there, perching on the shrouds for vespers, all goes well. Then, out of the blue, in an act of apparently random violence, the Mariner shoots the albatross with his crossbow. This seems to trigger a sequence of horrific events. The ship is becalmed in the Pacific, "As idle as a painted Ship/Upon a painted Ocean." The crew, dying of thirst, blame the Mariner for shooting the albatross, and the ship that they think is bringing help turns out to be a spectral vessel containing two animate corpses playing dice. That night, all the crew except the Mariner drop dead and he is left "Alone, alone, all all alone/Alone on the wide wide Sea." While admiring water-snakes, he feels a sudden liberation and sleeps. Rain falls, the dead crew stir and begin to sail the ship. In a trance, the Mariner hears two voices discussing his plight. He wakes, but does not dare look at the dead men standing "together on the deck,/For a charnel-dungeon fitter."

As the ship reaches home, the Mariner sees the spirits of the dead rising, and just as the pilot boat reaches him the ship sinks and the Mariner is rescued and lives to tell his tale.

The parts of the narrative that take place in the Antarctic are brief but important. The central difficulty for interpretations of the poem is that either the albatross must be made to represent something so essential that the Mariner's terrible punishment is justified or the "Rime" is about arbitrary and unjustified suffering, which is difficult to interpret without a context. Theories abound about the significance of the albatross and the source of the Mariner's guilt, which is out of all proportion to the crime of killing a bird; shooting the albatross can be a symbol of British colonial abuses of human rights, or the Mariner can be a Christ figure who suffers for the sins of the world. In either case the polar setting is not coincidental, and it seems to work against readings in terms of the slave trade and colonial guilt. If the killing of the albatross represents the abuse of colonized peoples, why would Coleridge choose for a setting the only uninhabited continent? Readings in terms of the Romantic interest in ecology may work better, allowing "the land of mist and snow" to occupy fully the position of importance that Coleridge gives it. Whatever the political or philosophical setting of the poem, the albatross is clearly a figure of primal innocence and clearly also closely associated with the Antarctic, particularly as a "spirit who bideth by himself/In the land of mist and snow" acts as the dead bird's avenger and guardian angel.

There are many possible sources in contemporary travel writing for the voyage itself and the killing of an albatross (one caught on the *Bounty* expedition was turned into a pie, a less ignominious end than the one on Douglas Mawson's 1930s expedition brained by a well-aimed tin of Spam), but no precedent for the stark and pared-down moral drama of the story. Coleridge's use of the polar setting is not dictated by his sources; it is a spontaneous and original artistic investment in Antarctica. The reasons for this are complex, but we can guess at some of them. Coleridge was fascinated by wintry weather in all landscapes, as the famous "Frost at Midnight" attests, and it is logical that someone inspired by the transformative effects of ice and snow in a domestic setting would find the idea of a permanently alien and monochrome landscape deeply appealing. The letters from Coleridge's 1799 walking tour in Germany show his passionate response to ice. He wrote to his wife on January 14:

> But when first the Ice fell on the Lake, & the whole Lake was frozen, one huge piece of thick transparent Glass, O my God! what sublime scenery have I beheld. —Of a morning when I have seen the little lake covered with Mist; when the Sun peeped over the Hill, the Mist broke in the middle; and at last stood as the waters of the red Sea are said to have done when the Israelites passed—& between these two walls of Mist the Sunlight burnt upon the Ice in a strait road of golden Fire, all across the lake—intolerably bright, & the walls of Mist partaking of the light in a multitude of colours. —About a month ago the vehemence of the Wind had shattered the Ice—part of it, quite smattered, was driven to shore & had frozen anew; this was of a deep blue & represented an agitated sea—the water, that ran up between the great islands of Ice, shone of a yellow green (it was at sunset) and all the scattered islands of smooth ice were blood; intensely bright Blood.

If the effect of a hard frost on the German countryside is to make it as wonderful as the parting of the Red Sea and as strange as islands of blood in a yellow green sea, then Antarctica, where the ice is so deep that the sea has frozen to the seabed and the Southern Lights sweep the skies, can easily figure as a place of profound enchantment. Being uninhabited and only very recently known to Westerners, Antarctica's strangeness was far more compelling than that of the Arctic, which had been part of the European geographical imagination for the previous millennium. Captain Cook and his successors had begun to map the Antarctic, but on 1790s world maps it is marked by a few hesitant squiggles and an entirely speculative dotted line which soon stutters into blankness. Coleridge made the albatross the spirit of the place that began at the limit of knowledge, and as such it is appropriate that readers still find its significance hard to explain. The Mariner's violence appears random and compulsive, an enactment of an unfocussed reflex of destruction. The Antarctic setting functions partly to intensify the Mariner's crime, placing this arbitrary violence against the background of the place where Earth seems most like Heaven, most like the numinous and intensely meaningful landscapes of the Hebrew Bible where God himself acted and left signs of his action. Coleridge may begin the tradition of imagining Antarctica as pristine Romantic nature, a landscape embodying originary purity.

Again, we encounter the polar regions as unearthly, other-worldly; fit settings for events of biblical proportion in an era that no longer looks for miracles at home. Coleridge himself was instrumental in introducing German theologies that questioned the literal truth and philosophical status of the Bible to the English, and this movement towards replacing conventional ideas of religious truth with the self-evident glories of landscape is one of the defining features of early Romanticism. The next generation of English writers were deeply critical.

Mary Shelley's novel *Frankenstein* is another famous Romantic work that engages with polar travel writing. As with the "Rime of the Ancient Mariner," we can only now see the novel through the multitude of literary, colloquial and visual interpretations that throng the two centuries since its publication. Those who have not read *Frankenstein* nevertheless know that it is about a scientist who gets carried away by his own powers and creates a monster from several corpses, which breaks from his control and terrorizes communities wherever it goes. Those who have read it know that the monster or creature has no name because its misguided creator, Victor Frankenstein, fails in his part as creator and parent to give it one, and that Frankenstein and the Creature are psychological doubles, playing out each other's repressions and worst fears.

The Creature, although hideous—because only God can make a human in His own image—is initially benevolent and utterly without knowledge of any kind, and follows his horrified Creator around like

a toddler demanding affection and attention. It is only when Victor
fails in this most basic parental duty and other people flee him in
terror that the Creature becomes warped and decides that if he is to
be treated as a monster he will behave like one, and sets out to kill all
Victor's family in an attempt to reduce Victor to the loveless isolation
he must himself endure. Victor's refusal to create a female Creature as
a companion for his rejected child triggers the final descent into
psychopathy (for both Creature and creator), and the chase is inverted
as the Creature lures the vengeful Victor into the High Arctic for the
final showdown. There, wandering frost-bitten and emaciated on the
polar ice, Victor encounters an English ship heading for the North
Pole. He tells his story to the Captain, Robert Walton, who rapidly
becomes his dearest friend and another double. Because Victor dies on
board, it is Walton who takes charge of his narrative and sends it home
in letters to his sister, prefacing his own account of the meeting with
Victor Frankenstein and concluding with his account of Victor's
death and the end of the voyage. It is this frame narrative which is of
most interest here.

Frankenstein opens with a letter from Walton to his sister, written
in St. Petersburg on his way north. Walton describes his expectations
of the North Pole in terms that foreshadow Frankenstein's desire to
create new life:

> Inspirited by this wind of promise, my day dreams become more
> fervent and vivid. I try in vain to be persuaded that the pole is the seat
> of frost and desolation; it ever presents itself to my imagination as the
> region of beauty and delight. There, Margaret, the sun is for ever visible;
> its broad disk just skirting the horizon, and diffusing a perpetual
> splendour . . . there snow and frost are banished; and, sailing over a calm
> sea, we may be wafted to a land surpassing in wonders and beauty every
> region hitherto discovered on the habitable globe. . . . What may not
> be unexpected in a country of eternal light? I may there discover the
> wondrous power which attracts the needle. . . . I shall satiate my ardent
> curiosity with the sight of a part of the world never before visited, and
> may tread a land never before imprinted by the foot of man.

The wildly unrealistic ideas expressed here, the readiness to act on the basis of fantasy and the passionate ambition for self-aggrandizement all establish Walton's similarity to Frankenstein. Both are scientists working alone and without reference to recent scientific developments or established views, and both end by endangering others through obstinate commitment to idiosyncratic ideas. Mary Shelley appears to be equating the desire to reach the North Pole with the desire to animate the dead. In the context of the many appalling deaths and frequent incidence of sociopathic behavior on polar expeditions, this may not be as odd as it first seems. Passing similarities between the two men include a belief in the redemptive powers of natural beauty, which Walton describes to his sister after taking the dying man on board:

> Even broken in spirit as he is, no one can feel more deeply than he does the beauties of nature. The starry sky, the sea, and every sight afforded by these wonderful regions, seems still to have the power of elevating his soul from earth. Such a man has a double existence: he may suffer misery, and be overwhelmed by disappointments; yet when he has retired into himself, he will be like a celestial spirit, that has a halo around him, within whose circle no grief or folly ventures.

This shows how deeply Walton and Frankenstein are involved in mutual self-deception. It is patently ludicrous to say that Frankenstein's capacity for Romantic landscape appreciation protects "his circle" from grief and folly when his foolish actions have directly caused the murders of his best friend, wife and baby brother, the wrongful execution of the family nurse and the terrorizing of several idyllic mountain and island communities. Such a man does indeed have a double existence as the originator and victim of these disasters, but Shelley is clear that his sense of "elevation" and moral purity has no validity whatsoever. Walton's inability to see that Victor is the author of his own misfortunes, dangerous as well as endangered, reflects his own parallel failings. Like Victor, Walton continues to believe in his own moral superiority as—ignoring all the signs that the expedition is in immediate and serious danger—he persists in heading north until the crew, driven to desperation by their conviction that their captain is not sane, rebel. As he draws the novel to a close, Walton writes,

> I am surrounded by mountains of ice, which admit of no escape, and threaten every moment to crush my vessel....You will not hear of my destruction, and you will anxiously await my return.Years will pass, and you will have visitings of despair, and yet be tortured by hope.

This is exactly what did happen to Lady Franklin thirty years later and to hundreds of poorer and less vociferous wives, parents and siblings over centuries of Arctic exploration. Unlike almost all real explorers in similar situations, Walton is as complacent as Frankenstein about the suffering his ambitions inflict on others, and the two men begin to work together in an attempt to ensure that Walton's aims are not defeated as Frankenstein's have been. At last the crew, many of who have "already found a grave amidst this scene of desolation" send a deputation to Walton to make him promise that, in the unlikely event of the ice opening and escape being possible, he will make all speed for home rather than continuing north into further danger with wholly inadequate supplies and equipment. The dying Frankenstein hears this, and is roused to his last great rhetorical effort (which, as the Oxford edition points out, echoes a speech in Dante's *Inferno* by Ulysses, who is found in the part of Hell reserved for evil counselors). He concludes:

> Oh! be men, or be more than men. Be steady to your purposes, and firm as rock. This ice is not made of such stuff as your hearts might be; it is mutable, cannot withstand you if you say that it shall not. Do not return to your families with the stigma of disgrace marked on your brows. Return as heroes who have fought and conquered, and who know not what it is to turn their backs on the foe.

This, like Walton's account of Frankenstein's moral elevation, is grandiloquent nonsense, using the rhetoric of heroism to dangerous ends. It is idiotic to suggest that ice is mutable and cannot withstand determined sailors. Common sense as well as centuries of polar travel indicate that ice is intractable and dangerous, metaphorically as well as literally. The logical and inevitable end of this approach to polar travel is slow and messy death; as we have seen, those who succeed work around the ice, regarding it as immutable and treating it with respect, while those who set out to defeat it by willpower rarely make it home. Frankenstein's speech here is so overblown as to be almost a parody of heroic polar travel writing, and it is interesting that Mary Shelley identifies her mad scientist so closely with the worst excesses of polar exploration. She was very interested in the major scientific developments of her day and not in any sense ideologically opposed to science per se, and nor is there any reason to believe that she regarded polar exploration as intrinsically wrong. The point here is both a feminist view that the masculine desire for self-aggrandizement— even and perhaps especially in the name of the family—is often destructive of the very women and children in whose name it is carried out (as Shackleton said to his wife after turning back within eighty miles of the South Pole, "I thought you'd rather have a live donkey than a dead lion"), and that the rhetoric of Romanticism can serve as a cover for iniquitous proceedings.

Frankenstein and Walton view the glaciers and snowy peaks of the Alps and the Arctic ice as compellingly beautiful and heavenly places to which they are irresistibly drawn. As for Coleridge and Thomson, in *Frankenstein* these white landscapes work as screens for the projection of high moral drama which has little to do with community life. Victor and his Creature play out their crucial interactions high on the Alpine glaciers and, at last, in the northern reaches of the Arctic ice, while Walton's extreme philosophical position is finally tested to destruction against the stark background of the frozen sea. Shelley differs from the other writers in presenting these literal and metaphorical journeys as a kind of abandonment, a retreat from the real and important world of love and care for individuals into an arid and intrinsically masculine desert of the imagination. In the context of English Romanticism, this is a very questionable idea, but in relation to polar exploration it would be hard to deny its validity. Over and over again, Antarctica and the Arctic figure as places where men fantasize escaping from the complex demands of life in society. It is an obvious criticism of this trope that expeditions take society with them, but Shelley's accusation that the fantasy itself constitutes an abdication of moral responsibility is both original and convincing. The Creature, the abandoned child gone to the bad, is left to set himself on fire in an act of vengeful self-destruction. He appears in Walton's cabin, keening with regret and guilt over Frankenstein's body, and announces his plans:

> "I shall quit your vessel on the ice-raft which brought me hither, and shall seek the most northern extremity of the globe; I shall collect my funeral pile, and consume to ashes this miserable frame, that its remains may afford no light to any curious and unhallowed wretch, who would create another such as I have been. . . . I shall ascend my funeral pile triumphantly, and exult in the agony of the torturing flames. The light of that conflagration will fade away; my ashes will be swept into the sea by the winds. My spirit will sleep in peace; or if it thinks, it will not surely think thus. Farewell."

By committing such a spectacular suicide at the North Pole, the Creature in some sense enacts Walton's ultimate ambition of heroic self-destruction as well as Frankenstein's of the Creature's death. The reviled and misbegotten child of flawed ambition has his ultimate revenge in proving himself able to withstand the polar ice as those of woman born cannot.

XVII
Discovered by Pooh: Children's Fiction Goes to the Poles

Given the importance of polar exploration to national identity in the late nineteenth and early twentieth centuries, it is not surprising to find that it figures more in children's literature than in that for adults. There was almost no need for fiction about Arctic and Antarctic travel in years when the newspapers were full of the search for Franklin and the death of Scott. But children's fiction, simply by virtue of being written by adults, is inescapably didactic whether it imparts subversion or unthinking patriotism, and so the discourse of polar exploration was passed on, through Sunday school books on Franklin and also through more complex texts. To quote E. C. Buley's *Into the Polar Seas: The Story of Sir John Franklin*, published by the Sunday School Union in 1908, "Though John Franklin came of no seafaring stock, he had many generations of honest British yeoman ancestry behind him, and so came of a race not easily moved from its purpose."

Between the search for Franklin in the 1850s and the post-war apotheosis of Scott in the 1930s, English children's fiction blossomed. The price of books fell with the size of families, so that, among the literate middle classes, there was more disposable income and leisure time to be given to fewer children. Over the same period, trends in childcare and attitudes to childhood changed. The Victorian idolization of "family life," which usually emphasized the parents' role rather than the child's experience, gave way to the Edwardian obsession with childhood as the golden and perfect time in life. A sequence of excellent writers constructed child-centered fantasy worlds which delighted adults as much as children, and the children's authors of the 1950s were still harking back to the fin-de-siècle Golden Age. It seems odd that the canon of children's literature from *The Hunting of the Snark* to *The Lion, the Witch and the Wardrobe* should ceaselessly revisit the highest latitudes when adult fiction barely acknowledges their existence, but there is clearly some symbiosis between polar exploration and the adult idealization of children's worlds.

The most obvious connection, and one arguably born out by Peter Pan's association with the Scott expedition, is that both polar expeditions and the settings of fantasy fiction for children are ostensibly asexual or pre-sexual environments. It is perhaps no coincidence that J. M. Barrie, the author of *Peter Pan*, was Robert Scott's closest friend and that Scott expressed his aspirations for his son by naming him after Barrie's hero. It is not hard to make connections, as Francis Spufford does, between Peter Pan's puckish announcement that "To die will be an awfully big adventure" and Scott summing up Oates' suicide as "the act of a brave man and an English gentleman." It is easy to see Scott's men as Peter Pan's Lost Boys, escaping to a simple world where boys make all the rules (and believe more in fairies than women). Barrie offered his dead friend as a model to the students of St. Andrews in his address on becoming Rector of the university in 1922, telling them, many of whom had been through the Great War and then returned to their studies, "I think it may uplift you all to stand for a moment by that tent and listen, as he says, to their songs and cheery conversation." He went on to compare Scott explicitly to the eternally youthful (or dead) Peter Pan:

> When I think of Scott I remember the strange Alpine story of the youth who fell down a glacier and was lost, and of how a scientific companion, one of several who accompanied him, all young, computed that the body would again appear at a certain date and place many years afterwards. When that time came round some of the survivors returned to the glacier to see if the prediction would be fulfilled; all old men now; and the body reappeared as young as the day he left them. So Scott and his comrades emerge out of the white immensities always young.

They may emerge "always young," and the evidence from the exhumations of the Arctic dead suggests that they would be recognizably themselves and recognizably youthful, but Barrie bizarrely glosses over the fact that they are also always dead, as if his need for them to be alive effects a resurrection. This casts light on the children's literature of the day because it shows how much the prizing of youth is to do with the abandoned hopes of adulthood rather than the celebration of present childhood, a trope which is particularly marked in those whose childhoods were divided from their maturity by war. Childhood is by definition a dynamic time, shaped by a rapid succession of milestones on the way to less changeful years, but Scott's beloved Barrie and his fellow writers glorify unnaturally static children, and it is not surprising that so many of the fantasy children's books of these years end in death. Better, it seems, to be young and dead than to live to maturity. In the aftermath of the First World War, it is not a surprising sentiment, but coming from a writer for children it is distinctly sinister. This craving for frozen childhood is one that can be traced through the great English children's books from Lewis Carroll to C. S. Lewis.

Parodying the Poles: The Snark and Pooh Take on Franklin and Scott

The Hunting of the Snark (1876), like most of Lewis Carroll's work, is open to innumerable interpretations, and it would be a rash critic who suggested any one was definitive. The long, narrative nonsense poem is clearly a parody of Coleridge's "Rime of the Ancient Mariner," and also lends itself readily to readings grounded in backgrounds from psychoanalysis to mathematical logic. Nevertheless, coming from the history of polar exploration, it is hard to avoid seeing Franklin's expedition behind the Baker's

> . . . forty two boxes, all carefully packed,
> With his name painted clearly on each:
> But, since he omitted to mention the fact,
> They were all left behind on the beach.

Franklin's heaps of food and equipment were left behind, piled on the beach at Resolution Bay to act as a monitory but welcome resource for generations of explorers. The bizarre luggage carried by his men comes to mind again when the crew,

> Land at last with their boxes, portmanteaus, and bags:
> Yet at first sight the crew were not pleased with the view
> Which consisted of chasms and crags.

The "large map representing the sea,/Without the least vestige of land" (i.e., "a perfect and absolute blank") is exactly what most eighteenth- and nineteenth-century polar expeditions had to navigate by, and where they had more detail they would often have been better served by blankness. This is a bleak parody of nineteenth-century geography and explorers' misplaced confidence in "Mercator's North Poles and Equators,/Tropics, Zones and Meridian Lines" to ward off butchery and starvation. The "mustard and cress" with which the Baker is roused when he faints was grown on damp cloth below decks and used sparingly to treat severe cases of scurvy from the beginning of the nineteenth century until the discovery of vitamins after the First World War. Again, Carroll's reference to this is parodic because it did not work; a teaspoonful of etiolated cress is as likely to revive someone unconscious as it is to cure severe scurvy. In this reading, the point about the random and nonsensical behavior of the Snark hunters is that it is as random and nonsensical as it seems, but it is also standard practice on contemporary polar expeditions, exemplified by Franklin's. The recommended means of catching the mysterious Snark are very similar to those apparently used by Crozier's men—looking for nothing less than the means of survival—seeking a route south after abandoning their ships:

> They sought it with thimbles, they sought it with care;
> They pursued it with forks and hope;
> They threatened its life with a railway share;
> They charmed it with smiles and with soap.

Whatever a Snark turns out to be, these seem likely to be about as useful as, and much like, the curtain poles, silver cutlery and hairbrushes that Franklin's crew dropped on their death march along the shores of King William Island. There were certainly forks, soap and hope (the latter carried in defiance of common sense as well as category) and there may well have been thimbles and railway shares, since there were evening slippers and works of light fiction. The Banker's fate, after being menaced by the Bandersnatch, is unpleasantly similar to that of many officers who came to a bitter end:

> To the horror of all who were present that day,
> He uprose in full evening dress,
> And with senseless grimaces endeavoured to say
> What his tongue could no longer express.

> Down he sank in a chair—ran his hands through his hair—
> And chanted in mimsiest tones
> Words whose utter inanity proved his insanity,
> While he rattled a couple of bones.

As was all too frequent under such circumstances, the others follow the Bellman's suggestion that they "Leave him here to his fate—it is getting so late," and the Banker is left gibbering among the chasms and crags as the search for the Snark continues. Both Greely and Scott record the "wandering intellects" and sudden talkativeness that preceded death from starvation on these expeditions. In the context of the end of the Franklin expedition, when men were left by the wayside, very probably chanting and in something not far short of "full evening dress," if there were "a couple of bones" to rattle they were probably human bones from cannibalized colleagues. The horror underlying this entertaining poem has always been recognized, and the Snark, which turns out to be a Boojum, has been identified with everything from the Freudian mother-figure to the Industrial Revolution. It seems that another possible source is the unnerving tales carried back from King William Island throughout Carroll's adult life.

Although there is no evidence that Lewis Carroll took a particular interest in polar exploration, there is some biographical information to support this reading. Carroll (or Charles Dodgson, his real name) spent the summer of 1854 in Whitby, on the North Yorkshire coast. He went with a reading party from Oxford, where Carroll was then an undergraduate, and, according to his friend Thomas Fowler, "used to sit on a rock on the beach, telling stories to a circle of eager young listeners of both sexes." It was in the autumn of 1854 that John Rae returned to London to write his reports to the *Times* and the Royal Geographical Society, and public excitement about Franklin was at its height. Several search expeditions were in the Arctic while Carroll was sitting on the beach at Whitby, and most of them had called at the major whaling port on the way, collecting crew, provisions and/or expertise from the men whose business it was to sail the Arctic seas year after year. Many polar explorers' ships were adapted whaling vessels from Whitby, and the town was more closely connected with the Arctic than anywhere else in Europe. Carroll certainly joined in with local life—the one surviving letter from this time describes the "feast" given for three hundred children in the grounds of the abbey, at which Carroll and a friend served currant bread and organized games—so it is highly unlikely that he did not hear about the comings and goings of Arctic ships in general and Franklin's in particular. Many of the children he befriended would have been the sons and daughters of whalers who made annual voyages to the Arctic, and these encounters probably taught Lewis Carroll something about sailing in high latitudes. He could not have read the newspapers over the next few years without learning more, and it seems quite possible that the ill-fated hunt for the Snark owes something to the disastrous quest for the Northwest Passage.

A very different work for children, *Winnie the Pooh*, was published in 1926, when the post-war enthusiasm for the Scott expedition was at its height. A. A. Milne was already a successful journalist and playwright (and friend of J. M. Barrie), and was also known for his pacifism. Milne's subversive approach to military life is clear from his own account of his work during the war, although he spent weeks in the trenches in northern France and saw several of his friends, colleagues and subordinates blown up before his eyes. It was part of his work to inspect his men's guns:

Sometimes at my request a man would open the breech and put a dirty thumb-nail at one end while I squinted down the other, and if I had seen a mouse crawling about inside I should have known that something was wrong. . . . I never, as they say, fired a shot in anger, and only twelve under the impetus of any other emotion. These all missed the musketry instructor, but hit the Isle of Wight. It was he who was angry.

There is something distinctly Pooh-ish about this adamant good cheer and public refusal to take the nastiest episodes seriously. It is impossible to imagine anyone on the Scott expedition finding this at all funny—or at least, impossible to imagine Scott tolerating anyone who did. In the wake of Frederick Crew's books *The Pooh Perplex* and *The Postmodern Pooh*, one is reluctant to embark on a lengthy analysis of militarism and modernity at Pooh Corner. Nevertheless, it is possible for the attuned reader to find distinct similarities between Scott's attempt on the South Pole and Christopher Robin's on the North Pole. From Pooh's preparations for the Adventure ("he brushed the honey off his nose with the back of his paw, and spruced himself up as well as he could, so as to look Ready for Anything") to Christopher Robin's happy-go-lucky approach to food ("I think," said Christopher Robin, "that we ought to eat all our Provisions now, so that we shan't have so much to carry"), Scott's influence is apparent. Eeyore can remind one of the relentlessly virtuous Wilson ("A little Consideration, a little Thought for Others, makes all the difference"). Meanwhile, the uncertainty about what the pole is actually for ("'It's just a thing that you discover,' said Christopher Robin carelessly, not being quite sure himself"), how to recognize it once found ("I suppose it's just a pole stuck in the ground?") and what to do next ("Then they all went home again.") arguably makes a more serious point about the triviality and even childishness of the whole endeavor.

One of the appeals of the Pooh books to adults is that Milne does not fetishize childhood; his children are not in the least concerned with sexuality or redemption because they are too busy being children engaged in appropriately infantile pursuits. The inclusion of polar exploration in these childish games might give a moment's pause for thought, especially as Christopher Robin laboriously spells out, "North Pole Dicsovered by Pooh Pooh Found It." The work seems reminiscent of all the tablets and plaques in the Far North and in Antarctica, chiseled out by frozen fingers and announcing proudly that such and such an island/point furthest north/river/coastline was "discovered" by the most senior survivor of whichever benighted group it was in the name of whichever (largely uninterested) monarch happened to be occupying the throne in London/Paris/Copenhagen/Moscow. It is Milne's sense that such announcements are generic and interchangeable that makes this funny. Christopher Robin knows what the important bits of polar exploring entail, and he knows how to go about it. One could be left wondering quite how different this is from the real thing.

Ice Maidens and Snow Queens

One of Lewis Carroll's friends was another, very different, children's writer and a clergyman, George MacDonald. MacDonald's books were very popular in the nineteenth century, but, for reasons which will become clear, fell from favor (although two were still in print in paperback in the 1980s). Where Charles Dodgson's Christianity would be impossible to deduce from Lewis Carroll's fantasy worlds of random violence, MacDonald's books are firmly in the Victorian tradition of improving allegory. As such, they purvey all the social ideals that later generations have found both powerful and distasteful. Good children are characterized by unthinking obedience, deference to their elders, and abasement before adults and children of higher social class than themselves. Their reward is in Heaven because they would not dream of seeking earthly satisfactions. Bad children insist on thinking for themselves and attending to their own needs and interests, and they must be taught a lesson. Increasing maturity brings wider opportunities to behave well, but in general, adults are morally disabled by compromise, and it is better to die young.

What is interesting about this fairly conventional ideology in relation to polar travel is that the children's Heaven is Arctic. In *At the Back of the North Wind*, George MacDonald's Arctic is a mythical space of glittering moral cleanliness (like J. M. Barrie's idea of the Antarctic). It is troubling, but perhaps inevitable, to find that one of the forces behind the English literary fascination with the poles is an ideology that regards the Arctic and Antarctic as the destinations at the end of the road to racial and sexual purity. No torrid indulgences here, no messy female bodies and no Oriental luxury. MacDonald's Arctic, setting the tone for a whole genre of muscular Christian Boys' Own polar adventures, resembles a mystically clean bathroom, all gleaming white surfaces and no germs anywhere.

At the Back of the North Wind is a disturbing book, a precursor of *The Lion, the Witch and the Wardrobe* in its celebration of death in childhood and also in its use of the Arctic in this context. The hero is an unnaturally virtuous little boy called Diamond (his goodness is prized above diamonds and he glistens with purity). Diamond's father is a poor but deserving cab driver, and Diamond sleeps in the stable loft where North Wind, an icily beautiful, stern, shape-changing woman starts to visit him at night. North Wind takes Diamond with her as she swirls about her business of sinking ships, felling trees and harrying people outdoors. Sometimes he is "nestling close to her grand bosom" and sometimes riding in a nest in her hair, and she occasionally allows him to help the distressed. North Wind is a kind of moral avenger whose identity remains hazy—she sinks ships because she must rather than because she wants to, but corrects and punishes faults from bad temper to drunkenness—and at last she takes Diamond to the country "at her back." She places him on a yacht until they come to the icebergs, and then hides him on a "much larger vessel . . . on its way to the North Pole." North Wind calls Diamond on deck to see "huge masses of floating ice, looking like cathedrals, and castles, and crags" and the sun circling the horizon, and then she seizes him and hurries him into a cave on one of the icebergs, which is drifting north. He is "enraptured with the colour of the air inside the cave" which is "a deep, dazzling, lovely blue, deeper than the deepest blue of the sky." North Wind, assuring him that she will return, melts away, and Diamond passes his time looking at the cave and the sea, "ever sparkling in the sun," until at last the Promised Land comes into view:

> . . . he spied, far off upon the horizon, a shining peak that rose into the sky like the top of some tremendous iceberg; and his vessel was bearing him straight towards it. As it went on the peak rose and rose higher and higher above the horizon; and other peaks rose after it, with sharp edges and jagged ridges connecting them. Diamond thought this must be the place he was going to; and he was right; for the mountains rose and rose, till he saw the line of the coast at their feet, and at length the iceberg drove into a little bay, all around which were lofty precipices with snow on their tops, and streaks of ice down their sides. The berg floated slowly up to a projecting rock. Diamond stepped on shore, and without looking behind him began to follow a natural path which led windingly towards the top of the precipice.

At the top he finds North Wind, who commands him to walk through her. As he does so, "the cold stung him like fire" and "he felt swallowed up in whiteness," but he revives to a temperate (and rather dull) place where a singing river runs over grass and he feels "still and quiet and patient and contented." Even the narrator admits that much is lacking in this modest afterlife, and after a while Diamond misses his mother unbearably and goes in search of North Wind, who takes him home. Needless to say, he wakes to find he has been dangerously ill, but he is spared for several years of sweetness and light, cheering his parents in their misfortunes and unwittingly teaching Christianity to the dissolute, before he meets the narrator (who is assailed by "a gush of reverence" on hearing Diamond speak of North Wind). North Wind begins to visit Diamond again and he remains tired and cold for several days, until he is found dead by his bedroom door one morning.

The intriguing thing about this strange and somewhat beguiling fable is that MacDonald feels no need to romanticize or exaggerate the Arctic landscape to turn it into heaven. In a text that includes shape-shifting, time travel and several coded dreams, the North Pole is simply described in terms that could easily have been gleaned from almost any voyage account, and this simple description is assumed to be enough to portray the place of salvation. Coldness becomes the sign of imminent redemption as well as bodily death, as if the holiness of the Arctic is self-evident. One function of this geographical rather than metaphysical location of heaven is to elide the boundary between life and death, which is one reason that the story is a little creepy. Children are offered a version of death which is metaphysically identical to life—Diamond can even see his family by climbing a tree at the Back of the North Wind, and meets child angels forever the age they reached in life—suggesting that dying young is more or less the same as staying young. In an era of relatively high child mortality and great fascination for the outposts of empire, it is possible to see why combining the two to reincorporate dead children into the body politic was attractive, but that does not grant MacDonald's project intellectual or pedagogical integrity.

C. S. Lewis was unusually enthusiastic about George MacDonald, whom he respected both as a children's writer and as a popular theologian, and the White Witch of Narnia obviously owes much to North Wind as well as to Hans Christian Andersen's Snow Queen (though her equipage is distinctly reminiscent of the Norse prophetess of Herjolfsness). She appears in a sledge driven by a dwarf dressed in polar bears' fur and drawn by reindeer whose "hair was so white that even the snow hardly looked white compared with them; their branching horns were gilded and shone like something on fire when the sunrise caught them." She herself is "a great lady, taller than any woman that Edmund had ever seen" and "covered in white fur up to her throat." She holds a gold wand and wears a gold crown and, "Her face was white—not merely pale, but white like snow or paper or icing sugar, except for her very red mouth. It was a beautiful face in other respects, but proud and cold and stern." Like North Wind and Andersen's Snow Queen, the White Witch is a female figure whose Arctic identity makes her dangerous and uncontrollable and irresistibly attractive. All three women have excessively long, luxuriant

hair which fascinates both the (adult male) narrators and the little boys
who have adventures, and all three use their unnatural beauty to lure
the boys to follow them into fantastic frozen worlds. They could be
said to epitomize the predatory female sexuality from which polar
exploration offers an escape.

It is interesting—although perhaps not surprising—that the same
writers who distrust adult sexuality so much that they present death
as preferable to maturity are also patently excited by these icy, punitive
and very grown-up women. As Francis Spufford writes, "North Wind
has a distinctly erotic physical presence." At their first encounter, she
sweeps the bedclothes from Diamond and then tells him, "I am sorry
I was forced to be so rough with you." "The boy" is "entranced by her
mighty beauty," and the next time she comes to him, he wakes to see
"a gigantic, powerful, but most lovely arm—with a hand whose

fingers were nothing the less ladylike that they could have strangled a boa constrictor, or choked a tigress off its prey—stretched down through a big hole in the roof." MacDonald's lingering anatomy of North Wind is reminiscent of Flaubert's of Emma Bovary or Hardy's of Tess of the D'Urbervilles, both men in love with their heroines. The difference is that Emma and Tess are both flawed and foolish (which is part of their attraction), while North Wind is overpoweringly sexual, the fantasy figure who combines extreme femininity (she is "nothing the less ladylike") with the capacity to sink ships and strangle boa constrictors with her bare hands. In the woodcuts illustrating the first edition, she is often naked but for her swirling hair, a statuesque and sensual figure who makes a great contrast to the downcast, girlish women in crinolines and caps who represent Diamond's mother and aunt.

Lewis, writing after Freud, is much more circumspect, but even so the White Witch draws Edmund with her beauty and then seduces him with magic Turkish Delight. The Witch, who keeps calling Edmund "Son of Adam" to remind us of his and our fallen nature, knows that she can now do anything she likes with Edmund because "this was enchanted Turkish Delight and that anyone who had once tasted it would want more and more of it, and would even, if they were allowed, go on eating it till they killed themselves." Edmund is now in her thrall as Diamond is in the less sinister North Wind's and Kay in the Snow Queen's.

The Arctic seduces little boys with a combination of purity and sexuality that no real woman will ever be able to rival, and when we remember how many adults reveled in children's fiction in the late nineteenth and early twentieth centuries, this provides a context for the Edwardian and Victorian cultures of polar exploration. Apsley Cherry-Garrard's *The Worst Journey in the World* repeatedly describes Antarctic expeditions as marriages, in which the participants undertake to support and tolerate one another through hell and high water. This sense that polar travel can be a substitute for adult sexuality fits in with children's writers' fascination for the topic. Jackie Wullschlager writes in *Inventing Wonderland* that, "The settings of the

Victorian and Edwardian children's classics . . . point to one of the strongest influences on the Victorian and Edwardian cult of childhood and on children's books: the regressive desire for a pre-industrial, rural world and the identification of the child with purity, a pre-sexual life, moral simplicity."

This pre-industrial world in which one can aspire to purity, asexuality and moral simplicity is exactly what many polar explorers hoped for in the Arctic and Antarctic—like Richard Byrd's longing for peace and simplicity alone in his hut miles from the Antarctic Little America, the intransigent opposition of the Ronne Expedition to Jennie Darlington's presence on the ice, or indeed the aspirations of the Celtic hermits who navigated the North Atlantic in search of somewhere remote enough for perpetual prayer. The polar regions seem to offer a simplified world in which things are literally black and white, a pure and gleaming land where there are no temptations or distractions from the quest for truth of one kind or another. In fact, of course, the tensions of group life and the stresses of physical discomfort and frequent danger encourage aggression and triviality, and the isolation of most polar expeditions brings out the worst in anxious travelers. In any case, the very longing for purity, for a return to a perceived childhood innocence and simplicity, carries the seeds of its own destruction. Children do not fantasize about being pre-sexual because they do not know that they are, and so an adult purveying such a fantasy is doing so with a knowingness that undermines it. It is no more possible to escape maturity than it is to achieve perpetual childhood. Human nature is not redeemed by ice. As Wordsworth, who knew all about childhood and the landscapes of the mind, wrote,

> Not in Utopia, subterraneous fields,
> Or some secreted Island Heaven knows where;
>   But in the very world which is the world
> Of all of us, the place on which, in the end,
> We find our happiness, or not at all.

EPILOGUE
The End of the Road

As English literary culture came to celebrate the polar regions and to establish a definitive polar aesthetic, something began to happen to the ends of the earth.

The poles will remain epistemologically challenging, places that are not quite places but which nevertheless define spatial relationships across the rest of the globe. The poles are, however ambiguously, there, and without them, no kind of cartography or navigation would be possible. This aspect of polar strangeness, the oddity of places which are obviously spatial and yet never quite present, will not change unless and until the relationship between the earth and the sun changes. But while the poles will continue to have one six-month night and one six-month day, and to be colder than anywhere else, the complementary weirdness of frozen land and seascapes is coming to an end.

The ice in the Arctic ocean has thinned by 40 percent in the last thirty years, and both this and the rising temperatures that cause it mean that most Arctic flora and fauna are threatened with imminent extinction. The evidence for ecological damage to the far south is less clear-cut, but scientists are increasingly convinced that rises in sea temperature and atmospheric temperature are greatly accelerating the fragmentation of the ice shelves and the melting of the sea ice, again endangering the viability of unique and little-known sea-creatures. In December 2003, the chair of the Inuit Circumpolar Conference, which represents all the Inuit living within the Arctic Circle, announced that the Conference was launching a human rights case against President George Bush's administration because of its refusal to take steps to limit damage to the polar environment through pollution and climate change. Traditional Inuit skills are becoming redundant as the ice melts, temperatures rise and snow is replaced by rain, and the thawing of the permafrost also endangers anything built upon it. The Bush administration is keen to drill for oil in the Arctic National Wildlife Refuge on Alaska's north coast, which many environmentalists believe will inaugurate the final phase in the destruction of the Arctic. The ice is melting, the ocean warming, and in the last few years rain has fallen in places where both human and animal inhabitants have evolved over thousands of years to rely on snow.

While Antarctica is better protected from direct pollution and destruction, it cannot be physically separated from the rest of the world as it may be in the Western imagination. There too, the ice is crumbling and melting and temperatures are rising to the irrecoverable detriment of an extraordinary environment. It is changing so fast that some species and landscapes will be gone before we can know about them, but the desire to know is also at the root of the problem. We burn oil in order to travel further and faster than we could without it, so that more people can see and know more about more of the world, and the result is that there is less of the world to see and know.

For centuries, we have dreamed and fantasized about the North and South Poles, using the inaccessibility and cartographical strangeness of the still points of the turning world as a basis for imagining various kinds of heaven and hell on earth. For everyone who has written about polar travel, from the early medieval monks to workers on the British Antarctic Survey who keep Internet diaries, the Arctic and Antarctic are hauntingly beautiful, even in the seventeenth and eighteenth centuries when conventional ideas of natural beauty celebrated the highly domesticated rolling landscapes of southern England and shrank in horror from dramatic scenery and unproductive land. The destruction of this beauty and the loss of the cultural aesthetic that has grown to celebrate it is surely not the worst consequence of environmental change, but it may be among the more painful for Europeans and North Americans. The places that we long to see for ourselves are being obliterated by the mining and burning of the oil that takes us there. It is not possible to travel without participating in the destruction of the imagination's most precious destination. Antarctica and the Arctic are nearly over, and with them the defining tension of places that are beautiful to look at and hard to survive. They will exist only in memory and imagination.

FURTHER READING

Introduction: A Brief History of Polar Exploration

Berton, Pierre, *The Arctic Grail: the Quest for the North West Passage and the North Pole, 1818-1909*. New York: Viking, 1988

Beste, George, *The Three Voyages of Martin Frobisher*. London: Hakluyt Society (1578), 1867

Bockstoce, John R., *Whales, Ice and Men: the History of Whaling in the Western Arctic*. Seattle: University of Washington Press, 1986

Brody, Hugh, *The People's Land: Eskimos and Whites in the Eastern Arctic*. Harmondsworth: Penguin, 1975

Brody, Hugh, *Living Arctic: Hunters of the Canadian North*. London: Faber, 1988

Davis, John, *The Voyages and Works of John Davis*, ed. A. H. Markham. London: Hakluyt Society, 1880

Feeney, Robert E., *Polar Journeys: the Role of Food and Nutrition in Early Exploration*. Fairbanks: American Chemical Society, University of Alaska Press, 1997

Fleming, Fergus, *Barrow's Boys*. Cambridge: Granta, 2001

Hudson, Henry, *Henry Hudson the Navigator, the Original Documents in Which His Career is Recorded, Collected, Partly Translated and Annotated by G. M. Asher*. London: Hakluyt Society, 1860

Kemp, Peter, *The British Sailor: a Social History of the Lower Deck*. London: Dent, 1970

Kirwan, Laurence, *The White Road: a Survey of Polar Exploration*. London: Hollis and Carter, 1959

Lopez, Barry, *Arctic Dreams: Imagination and Desire in a Northern Landscape*. London: Macmillan, 1986

Mackay, David, *In the Wake of Cook: Exploration, Science and Empire, 1780-1801*. London: Croom Helm, 1985

Mawson, Douglas, *Home of the Blizzard*. London: Heinemann, 1915

Moss, John, *Enduring Dreams: An Exploration of Arctic Landscape*. Concord, Ontario: Anansi Press, 1996

Mountfield, David, *A History of Polar Exploration*. London: Hamlyn, 1974

Neale, Jonathan, *The Cutlass and the Lash: Mutiny and Discipline in Nelson's Navy*. London: Pluto Press, 1985

Nuttall, Mark, *Arctic Homeland: Kinship, Community and Development in Northwest Greenland*. London: Belhaven in association with Scott Polar Research Institute, 1992

Rediker, Marcus, *Between the Devil and the Deep Blue Sea: Merchant Seamen, Pirates and the Anglo-American Maritime World 1700-1750*. Cambridge: Cambridge University Press, 1987

Shackleton, Ernest, *South: the Story of Shackleton's 1914-1917 Expedition*. London: Heinemann, 1922

Simpson-Housley, Paul, *Antarctica: Exploration, Perception and Metaphor*. London: Routledge, 1992

Williams, Glyndwr, *The British Search for the Northwest Passage in the Eighteenth Century*. London: Longmans for The Royal Commonwealth Society, 1962

Part One: Making a Home

Berglund, Joel, "The Decline of the Norse Settlements in Greenland." *Arctic Anthropology* 23 (1986): 109-35

Bobe, Louis, "History of the Trade and Colonization until 1870." In *The Colonization of Greenland and its History until 1929*, ed. Gustav Rasmussen *et al* Gudmund Hatt 3, 77-165. Copenhagen: C. A. Reitzel, 1929

Clausen, B. L., ed., *Viking Voyages to North America*. Odense, 1993

Crantz, David, *The History of Greenland*. London: Brethren's Society for the Furtherance of the Gospel, 1767

Egede, Hans, *A Description of Greenland*. London, 1745

Graah, W. A., *Narrative of an Expedition to the East Coast of Greenland. . . in Search of the Lost Colonies*. Trans G. G. Macdougall, London: Murray, 1837

Ingstad, Anne Stine, *The Discovery of the Norse Settlements in America*. Oslo, 1977

Ingstad, Helge, *Land under the Pole Star*. London: Jonathan Cape, 1966

Ingstad, Helge, *Westward to Vinland*. Trans Erik J Friis. London: Book Club Associates, 1974

Keller, Christian, "Vikings in the West Atlantic." *Acta Archaeologica* 61 (1990): 126-146

Krogh, Knud, *Viking Greenland*. Copenhagen, 1967

de Laguna, Frederica, *Voyage to Greenland: a Personal Initiation into Anthropology*. New York: Norton, 1977

McGovern, Thomas, "Economics of Extinction in Norse Greenland." In *Climate and History: Studies in Past Climates and Their Impact on Man*, eds. T. M. Wrigley, M. J. Ingram, and G. Farmer, 404-434. Cambridge: Cambridge University Press, 1980

Morris, C. D., and D. J. Rackham, eds., *Norse and Later Settlement and Subsistence in the North Atlantic*. Glasgow: Department of Archaeology, University of Glasgow, 1993

Norlund, Poul, *Viking Settlers in Greenland*. Cambridge: Cambridge University Press, 1936

Quinn, David B., *North America from Earliest Discovery to First Settlements*. New York: Harper and Row, 1977

Seaver, Kristen A., *The Frozen Echo: Greenland and the Exploration of North America c.a. AD 1000-1500*. Stanford: Stanford University Press, 1996

The Vinland Sagas: the Norse Discovery of America: Graenlendinga Saga and Eirik's Saga. Trans. Magnus Magnusson and Hermann Palsson. Harmondsworth: Penguin, 1965

Part Two: The Long Dark Night

Byrd, Richard, *Alone.* London: George Putnam and Sons, 1938

Nansen, Friedrich, *Farthest North.* London: Constable, 1897

Parry, William Edward, *Journal of a Voyage for the Discovery of the North West Passage.* London: Murray, 1821

Ross, James, *Narrative of the Second Voyage of Captain Ross to the Arctic Regions, in the Years 1829-30-31-32-33.* London: Murray, 1834

Part Three: The Bitter End

Amundsen, R., *The South Pole.* Trans. A. G. Chater, 2 vols. London: Murray, 1912

The Andrée diaries: being the diaries and records of S. A. Andrée, Nils Strindberg and Knut Fraenkel, written during their balloon expedition to the North Pole in 1897 and discovered on White Island in 1930, together with a complete record of the expedition and discovery; authorized tr. from the official Swedish edition by Edward Adams-Ray. London: John Lane, 1931

Cherry-Garrard, Apsley, *The Worst Journey in the World: Antarctic 1910-13.* London: Picador, 1994

Greely, Adolphus W., *Three Years of Arctic Service: an Account of the Lady Franklin Bay Expedition of 1881-84.* London: Murray, 1886

Huntford, Roland, *The Last Place on Earth: Scott and Amundsen's Race to the South Pole.* London: Abacus, 2000

Jones, Max, *The Last Great Quest: Captain Scott's Antarctic Sacrifice.* Oxford: Oxford University Press, 2003

Ponting, Herbert G., *The Great White South: Being an Account of Experiences with Captain Scott's South Pole Expedition and of the Nature Life of the Antarctic.* London: Duckworth, 1921

Scott, Robert F., *Scott's Last Expedition*, ed. Leonard Huxley. London: Smith, Elder and Co., 1913

Spufford, Francis, *I May Be Some Time: Ice and the English Imagination.* London: Faber, 1996

Part Four: Visiting the Dead

Beattie, Owen, and John Geiger, *Frozen in Time: the Fate of the Franklin Expedition.* London: Bloomsbury, 1987

Blake, E. Vale, *Arctic Experiences: Containing Capt. George E. Tyson's Wonderful Drift on the Ice-floe, a History of the Polaris Expedition, the Cruise of the Tigress, and Rescue of the Polaris Survivors.* New York: Harper & Brothers, 1874

Cookman, Scott, *Ice Blink: the Tragic Fate of Sir John Franklin's Lost Polar Expedition*. Chichester: Wiley, 2000

Delgado, James P., *Across the Top of the World: the Quest for the Northwest Passage*. London: British Museum Press, 1999

Franklin, John, *Narrative of a Journey to the Shores of the Polar Sea, in the Years 1819-20-21-22*. London: Murray, 1824

Franklin, John, *Narrative of a Second Expedition to the Shores of the Polar Sea, in the Years 1825, 1826, and 1827*. London: Murray, 1828

Kent Kane, Elisha, *Arctic Explorations in Search of Sir John Franklin*. London/New York: T. Nelson, 1876

Kilgour, Maggie, *From Communion to Cannibalism: An Anatomy of Metaphors of Incorporation*. Princeton: Princeton University Press, 1990

Loomis, Chauncey C., *Weird and Tragic Shores: the Story of Charles Francis Hall, Explorer*. London: Macmillan, 1972

M'Clintock, Sir F. Leopold, *Fate of Sir John Franklin: the Voyage of the 'Fox' in the Arctic Seas in Search of Franklin and His Companions*. London: John Murray, 1881

McGoogan, Ken, *Fatal Passage: the Untold Story of John Rae, the Arctic Adventurer Who Discovered the Fate of Franklin*. Toronto: Harper Collins, 2002

Woodman, David C., *Unravelling the Franklin Mystery: Inuit Testimony*. Montreal/London: McGill–Queen's University Press, 1991

Part Five: Women at the Ends of the Earth

Brown, Jennifer S. H., *Strangers in Blood: Fur Trade Company Families in Indian Country*. Vancouver: University of British Columbia Press, 1980

Burley, Edith, *Servants of the Honourable Company: Work, Discipline and Conflict in the Hudson's Bay Company 1770-1870*, Oxford: Oxford University Press, 1997

Darlington, Jenny, *My Antarctic Honeymoon: a Year at the Bottom of the World*. London: F. Muller, 1957

Hargrave, Letitia, *The Letters of Letitia Hargrave*, ed. Margaret Arnett MacLeod. Toronto: Champlain Society, 1947

Hutchison, Isobel Wylie, *On Greenland's Closed Shore: the Fairyland of the Arctic*. Edinburgh: William Blackwood & Sons, 1930

Kirk, Sylvia Van, *Many Tender Ties: Women in Fur Trade Society in Western Canada, 1670-1870*. Montreal: McGill–Queen's University Press, 1988

Mancke, Elizabeth, *A Company of Businessmen: The Hudson's Bay Company and Long Distance Trade 1670-1730*. Winnipeg: Rupert's Land Research Centre, 1988

Newman, Peter C., *Company of Adventurers: the Story of the Hudson Bay Company*. Ottawa: Penguin Books Canada, 1985

Ronne, Finn, *Antarctic Conquest: the Story of the Ronne Expedition, 1946-1948*. New York: Putnam's Sons, 1949

For more general discussion of women's writing and the polar regions, see:

Atwood, Margaret, *Strange Things: the Malevolent North in Canadian Literature*. Oxford: Clarendon Press, 1995

Diski, Jenny, *Skating to Antarctica*. London: Granta, 1997

Wheeler, Sara, *Terra Incognita: Travels in Antarctica*. London: Jonathan Cape, 1996

Part Six: Literature on Ice
English Poetry:
Bohls, Elizabeth, *Women Travel Writers and the Language of Aesthetics, 1716-1818*. Cambridge: Cambridge University Press, 1995

Coleridge, S. T. and William Wordsworth, *Lyrical Ballads*, ed. R. L. Brett and A. R. Jones. London: Routledge, 1991

Donne, John, *The Divine Poems*. 2nd ed., ed. Helen Gardner. Oxford: Clarendon Press, 1978

Shelley, Mary, *Frankenstein, or, The Modern Prometheus: the 1818 Text*, ed. Marilyn Butler. Oxford: Oxford University Press, 1994

Thomson, James, *The Seasons*, ed. James Sambrook. Oxford: Oxford University Press, 1981

Children's Fiction:
Barrie, J. M., *Courage*. London: Hodder and Stoughton, 1922

Barrie, J. M., *Peter Pan in Kensington Gardens; Peter and Wendy*, ed. Peter Hollindale. Oxford: Oxford University Press, 1991

Carroll, Lewis, *The Annotated Snark: the Full Text of Lewis Carroll's Great Nonsense Epic The Hunting of the Snark*, ed. Martin Gardner. Harmondsworth: Penguin, 1973

Carroll, Lewis, *The Letters of Lewis Carroll*, ed. Morton N. Cohen and Roger Lancelyn Green. London: Macmillan, 1979

Huxley, Francis, *The Raven and the Writing Desk*. London: Thames and Hudson, 1976

Lewis, C. S., *The Lion, the Witch and the Wardrobe*. London: HarperCollins, (1950) 1991

Macdonald, George, *At the Back of the North Wind*. London, 1871

Milne, A. A., *An Expotition to the North Pole*. Illustrated by E. H. Shepard. London: Methuen, 1991

Milne, Christopher, *The Enchanted Places*. London: Eyre Methuen, 1974

Rose, Jacqueline, *The Case of Peter Pan, or, The Impossibility of Children's Fiction*. Philadelphia: University of Pennsylvania Press, 1993

Thwaite, Ann, *A. A. Milne: His Life*. London: Faber, 1990

Wullschläger, Jackie, *Inventing Wonderland: the Lives and Fantasies of Lewis Carroll, Edward Lear, J. M. Barrie, Kenneth Grahame and A. A. Milne*. London: Methuen, 1995

INDEX

ACKNOWLEDGEMENTS

This book has been brewing for so long that almost everyone I know has contributed to it in some way. In or passing through the Oxford English Faculty I would like to thank James Treadwell for encouraging my interest and sharing my fascination; Lucy Newlyn, who supervised my doctorate; Kate Flint, who very kindly read my thesis when she had other things to do and four years later produced a generous and constructive reader's report; and Heather O'Donoghue, whose lovely Old Norse seminars fed my interest in northernness for several years. I thank John Geiger for his generosity and interest in the project as well as permission to reprint the Torrington photograph. Needless to say, all errors are my own.

Much of the initial research was done as part of my doctoral thesis, which was funded by the Arts and Humanities Research Board between 1997 and 2001. I thank the Randall McIver trust for funding my research at Lady Margaret Hall from 2001 to 2004. The staff of the Upper Reading Room in the Bodleian Library and at Rhodes House Library in Oxford produced hundreds of books with good cheer, while the Scott Polar Research Institute in Cambridge was an invaluable resource. A Vaughn Cornish award from Oxford University enabled me to travel north, where Terje and Anne Brundtland provided hospitality and inspiration in Tromsø. I am grateful to Sinead Mooney, whose joke became the book's British title, and to Kathy MacDonald, whose companionship in Iceland and the Faroes was beyond compare and whose interest ever since is a constant pleasure. Finally, I thank Anthony for his stimulating company and unstinting support, and Max, who is no help with writing but the light of the rest of life. This book is dedicated to them, and in loving memory of Kenneth Gummersall, 1916–2003.

Sarah Moss